WACO-McLENNAN COUNTY
1717 AUSTIN AVE
WACO TX 76701

SOCKS
FROM AROUND NORWAY

NINA GRANLUND SÆTHER

SOCKS
FROM AROUND NORWAY

*Over 40 Traditional Knitting Patterns
Inspired by Norwegian Folk-Art Collections*

TRAFALGAR SQUARE
North Pomfret, Vermont

First published in the United States of
America in 2019 by
Trafalgar Square Books
North Pomfret, Vermont 05053

Originally published in Norwegian as
Sokker fra hele Norge.

Copyright © 2017 Cappelen Damm AS
English translation © 2018 Trafalgar Square
Books

All rights reserved. No part of this book may be reproduced, by any means, without written permission of the publisher, except by a reviewer quoting brief excerpts for a review in a magazine or newspaper or on a website.

ISBN: 978-1-57076-922-1

Library of Congress Control Number: 2018961115

Interior Design: Sissel Holt Boniface
Photography: Guri Pfeifer; for exceptions, see page 199.
Charts: Denise Samson
Translation into English: Carol Huebscher Rhoades

Printed in China

10 9 8 7 6 5 4 3 2 1

CONTENTS

- 6   Preface
- 8   Read Before You Begin
- 8   Needles
- 8   Abbreviations
- 8   Yarn and Reinforcing Thread
- 8   Gauge (Tension)
- 8   Sizes
- 9   Casting On
- 9   Two-Color Stranded Knitting
- 9   Yarn Floats
- 9   Two-End (Twined) Braid
- 10   Entrelac
- 11   Abbreviations
- 12   Heels
- 13   Hourglass Heel
- 14   Gusset Heel
- 16   Band Heel with Short Heel Flap
- 18   Band Heel with Long Heel Flap
- 19   Shaped Common Heel
- 20   Afterthought Heel
- 21   Reinforcing the Heel
- 22   Toe Shaping
- 22   Star Toe
- 22   Wedge Toe
- 22   Weaving in Yarn Ends
- 23   Garment Care
- 24   Striped Socks from Østfold
- 28   Star Socks
- 34   Rose Stockings from Asker
- 38   Oslo Socks
- 42   Stockings from 1868
- 46   Rose Ankle Socks
- 50   Striped Stockings from Glåmdalen
- 54   Color Party
- 58   Stockings from Valdres
- 62   Stockings from Gausdal
- 66   Barleycorn (*Byggkorn*) Socks from Numedal
- 70   Halling Socks
- 74   Larvik Socks
- 78   Long Lace Stockings
- 84   Telemark Socks
- 88   Cable Socks from Tinn
- 92   Setesdal *Krot* Socks
- 96   Zigzag Pattern Socks
- 100   Cable Stockings from Marnardal
- 104   Leftover Party
- 108   Bridegroom's Socks from Vindafjord
- 112   Rose Socks with Lace Patterns
- 118   Stockings from Voss
- 122   Short *Skakareiker* Socks from Austevoll
- 126   *Kroneleistar* from Øygarden
- 130   Hardanger Socks
- 134   Sunnfjord Socks
- 138   Spiral Socks from Nordfjord
- 142   Children's Socks from Nordmøre
- 146   Socks from Budalen
- 150   *Ragg* Socks from Hitra
- 154   Striped Socks from Orkladalen
- 158   Maria's Stockings from Lierne
- 164   Trønder Socks
- 168   Children's Socks from Helgeland
- 172   Entrelac Stockings from Helgeland
- 176   Spider Socks from Troms
- 180   Sports Socks from Alta
- 184   Shell Pattern
- 188   Heart Socks
- 192   Socks with Larger Lice Pattern
- 196   Yarn Information
- 198   Bibliography
- 199   Photography Credits

PREFACE

From Old Stockings to New Socks

I'm unusually fascinated by old textiles. They might be yellowed by fire, full of holes and torn, and maybe even a little moth-eaten, but they catch my eye nevertheless. Every garment had hours of work behind it. Before knitting could begin, the wool had to be carded and spun into yarn. It might also have to be dyed. An experienced spinner can usually produce about 3.5 ounces / 100 grams of yarn in an hour. After that, hours and hours of knitting ensued. The finer and thinner the yarn, the more time it took.

There was little light inside during wintertime. There might only have been light from the fireplace to see by, or a little tallow candle to help. Hanna Winsnes recommended that servant girls knit if there wasn't enough light for other work.

Nevertheless, unbelievably beautiful textiles were created—both well-needed everyday clothing and beautifully decorated fine garments. The clothes made for confirmations and weddings were later worn for festive occasions or for going to church on Sundays. When fine garments wore out, they became everyday clothes. And when it was no longer possible to darn or patch them, the fabric was taken to the woolen mills that popped up at the end of the nineteenth century. The former owner might get a few pennies or maybe some new yarn from the shoddy mill in return. For that reason, few old textiles are preserved.

In this book, I have tried to showcase a few of the stockings from past times that still remain—preserved both in museums and in private collections. I have found a number of lovely well-kept treasures. In writing this book, I wanted to share some of the textile knowledge our foremothers, and some forefathers, had. This is cultural history and women's history specific to Norway—knowledge that I think is important in our globalized times. I've also tried to convey the specifics of regional names and colloquial language.

Creative women stand behind most of the stockings I have included. Individual districts have strong, distinctive traditions. In working on this book, I have, among other things, shown how clever and industrious people were at knitting cable pattern stockings, particularly in Telemark and Agder. The yarn is so fine and the techniques so advanced that it's genuinely difficult to recreate them today. Other places have stockings made with the finest stripe compositions or eight-petal roses. In Numedal, the so-called *byggkorn* pattern was often used—a fun but almost forgotten technique. I've tried to include something from each of Norway's provinces. Some places have so much exciting work available that it was difficult to choose.

You will find mostly patterns for women's socks, but also a couple pairs of children's and men's socks in this book. Some of the stockings are quick to knit, others take time and patience. My goal wasn't to copy the original textiles exactly, but most of the patterns were inspired by preserved materials. It's been more important for me to note the pattern motifs and details, and use what I've learned in new designs for today.

Nina Granlund Sæther

Nina Granlund Sæther on the internet:
www.hjertebank.no
Facebook: Hjertebank Nina Granlund Sæther
Instagram: @ninagranlundsather

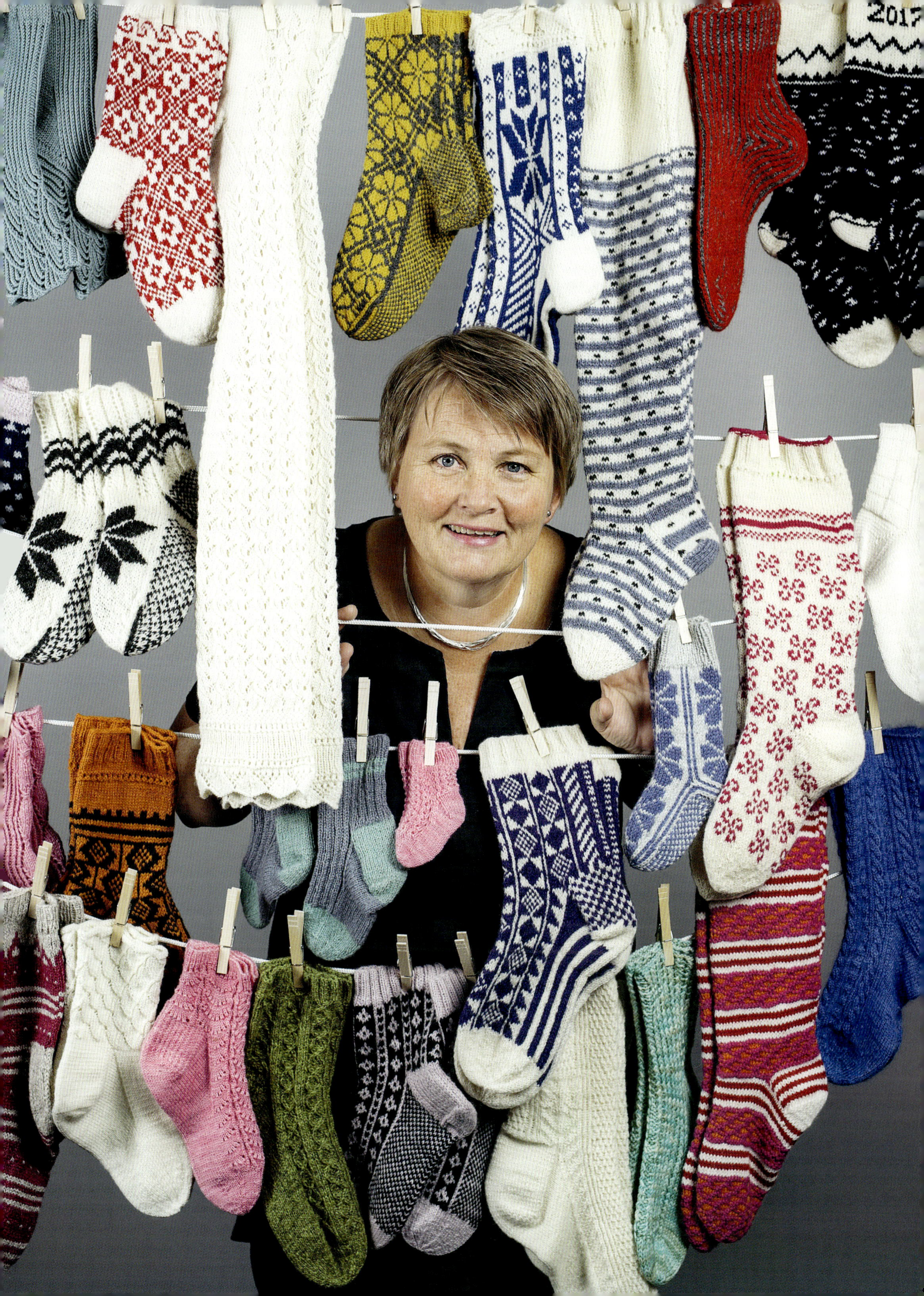

READ BEFORE YOU BEGIN

Needles
All the socks and stockings in this book are knitted with five double-pointed needles (dpn) and worked from the cuff down. Of course, you can work with a long magic loop circular needle instead; just remember that the patterns are written with double-points in mind. The stitches are usually divided with the same number on each needle but sometimes there will be more stitches on the instep than the sole.

The beginning and end of the round is at the center back of the leg or centered on the sole. The first needle holds the stitches for the left half of the back, the second needle has half of the left front; half of the right front stitches are on the third needle, and the fourth needle has the right half of the back.

I have divided the patterns into three sections: the left, heel, and foot. The leg usually begins with ribbing or an edging, and the foot ends with the toe shaping.

Yarn and Reinforcing Thread
The patterns include yarn suggestions. Feel free to substitute yarn but adhere to the given gauge if you want the same results.

There are various yarn qualities suitable for socks. Sock yarns have a percentage of polyamide (nylon) or polyester for durability. These yarns are usually superwash-treated so the wool won't felt.

Norwegian Spelsau wool was the usual choice of yarn in previous times. Spelsau fleece has both a soft undercoat and a strong, long outer coat. This combination makes the yarn especially durable. Today, many small mills market yarn from this wool.

Both horse and goat hair have been used to reinforce heels and soles on ragg socks (the word *ragg* refers to thick, shaggy goat hair). Women's hair was also used for reinforcement. Although we now prefer to use sock yarn strengthened with nylon, you might not want to use wool blended with other fibers. You can, instead, add in another strong thread, either for the whole sock or only for heels and perhaps the toes.

Finely-spun Spelsau yarn, such as Røros embroidery yarn, is a good choice for this, but the knitted fabric will be somewhat stiffer. You could also use silk thread or nylon buttonhole thread, which comes in a wide choice of colors (look for it in fabric shops). That adds less bulk and is barely visible.

Gauge (Tension)
In order for finished garments to be the expected size, the gauge must be maintained. If you knit too loosely, your socks will be too big. In that case, try smaller needles. And vice versa: if your knitting is too tight, the socks will be too small, so you should try bigger needles.

Sizes
Some of the socks in this book are written for one size only—women's shoe size U. S. 6½-9½ / Euro 37-40. If you want smaller socks, you can work with finer yarn and smaller needles, or, for larger socks, choose a heavier yarn and bigger needles. You can also consult the various tables in the Heel section of the book (pages 12-19) for information about adjusting sizing.

In most cases, the foot length can be adjusted. The toe shaping measures 1¾-2¼ in / 4.5-6 cm long for adults and somewhat less for children's socks.

If your socks are a bit too large, you can lightly felt them if you've used pure, untreated wool. Previously, it was common to felt socks to make them both warmer and more durable.

Shoe Sizes

U. S. / Euro	Foot Length	Approx. Age
1½-5½ / 17-21	4-4¾ in / 10-12 cm	1-2 years
6-9½ 22-26	5¼-6¼ in / 13-16 cm	2-4 years
10½-13½ / 27-31	6¾-7½ in / 17-19 cm	5-6 years
1-4 / 32-36	8-8¾ in / 20-22 cm	7-10 years
6½-9½ / 37-40	9-9¾ in / 23-25 cm	Women's
8-11 / 41-44	10¼-11 in / 26-28 cm	Men's
12-15 / 45-48	11½-12¼ in / 29-31 cm	Men's XL

Casting on

There are many ways to cast on. For socks, the cast-on should be firm but not too tight. Choose a cast-on you like.

Two-Color Stranded Knitting

When knitting patterns with two or more colors, it's important that the strands aren't reversed on the wrong side. If you change the arrangement of the yarns, you'll easily see the mistake on the right side.

Yarn Floats

If you leave long floats on the inside of your knitting, it'll be all too easy to catch a toe on one. For patterns where the float is more than 5-6 stitches, I recommend that you twist the strands around each other on the wrong side. Be careful not to stack the twists because that makes little blips on the right side.

Two-End (Twined) Braid

Some of the socks feature two-end braids (sometimes called Latvian or Estonian braids). You'll need two colors for a braid, blue and white, for example.
To make a braid, work as follows:

Rnd 1: (K1 blue, k1 white) around.
Rnd 2: Bring both strands to the RS. Begin with blue and purl 1 over the previous blue stitch. Keeping the blue on the RS, move it to the right, laying it OVER the white strand. *Now bring the white strand UNDER the blue and purl 1 over the previous white stitch. Move the white to the right and OVER the blue strand. Bring the blue strand UNDER the white and purl 1. Always work blue over blue and white over white. Move the blue to the right and OVER the white.*
Repeat these 2 stitches from * to * around. End with p1 white. Throughout, the strand you pick up always comes UNDER the strand you just purled with.
As you work, the yarns will twist together. Just move the twist down and wait until the next round when, with the twists in the opposite direction, they will disappear.

The second half of the chevron braid is formed by reversing the twisting of the yarns.
Rnd 3: Begin with *purl 1 blue over the previous blue stitches. Keep the strand on the RS and to the right. Now bring the white yarn OVER the blue and purl 1. Move white to the right and beneath the blue on the RS*. Bring the blue OVER the white, p1. Leave white on RS to the right and down.
Repeat these 2 stitches, from * to * around. End with p1 white. Throughout, the yarn to be used next comes OVER the previous strand.

If you've worked the second purl round correctly, the yarns will have untwisted by the end of the round.

Entrelac
It's advantageous, when working entrelac, to have the RS always facing you. This means that you will knit towards both the right and left. Check the internet for videos on this technique.

Begin by knitting a tier of half blocks and then build tiers of whole blocks after that.

Begin each block with slipping the first st so you will have a chain along the sides. The only exception is the first stitch of the half blocks—there's only one stitch and it has to be knitted.

First Tier of Half Blocks (worked from right to left—shown in blue in the photo below):
Work 1; turn, work 1 back.
Work 2; turn, work 2 back.
Work 3; turn, work 3 back.
Continue the same way until you have the right number of sts. End by knitting all the sts towards the left.
Now you've completed the first half block. Work half blocks all around.

First Tier of Whole Blocks (white in the photo below):
Begin by picking up and knitting sts through both loops of each chain along the right edge of the first half block. Pick up the number of sts given in the pattern.
Turn, work back to the right until 1 st remains. Work this st together with the 1st st of the half block to the right.
Turn, work leftwards across block.
Turn, work rightwards until 1 st remains. Work last st together with 1st st of the half block to the right.
Continue the same way until all the sts of the half block have been worked together with sts of the new block.
The next block is worked the same way. Begin by picking up new sts from left to right.
The last st is worked together with the 1st st of the half block to the right.
Turn and work towards the left. Continue as est until all the sts of the half block have been worked together with the sts in the new block.
Continue the same way all around.

Second Tier of Whole Blocks:
Now work from left to right.
Pick up and knit sts along the chain edge of the last whole block. Continue as before, working the last st of the new block together with the first st of the block to the left. This is done by slipping the last st of the new block, work 1st of block to left and pass slipped st over (or use ssk to join sts).
Turn, work to the left.
Continue as est until block is completed and work remaining blocks of tier the same way.

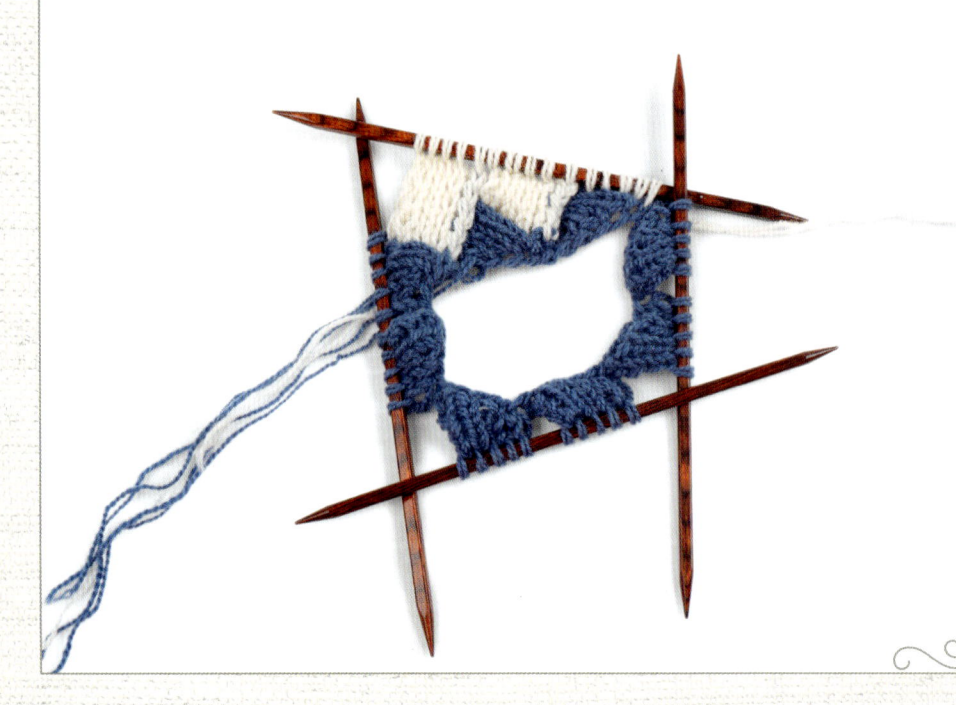

ABBREVIATIONS

BO	bind off (= British cast off)	p2tog	purl 2 stitches together = 1 stitch decreased
CC	contrast (pattern) color		
cm	centimeter(s)	pm	place marker
CO	cast on	psso	pass slipped st(s) over
dpn	double-pointed needles	rem	remain(s)(ing)
dst	double stitch (for German short rows)	rnd(s)	round(s)
est	established = continue pattern as set	RS	right side
in	inch(es)	sl	slip
k	knit	ssk	[slip 1 knitwise] 2 times, knit the 2 sts together through back loops = 1 stitch decreased; left-leaning decrease
k2tog or k3tog	knit 2 (3) together = 1 (2) stitches decreased; right-leaning decrease		
		st st	Stockinette (= British stocking stitch)
m	meter(s)	st(s)	stitch(es)
mm	millimeters	WS	wrong side
M1	make 1 = increase one stitch by picking up the yarn between two stitches with the left needle tip, from the front, and knitting directly into the back loop	wyb	with yarn held in back
		wyf	with yarn held in front
		yd	yard(s)
		yo	yarnover
MC	main (background) color		
p	purl		

HEELS

Feet are different. Some people have narrow feet and others have wide ones. The height over the instep also varies. Heels can be formed in many ways and the heel type we prefer often depends on what fits our feet best. At one point, in Norway, it was standard to use what we now call the "common" heel, with a slight diagonal at the back of the heel and a sewn, or sometimes knitted, seam at the center of the base. I've also selected a few other heel options.

Knitting heels isn't difficult but can be a little challenging the first time. Ask someone who's knitted heels before for help or check the internet, where you'll find many good instructional videos.

When preparing to knit the heel, I recommend using a length of scrap yarn or a circular needle as a holder for the instep stitches. This is because the stitches at each end will stretch less that way than if you leave them on two double-pointed needles. Using scrap yarn also helps avoid ugly holes or dropped stitches at the sides.

Chain Stitches
When making the heel flap, slip stitches at each side to form a chain along the edge. Slip the first st of each row purlwise.
The chain forms as you work back and forth on two needles. ❶

Picking Up and Knitting Stitches along a Heel Flap
You have several options for picking up stitches along a heel flap. For example, you can pick up the chain sts and place them directly on the needle without knitting them. This is the easiest method. You can also knit the sts with the working yarn. ❷ You can pick up and knit through either one or both loops of the chain. Each way works just as well. Personally, I prefer to pick up and knit stitches through both loops. You can pick up the sts through back loops (twisted) or knit them through back loops on the next round. ❸

12

HOURGLASS HEEL

This type of heel is worked back and forth with knit and purl stitches and shaped by working short rows. This means that the work is turned before the end of the row. Many people like this type of heel because it means you don't have to pick up stitches at the sides to work the foot.

How to Form the Hourglass Heel

After completing the leg, divide the stitches, placing instep stitches onto scrap yarn. These instep stitches will "rest" until the heel is complete.

Place the remaining stitches on one needle and work back and forth.
Row 1 (RS): Knit all the sts; turn.
Row 2: Sl 1, purl until 1 st rem; turn.
Row 3: Sl 1, knit until 1 st rem; turn.
Row 4: Sl 1, purl until 2 sts rem; turn.
Row 5: Sl 1, knit until 2 sts rem; turn.
Continue as est, with one st more rem at each side until approx. ⅓ of the sts rem at the center of the heel (see table to right).
The last row is worked on RS.

Sl 1, purl as many sts as were knitted on previous row. Pick up the strand between the last st and next st, twist it and then purl it together with the next st; turn.

Sl 1, knit as many sts as were purled on previous row. Pick up the strand between the last st and next st, twist it and then knit it together with the next st; turn.
Continue as est, repeating these 2 rows. Each row, you will have 1 more st before turning.
NOTE: Tighten the yarn a bit every time you turn to avoid holes.
Continue the same way with 1 more stitch on each row until the last row is worked over all the sts.

Now work around on all the stitches.

The following table can be used for socks that are shaped this way.

Total number of stitches	Stitches on instep	Stitches in center section of heel after decreasing
96	48	16
92	46	16
88	44	16
84	42	14
80	40	14
76	38	14
72	36	12
68	34	12
64	32	12
60	30	10
56	28	10
52	26	10
48	24	8
44	22	8
40	20	8
36	18	6
32	16	6
28	14	6
24	12	4
20	10	4

GUSSET HEEL

For a gusset heel, you first need to make a heel flap ending with a gusset at the base of the flap to follow the contour of your heel. The gusset's formed with short rows. Afterwards, pick up stitches along the sides of the heel flap and then decrease to eliminate the extra stitches at the same time as you begin the foot. The socks will then have a characteristic gusset at each side. This type of heel is particularly good if you have a high instep.

How to Form the Gusset Heel

After completing the leg, divide the stitches and place the instep stitches onto scrap yarn. These instep stitches will "rest" until the heel is complete.

Place the remaining stitches onto one needle and work back and forth. Begin with the WS facing you.
Row 1 (WS): Sl 1, purl to end of needle.
Row 2: Sl 1, knit to end of needle.
Repeat these 2 rows until the number of chains at each side of the flap is the same as half the stitch count on the needle (see table on next page).

Shaping the Heel

Row 1: Sl 1, purl until approx. ⅓ of the sts rem on the needle (see table—left side), p2tog, p1; turn.
Row 2: Sl 1, knit until approx. ⅓ of the sts rem on needle (see table—right side), ssk, k1; turn.
Row 3: Sl 1, purl until 1 st before gap, p2tog, p1; turn.
Row 4: Sl 1, knit until 1 st rem before gap, ssk, k1; turn.
Repeat Rows 3-4 until all the side sts have been eliminated.

Gusset Shaping

Divide the instep sts from the holder onto 2 dpn; divide the sole sts onto 2 dpn with half of the sts on each. With RS facing, begin working in the round. Begin rnd at center of sole. With Ndl 1, knit to flap; pick up and knit 1 st in each chain up side of flap. You can pick up the chain sts through back loops, or knit them through back loops on the next rnd. Work across the instep (the sts which had been "resting") with Ndls 2 and 3. Next, with Ndl 4, pick up and knit sts down opposite side of flap as for the first side. Knit to center of sole.

On the next rnd, begin decreasing to shape gusset: Knit until 2 sts rem on Ndl 1, k2tog. Work across instep sts on Ndls 2-3. On Ndl 4, ssk and then knit to end of rnd.
Work the next rnd without decreasing.
Repeat these 2 rnds until you have the same number sts as for the leg. Continue knitting foot without decreasing.

Total number of stitches	Stitches on heel flap	Chain stitches at each side of heel flap	Heel flap left side	Heel flap center	Heel flap right side
96	48	24	16	16	16
92	46	23	15	16	15
88	44	22	15	14	15
84	42	21	14	14	14
80	40	20	13	14	13
76	38	19	13	12	13
72	36	18	12	12	12
68	34	17	11	12	11
64	32	16	11	10	11
60	30	15	10	10	10
56	28	14	9	10	9
52	26	13	9	8	9
48	24	12	8	8	8
44	22	11	7	8	7
40	20	10	7	6	7
36	18	9	6	6	6
32	16	8	5	6	5
28	14	7	5	4	5
24	12	6	4	4	4
20	10	5	3	4	3

This chart can be used for socks shaped as for the Gusset Heel and on Band Heels with a long heel flap.

BAND HEEL WITH SHORT HEEL FLAP

Band heels can be made with either a short or long heel flap. Short flaps work best for people with low arches. As for a gusset heel, you first need to make a heel flap, ending with a gusset at the base of the flap to follow the contour of your heel. The gusset is formed with short rows. Afterwards, pick up stitches along the sides of the heel flap and then decrease to eliminate the extra stitches at the same time as you begin the foot.

How to Form the Band Heel
After completing the leg, divide the stitches and place the instep stitches onto scrap yarn. These instep stitches will "rest" until the heel is complete.

Place the remaining stitches onto one needle and work back and forth. Begin with the WS facing you.
Row 1 (WS): Sl 1, purl to end of needle.
Row 2: Sl 1, knit to end of needle.
Repeat these 2 rows until the number of chains at each side of the flap is the same as the appropriate count given on the table on next page.

Shaping the Heel
Row 1: Sl 1, purl until approx. ⅓ sts rem on the needle (see table—left side), p2tog; turn.
Row 2: Sl 1, knit until approx. ⅓ of the sts rem on needle (see table—right side), ssk; turn.
Row 3: Sl 1, purl until 1 st before gap, p2tog; turn.
Row 4: Sl 1, knit until 1 st before gap, ssk; turn.
Repeat Rows 3-4 until all the side sts have been eliminated.

Gusset Shaping
Divide the instep sts from the holder onto 2 dpn; divide the sole sts onto 2 dpn with half of the sts on each. With RS facing, begin working in the round. Begin rnd at center of sole. With Ndl 1, knit to flap; pick up and knit 1 st in each chain up side of flap. You can pick up the chain sts through back loops, or knit them through back loops on the next rnd. Work across the instep (the sts which had been "resting") with Ndls 2 and 3. Next, with Ndl 4, pick up and knit sts down opposite side of flap as for the first side. Knit to center of sole.

Total number of stitches	Stitches on heel flap	Chain stitches at each side of heel flap	Heel flap left side	Heel flap center	Heel flap right side
96	48	16	17	14	17
92	46	15	16	14	16
88	44	15	16	12	16
84	42	14	15	12	15
80	40	13	14	12	14
76	38	13	14	10	14
72	36	12	13	10	13
68	34	11	12	10	12
64	32	11	12	8	12
60	30	10	11	8	11
56	28	9	10	8	10
52	26	9	10	6	10
48	24	8	9	6	9
44	22	7	8	6	8
40	20	7	8	4	8
36	18	6	7	4	7
32	16	5	6	4	6
28	14	5	6	2	6
24	12	4	5	2	5

This chart can be used for socks shaped as for the Band Heel with a short heel flap.

BAND HEEL WITH LONG HEEL FLAP

Band heels with long flaps work well for those with either a high or low arch. The gusset is formed as for a band heel with a short heel flap, except the flap is worked until the number of chain stitches at each side equals half the number of stitches on the needle. Begin with a heel flap ending with a gusset at the base of the flap to follow the contour of your heel. It's formed with short rows. Afterwards, pick up stitches along the sides of the heel flap and then decrease to eliminate the extra stitches at the same time as you begin the foot. You can work the shaping one of two ways: either by making a gusset at each side as for a regular gusset heel or by centering the decreases on the sole.

How to Form the Band Heel
After completing the leg, divide the stitches and place the instep stitches onto scrap yarn. These instep stitches will "rest" until the heel is complete.

Place the remaining stitches onto one needle and work back and forth. Begin with the WS facing you.
Row 1 (WS): Sl 1, purl to end of needle.
Row 2: Sl 1, knit to end of needle.
Repeat these 2 rows until the number of chains at each side of the flap equals half the number of stitches in the heel flap. Use the same table as for the gusset heel on page 15.

Shaping the Heel
Now shape the band:
Row 1: Sl 1, purl until approx. ⅓ sts rem on the needle (see table—left side), p2tog; turn.
Row 2: Sl 1, knit until approx. ⅓ of the sts rem on needle (see table—right side), ssk; turn.
Row 3: Sl 1, purl until 1 st before gap, p2tog; turn.
Row 4: Sl 1, knit until 1 st rem before gap, ssk; turn.
Repeat Rows 3-4 until all the side sts have been eliminated.

Divide the instep sts from the holder onto 2 dpn; divide the sole sts onto 2 dpn with half of the sts on each. With RS facing, begin working in the round. Begin rnd at center of sole. With Ndl 1, knit to flap; pick up and knit 1 st in each chain up side of flap. You can pick up the chain sts through back loops, or knit them through back loops on the next rnd. Work across the instep (the sts which had been "resting") with Ndls 2 and 3. Next, with Ndl 4, pick up and knit sts down opposite side of flap as for the first side. Knit to center of sole.

See photo on page 12.

Gusset Shaping at the Sides
Knit until 2 sts remain on Ndl 1, k2tog. Work across Ndls 2-3. On Ndl 4, ssk, and knit to end of rnd. Do not decrease on the next rnd. Repeat these 2 rnds until you have the same number sts as for the leg. Continue knitting foot without decreasing.

Shaping on the Sole
Knit until 2 sts rem at the lower edge on the left side of the heel gusset, k2tog. Knit to end of needle. Work around to beginning of heel gusset, ssk before knitting the rest of the sts on the needle. Do not decrease on the next rnd. Repeat these 2 rnds until you have the same number sts as for the leg. Continue knitting foot without decreasing.

SHAPED COMMON HEEL

A gusset heel begins with a heel flap, shaped by a small gusset to follow the contour of a heel. This is made by decreasing some of the stitches and joining the rest at the center of the sole. Afterwards, stitches are picked up and knitted along each side of the heel flap. No extra stitches remain that need to be eliminated around the heel.

How to Form the Shaped Common Heel
After completing the flap, divide the stitches, placing the instep stitches on scrap yarn. These instep stitches will "rest" until the heel is complete. Common heels often have more stitches on the heel flap than on the instep—see chart.

Heel Flap
Divide the remaining stitches onto two dpn (Ndls A and B) and work back and forth. Begin with the RS facing you.
Row 1: Sl 1, knit rem sts on Ndls A and B.
Row 2: Sl 1, purl rem sts on Ndls A and B.
Repeat these 2 rows until the number of chains at each side of the flap matches the number given in the chart.

Shaping the Heel
Now you will shape the back by decreasing as follows:
Row 1: Sl 1, knit until 5 sts rem on Ndl A, k2tog, k3. On Ndl B, k3, ssk, knit to end of needle.
Row 2: Sl 1, purl to end of row.
Row 3: Sl 1, knit until 4 sts rem on Ndl A, k2tog, k2. On Ndl B, k2, ssk, knit to end of needle.
Row 4: Sl 1, purl to end of row.
Row 5: Sl 1, knit until 3 sts rem on Ndl A, k2tog, k1. On Ndl B, k1, ssk, knit to end of needle.
Row 6: Sl 1, purl to end of row.
Row 7: Sl 1, knit until 2 sts rem on Ndl A, k2tog. On Ndl B, ssk, knit to end of needle.
Row 8: Sl 1, purl to end of first needle. Yarn is now at center of heel flap.
Hold the two dpn with RS facing (so WS faces out on each side). Join the sets of sts with 3-needle BO: K2tog with 1 st from each needle, *k2tog with next st from each needle, pass first st over the second*. Repeat from * to * until 1 st loop rem.

Divide the instep sts onto 2 dpn. With RS facing and Ndl 1, beginning at the center of the sole, pick up and knit 1 st in each chain st on the side of the flap. You can pick up the chain sts through back loops or knit them tbl on the next rnd. Work the instep sts on Ndls 2-3 (those that had been "resting"). With Ndl 4, pick up and knit sts on opposite side of heel flap.

Total number of stitches	Stitches on instep	Stitches on heel flap	Chain stitches on each side of flap before decreasing
96	40	56	24
92	38	54	23
88	36	52	22
84	34	50	21
80	34	46	19
76	32	44	18
72	30	42	17
68	28	40	16
64	26	38	15
60	24	36	14
56	22	34	13
52	22	30	11
48	20	28	10
44	18	26	9
40	16	24	8
36	14	22	7
32	12	20	6

AFTERTHOUGHT HEEL

The afterthought heel is a good choice whenever your socks have heel patterning. The heel begins with a strand of scrap yarn knitted in (as for mitten thumbs) to mark the heel. After the foot is complete, you pick up stitches below and above the scrap yarn and knit in the round. You can work the heel with one or more colors.

How to Work the Afterthought Heel
Work until you reach the place for the heel. With a strand of smooth, contrast-color scrap yarn, knit half of the total number of stitches minus 2. For example, if the heel is to be worked over 20 stitches, knit 18 stitches with scrap yarn. This helps avoid holes at the sides of the heel. Place the stitches just knitted back on the left needle and knit with the working yarn. Continue working the foot.

After completing the foot, pick up the sts below and above the scrap yarn: begin 1 st to the right of the scrap yarn and end 1 st to the left of the scrap yarn so that you pick up a total of 20 sts. Turn and, with a second dpn, pick up sts as before. You should now have 40 sts around. Carefully remove the scrap yarn and divide the sts evenly onto 4 dpn.

Choose one of these two ways to shape the heel: wedge or a star-shape. These are exactly the same methods as used for toes. See the instructions on page 22.

NOTE: Some of the patterns in the book suggest modifications to these methods.

REINFORCING THE HEEL

The heel is the part of a sock that's the most likely to wear out. There are several techniques for reinforcing heels so they'll be stronger and more durable. You can knit with two colors, with reinforcing thread, doubled yarn, or knit a reinforced heel.

Reinforced Heel
Begin with WS facing you.
Row 1: Sl 1, purl to end of row.
Row 2: Sl 1, *k1, sl 1*; rep * to * to last st and end k1.
Repeat these 2 rows until you have the required number of chain sts on each side of the heel flap.
You can continue repeating these two rows for the gusset under the flap, or you can work it in st st.

Sewing in Reinforcing Thread
Another method for reinforcing the heel after the heel has been worked is to sew in reinforcing thread through the ridges on the wrong side, threading it in as if weaving in ends.

TOE SHAPING

There are a number of ways to shape toes; I've described two of the most common methods here. The length of the toe is between 1¼ and 2½ in / 4.5 and 6 cm for adult sizes and somewhat less for children.

Star Toe
Begin the round at the center of the sole.
Rnd 1: (K5, k2tog) around.
Rnds 2-6: Knit.
Rnd 7: (K4, k2tog) around.
Rnds 8-11: Knit.
Rnd 12: (K3, k2tog) around.
Rnds 13-15: Knit
Rnd 16: (K2, k2tog) around.
Rnds 17-18: Knit.
Rnd 19: (K1, k2tog) around.
Rnd 20: Knit.
Rnd 21: (K2tog) around.

Cut yarn and draw end through rem sts; tighten. If the beginning number of sts is not a multiple of 7, there will be one or more stitches left on the last needle of the first rnd. These extra stitches will be decreased on subsequent rounds.

Wedge Toe
Divide the sts with the same number on each of the 4 dpn. Begin at the center of the sole.
Rnd 1:
Ndl 1: Knit until 3 sts rem on needle, k2tog, k1.
Ndl 2: K1, ssk, knit to end of needle.
Ndl 3: Work as for Ndl 1.
Ndl 4: Work as for Ndl 2.
Rnd 2: Knit without decreasing.

Repeat these two rounds 4 times and then decrease on every rnd until 6 sts rem on each needle.

Slip the sts from Ndl 1 onto Ndl 4 and from Ndl 3 to Ndl 2 so there are 12 sts on each of the two needles. Turn the work inside out so the WS faces out. Holding the two needles together, push them out so you can work the 3-needle BO. If it's difficult to move the needles through the hole at the tip of the toe, you can move the sts onto scrap yarn before you turn the sock inside out and then place them back on the needles once the stitches are in place. Join the sets of stitches with 3-needle BO: K2tog with 1 st from each needle, *k2tog with next st from each needle, pass first st over the second*. Repeat from * to * until all sts have been joined. Cut yarn and draw end through rem st.

WEAVING IN YARN ENDS

It's important to weave in all ends well. Weave in on the wrong side by sewing through the ridges. Sew in one direction, turn, and sew back. Make sure the ends don't show on the right side.

GARMENT CARE

To ensure your socks are professionally finished, wash them in lukewarm water with a mild, wool-safe soap and then block them. You can buy a variety of sock blockers. If you don't have blockers, dry the socks flat. Pin out lace edgings, leaving pins in until socks are completely dry.

ØSTFOLD

Striped Socks from Østfold

By 1589, William Lee of Cambridge, England, had already invented a sock knitting machine that could produce several hundred stitches very quickly. An enormous demand for knitted goods spurred on technical innovations. However, Queen Elizabeth I and the British government didn't favor his invention and denied him a patent—the new machine would negatively affect the livelihoods of hand knitters.

After Lee's partner was executed in 1600, Lee fled to France and the French king did award Lee a patent, thus giving the French stocking industry a huge advantage.

The first knitting machines came to Norway in the 1700s. These machines were based on Lee's invention and used primarily for producing stockings and caps. Handworkers who operated the machines became known as "stocking weavers." Since then, hand and machine knitting have existed side by side.

A pair of socks from Østfold, catalogued in The Norwegian Institute of Bunad and Folk Costume, was most likely knitted by machine. The decreases on the foot are proof of that.

These socks were worn by a farmer from Askim (born in 1867), likely during what's known as "the neutrality guard" in 1905: at the turn of the century, there was a danger of war with Sweden, and several divisions of the army began keeping guard along the Swedish border. However, war was averted and the union between Norway and Sweden was dissolved in June of the same year.

The original socks were knitted in stockinette (stocking stitch) with black and white wool yarn. The inside is lined with loops sewn on with natural white wool. A brown cotton band is attached, with a metal clasp at the top of the leg. The band kept the socks from sliding down. These socks must have been especially warm because of the looped lining, and they were likely pulled on over shoes.

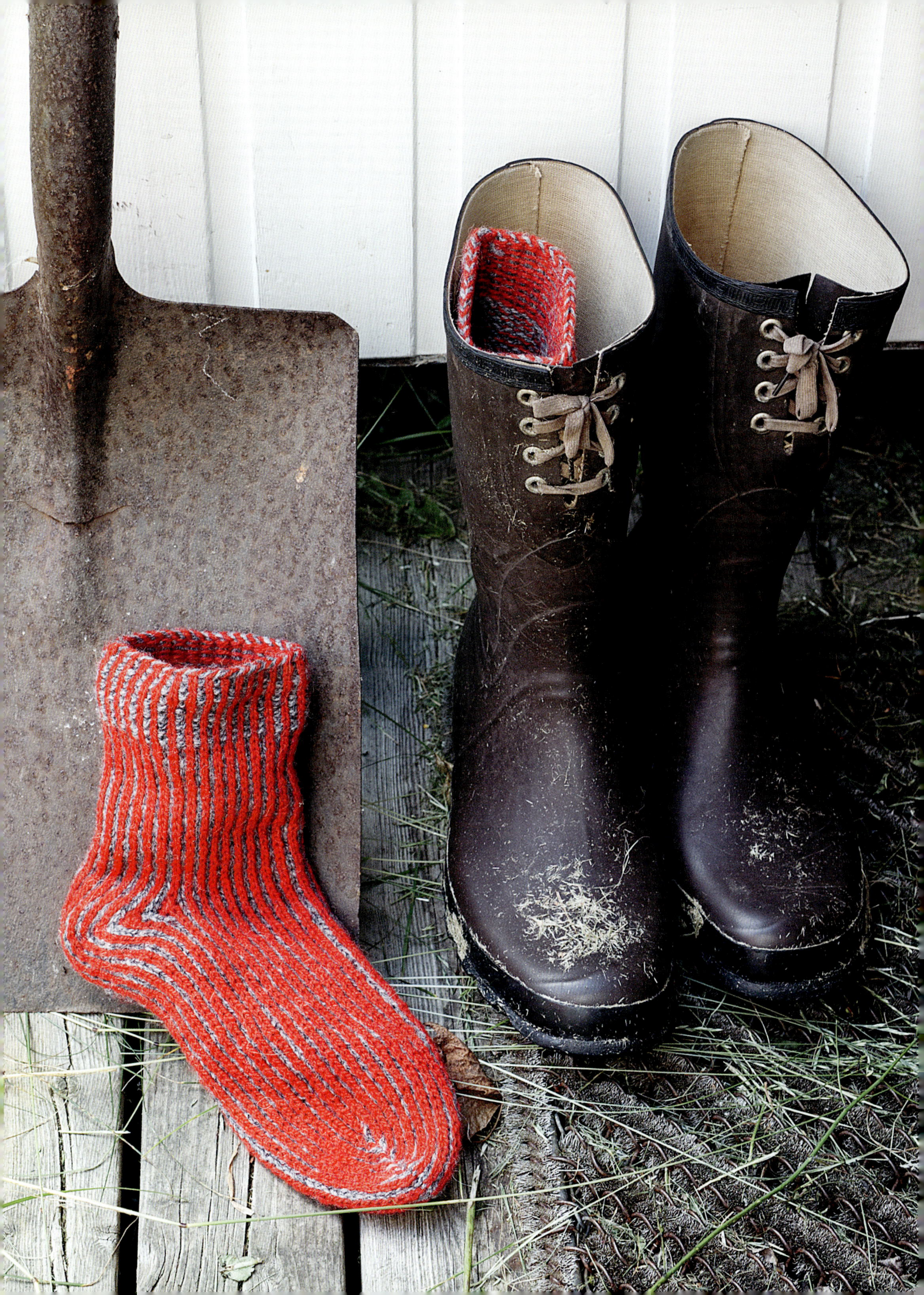

TOE

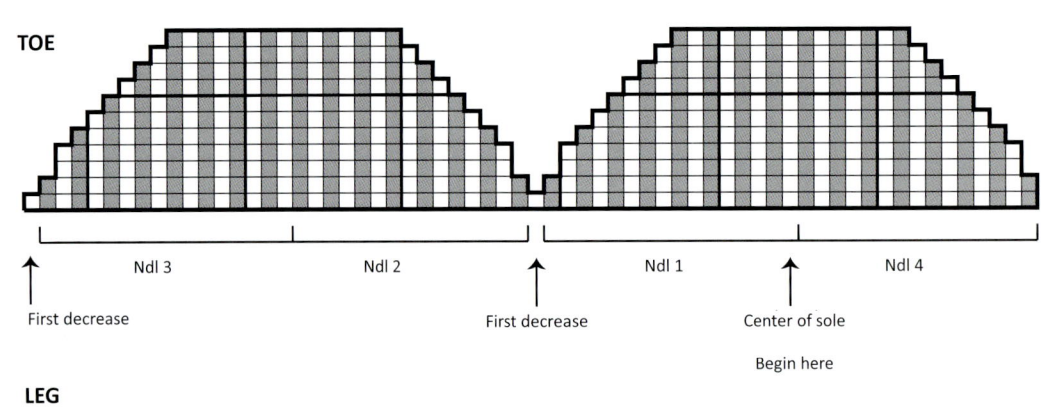

Ndl 3 | Ndl 2 | Ndl 1 | Ndl 4

↑ First decrease ↑ First decrease ↑ Center of sole

Begin here

LEG

Repeat

Ribbing

Repeat

☐ Red—knit
▨ Gray—knit
☒ Gray—purl

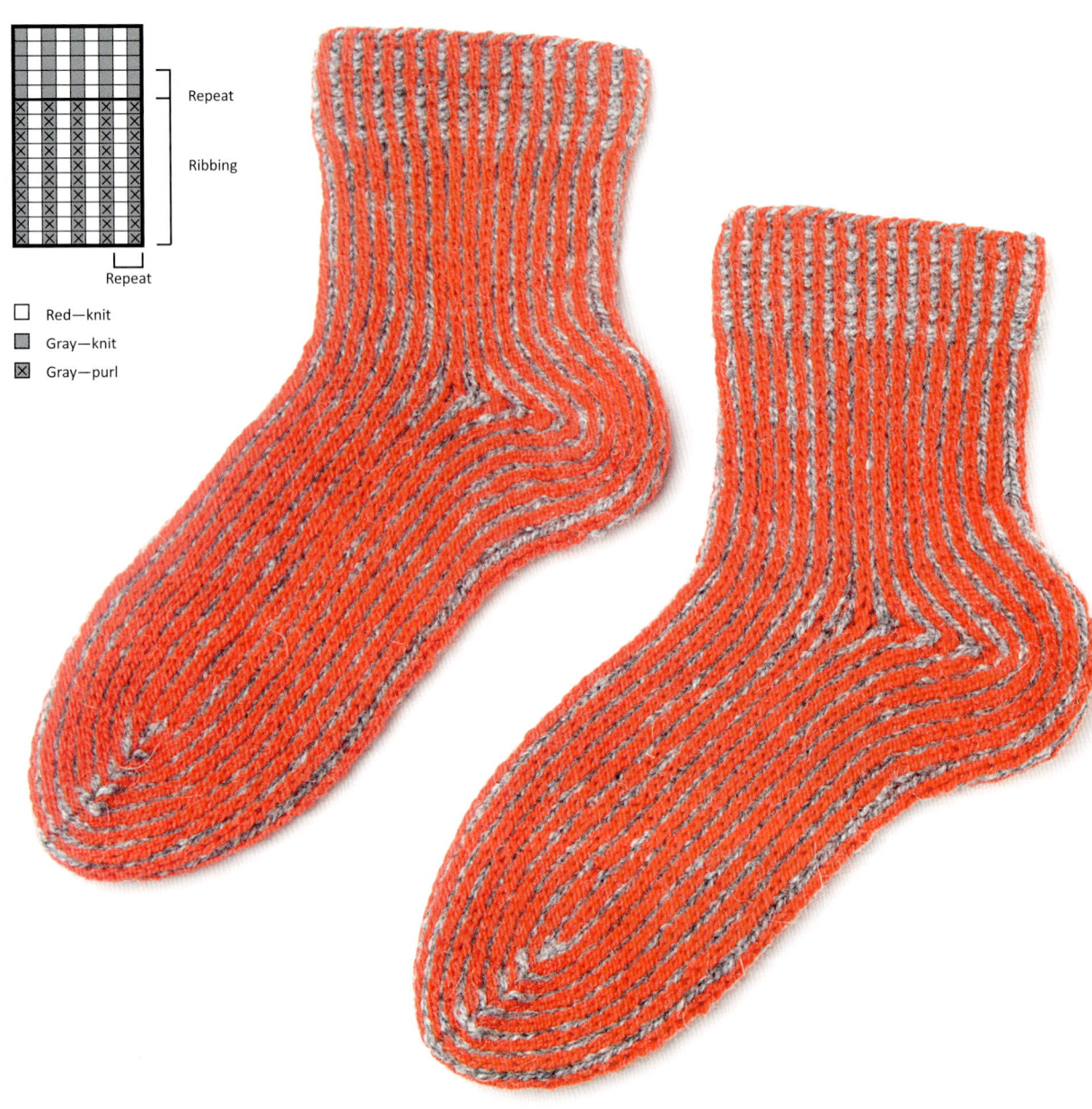

26

INSTRUCTIONS

Skill Level: Experienced

Sizes: Women's (Men's)

MATERIALS
Yarn: CYCA #2 (sport/4 ply), Fjord Sock from Hillesvåg Ullvarefabrikk (80% Norwegian wool, 20% nylon, 273 yd/250 m / 100 g)

Yarn Colors and Amounts:
Red 03505: 100 (100) g
Dark Gray 03130: 100 (100) g

Needles: U. S. size 2.5 (4) / 3 (3.5) mm: set of 5 dpn

Gauge: 30 (28) sts in pattern = 4 in / 10 cm. Adjust needle size to obtain correct gauge if necessary.

LEG
CO 64 sts, alternating Red and Gray, using two strands of each color as follows:
Make a slip knot with 2 strands of Red and another slip knot with 2 strands of Gray. Arrange the yarn so the two Red strands are between the two Gray strands and then CO 1 new st. Now bring the 2 Gray strands out between the 2 Red ones and CO 1 new st. Repeat until you have the right stitch count. (You can also cast on with Red only and then K1 Red, k1 Gray on the first rnd.)

(K1 Red (dominant color), p1 Gray) around for 10 rnds. Now work (k1 Red, k1 Gray) around until leg measures 5¼ in / 13 cm. See chart.

HOURGLASS HEEL
Divide the sts, placing 32 sts for the instep on scrap yarn. These sts will "rest" until the heel is finished.

Arrange rem 32 sts on one dpn and work back and forth with Red over Red and Gray over Gray.
Row 1: Knit across; turn.
Row 2: Sl 1, purl until 1 st rem; turn.
Row 3: Sl 1, knit until 1 st rem; turn.
Row 4: Sl 1, purl until 2 sts rem; turn.
Row 5: Sl 1, knit until 2 sts rem; turn.
Continue the same way with 1 less st before each turn until 18 sts rem at the center of the heel. Knit the last row.
Sl 1, purl as many sts as were last knitted (18). Pick up the strand between the last and next st, twist it and purl it tog with the next st; turn.
Sl 1, knit as many sts as last worked (18), Pick up the strand between the last st and the next, twist it and knit it together with the next st; turn.
Continue, repeating these 2 rows. You should have 1 more st each time before you turn.
NOTE: Tighten the yarn a bit each time you turn to avoid holes.
Continue with 1 st more on each row until you work across all 32 sts on the last row. There should be a total of 64 sts around.

Now work around on all sts until the foot is 7 (8¾) in / 18 (22) cm long or desired length before toe shaping.

WEDGE TOE
See chart: Decrease 1 red st at *each* side so that 31 sts each remain on instep and sole. Knit 1 rnd without decreasing.
Divide the sts, with 16 sts on Ndl 1 (begin counting at center of sole), 15 sts on Ndl 2, 16 sts on Ndl 3, and 15 sts on Ndl 4.
Ndl 1: Knit until 2 sts rem on needle, k2tog tbl with Red.
Ndl 2: K2tog with Red, knit to end of needle.
Ndl 3: Work as for Ndl 1.
Ndl 4: Work as for Ndl 2.
Knit 2 rnds without decreasing and then work as shown on the chart until 15 sts *each* rem on instep and sole. Move the sts for instep onto one dpn and the sole sts onto a second dpn.

Turn the work inside out so the WS faces out. Holding the two needles together, push them out so you can work the 3-needle BO. If it's difficult to move the needles through the hole at the tip of the toe, you can move the sts onto scrap yarn before you turn the sock inside out and then place them back on the needles once the stitches are in place.
With Gray, join the sets of stitches with 3-needle BO:
K2tog with 1 st from each needle, *k2tog with next st from each needle, pass first st over the second*. Repeat from * to * until all sts have been joined. Cut yarn and draw end through rem st.

FINISHING
Weave in all ends neatly on WS. Make the second sock the same way.

Star Socks

Many people believe the eight-petal rose motif is Norwegian, or that it comes from Selbu—hence its other name, the Selbu Rose. However, this isn't true. We have found eight-petal roses on the oldest known European knitted textiles, including Spanish pillow covers from the 11th century.

In the first printed pattern book, published at the beginning of the 14th century, you can also find eight-petal roses arranged in various compositions.

Here in Norway, we have a collection of exclusive nightshirts made at the end of the 15th century. The garments were knitted with expensive silk and are embellished with beautiful gold and silver embroidery. The background pattern has eight-petal roses arranged diagonally in block netting. Only knit and purl stitches were used to emphasize the pattern. We don't know where each garment was made, but they were most likely imported.

The eight-petal rose motif wasn't reserved for knitting alone. We can find it in woven and embroidered textiles, and it was also frequently used in woodwork. The pattern is based on an octagram and was used over large parts of the world.

The eight-petal roses in these socks are more condensed in shape than usual and look more star-like.

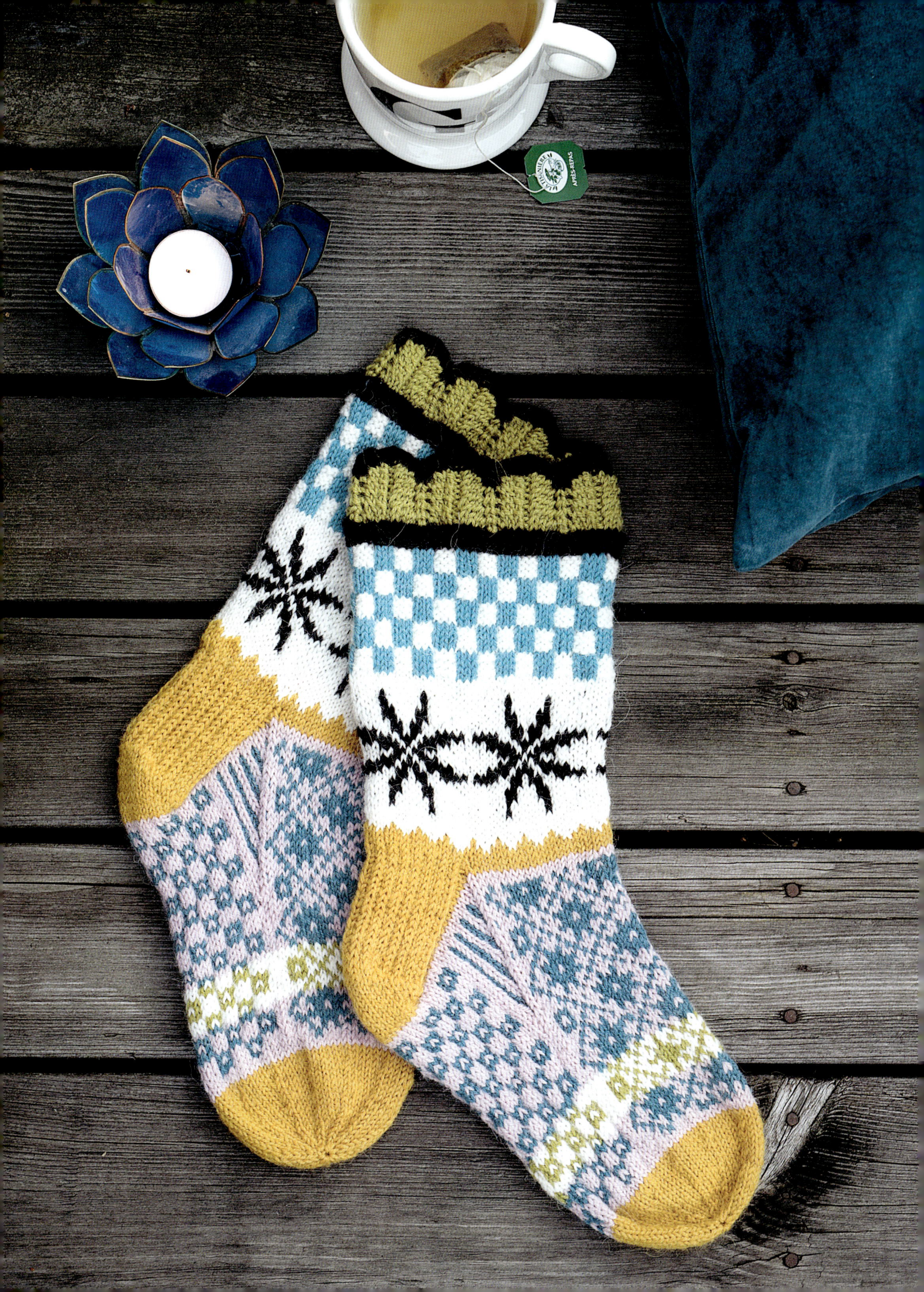

Color 1 (Black)—knit
Color 2 (Yellow-Green)—knit
Color 3 (Natural)—knit
Color 3 (Natural)—purl
Color 4 (Turquoise)—knit
Color 5 (Dark Sea Green)—knit
Color 6 (Gold)—knit
Color 7 (Light Pink)—knit

CHART 4
Women's large

CHART 4
Women's small

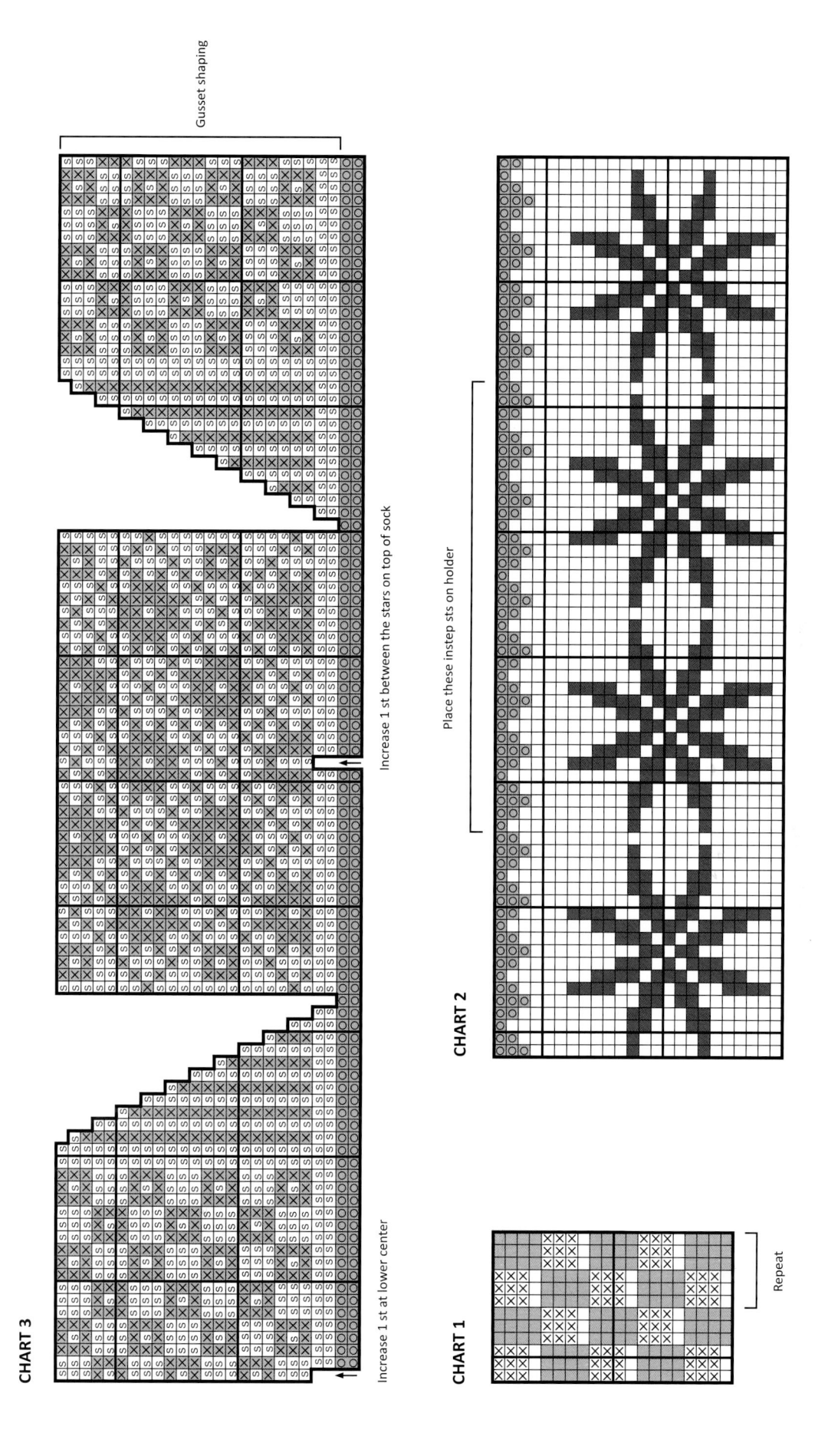

CHART 3

Gusset shaping

Increase 1 st between the stars on top of sock

Increase 1 st at lower center

CHART 2

Place these instep sts on holder

CHART 1

Repeat

INSTRUCTIONS

Skill Level: Experienced

Sizes: Women's small, U. S. shoe sizes 5-8 / Euro 35-38 (Women's large, U. S. sizes 8½-11 / Euro 39-42)

MATERIALS
Yarn: CYCA #1 (fingering/2 ply), Mini Sterk from Du Store Alpakka (40% alpaca, 40% Merino wool, 20% polyamide, 182 yd/166 m / 50 g)

Yarn Colors and Amounts:
A total of approx. 150 g
50 g each:
Black 809
Yellow-Green 843
Natural 806
Turquoise 834
Dark Sea Green 857
Golden Yellow 835
Light Pink 850

Needles: U. S. size 0 (1.5) / 2 (2.5) mm: set of 5 dpn

Gauge: 32 (30) sts in pattern = 4 in / 10 cm. Adjust needle size to obtain correct gauge if necessary.

LEG
With Black, CO 70 (80) sts. Divide sts as evenly as possible onto 4 dpn. Join, being careful not to twist cast-on row. Pm for beginning of rnd.
Rnd 1: *K2tog, k2, yo, k1, yo, k2, k2tog tbl, p1*; rep * to * around. The repeat is a multiple of 10 sts.
Rnd 2: *K9, p1*; rep from * to * around.
Change to Golden Yellow and rep Rnds 1-2 a total of 5 times.
Change to Black and knit 1 rnd, purl 1 rnd.
Eyelet Rnd: (K2tog, yo) around.
Knit 1 rnd.
Purl 1 rnd, increasing 2 sts evenly spaced on rnd for the small size and decreasing 2 sts evenly spaced for the large size = 72 (78) sts.

Change to Natural and Turquoise and work the block pattern as shown on Chart 1 (a total of 20 rnds).

Next, knit 1 rnd with Natural.
On the next rnd, decrease 0 (6) sts evenly spaced around = 72 (72) sts rem. Knit 1 more rnd Natural and then work the Star pattern as shown on Chart 2 (see note below), ending with the Zigzag panel with Golden Yellow.

NOTE: There are long yarn floats in this section, and it's important to remember to twist the strands around each other on the WS. Make sure the yarn twists don't stack vertically.

REINFORCED HEEL
Place the 36 (36) sts for instep on scrap yarn (see Chart 2). These sts will "rest" while you work the heel flap.

Place the rem 36 (36) sts on one dpn and work the heel flap back and forth with Golden Yellow. Begin with WS facing you.
Row 1 (WS): Sl 1 purlwise wyf, purl to end of row.
Row 2: Sl 1 purlwise wyb, *k1, sl 1 purlwise wyb*; rep * to * to last st, end k1.
Repeat these 2 rows until there are 18 chain sts on each side of flap.

Shaping Heel Gusset
Row 1: Sl 1, purl until 12 sts rem, p2tog, p1; turn.
Row 2: Sl 1, knit until 12 sts rem, ssk, k1; turn.
Row 3: Sl 1, purl until 1 st before gap, p2tog, p1; turn.
Row 4: Sl 1, knit until 1 st before gap, ssk, k1; turn.
Rep Rows 3-4 until all the side sts have been eliminated = 24 sts rem.

Divide the instep sts onto 2 dpn and divide the rem heel sts onto 2 dpn so you have half of each section on a needle. Now work in the round with RS facing you.

Begin rnd at center of heel. K12. Pick up and knit 1 st in each chain st along side of heel flap = 18 (18) sts. You can pick up the sts tbl or knit them tbl on next rnd. Knit across instep. Pick up and knit 1 st in each chain st of opposite side of flap = 18 (18) sts and knit to beginning of rnd at center of sole (12 sts).

On the next rnd, begin shaping the gusset: Knit until 2 sts rem on Ndl 1, k2tog. Work across Ndls 2-3. At beginning of Ndl 4, ssk and knit to end of rnd. Read notes before you start shaping the gusset.

Change to Pink and knit 1 rnd without decreasing.
Work following Chart 3 and continue decreasing on every other rnd as est.

NOTE 1: After working 2 rnds with Pink, increase 1 st at center of instep, between the two stars = 37 sts for instep. Also increase 1 st at center of sole—see Chart 3.

NOTE 2: Work all decreases for the gusset with Pink, both when you k2tog on Ndl 1 and, on Ndl 4, sl 1, k1 Pink, and then psso.

FOOT
After gusset is complete, 74 sts rem. Continue in pattern following Chart 4.
NOTE: There are two different charts, one for size Small and one for Large.
For Size Small: decrease 2 sts to 72 sts.

STAR TOE
Continue with Pink *at the same time* as you begin decreasing for the star toe:
Begin at the center of the sole.
Rnd 1: (K5, k2tog) around. The 2 (4) sts rem on Ndl 4 will be decreased in subsequent rnds.
Rnd 2: Knit.
Rnds 3-6: Change to Golden Yellow and knit.
Rnd 7: (K4, k2tog) around.
Rnds 8-11: Knit.
Rnd 12: (K3, k2tog) around.
Rnds 13-15: Knit
Rnd 16: (K2, k2tog) around.
Rnds 17-18: Knit.
Rnd 19: (K1, k2tog) around.
Rnd 20: Knit.
Rnd 21: (K2tog) around.

FINISHING
Cut yarn and draw end through rem sts; tighten. Weave in all ends neatly on WS. Make the second sock the same way.

AKERSHUS

Rose Stockings from Asker

In a bag of assorted woolens that were stored away, I found my father-in-law's old ski stockings. They were from a time when it was common to wear knickerbockers and patterned stockings for skiing and they likely came from the period right after the war or the beginning of the 1950s. Later on, he wore stretch ski pants—before knickerbockers once again became popular.

The stockings are knitted with natural sheep's black and white wool and are slightly felted. The heel (a type of common heel seamed at the center of the sole) is quite worn and darned with brown yarn. Someone also tried to repair the tip of the stockings.

I'm reasonably sure the stockings were knitted by my husband's grandmother, Otilie Sæther, née Rønsen (1880-1964). She was originally from Eidsvoll and came to Asker in 1905 when the Dikemark hospital was ready. She trained as a Red Cross sister and worked as a nurse, first in Dikemark and then at the Blakstad hospital. She often knitted stockings.

Patterned knickerbocker stockings were certainly popular when sports heroes were beginning to wear Selbu stockings. The Norwegian Olympic teams in 1948, 1952, 1960, and 1964 were outfitted with knitted garments from the Selbu Handcraft Association.

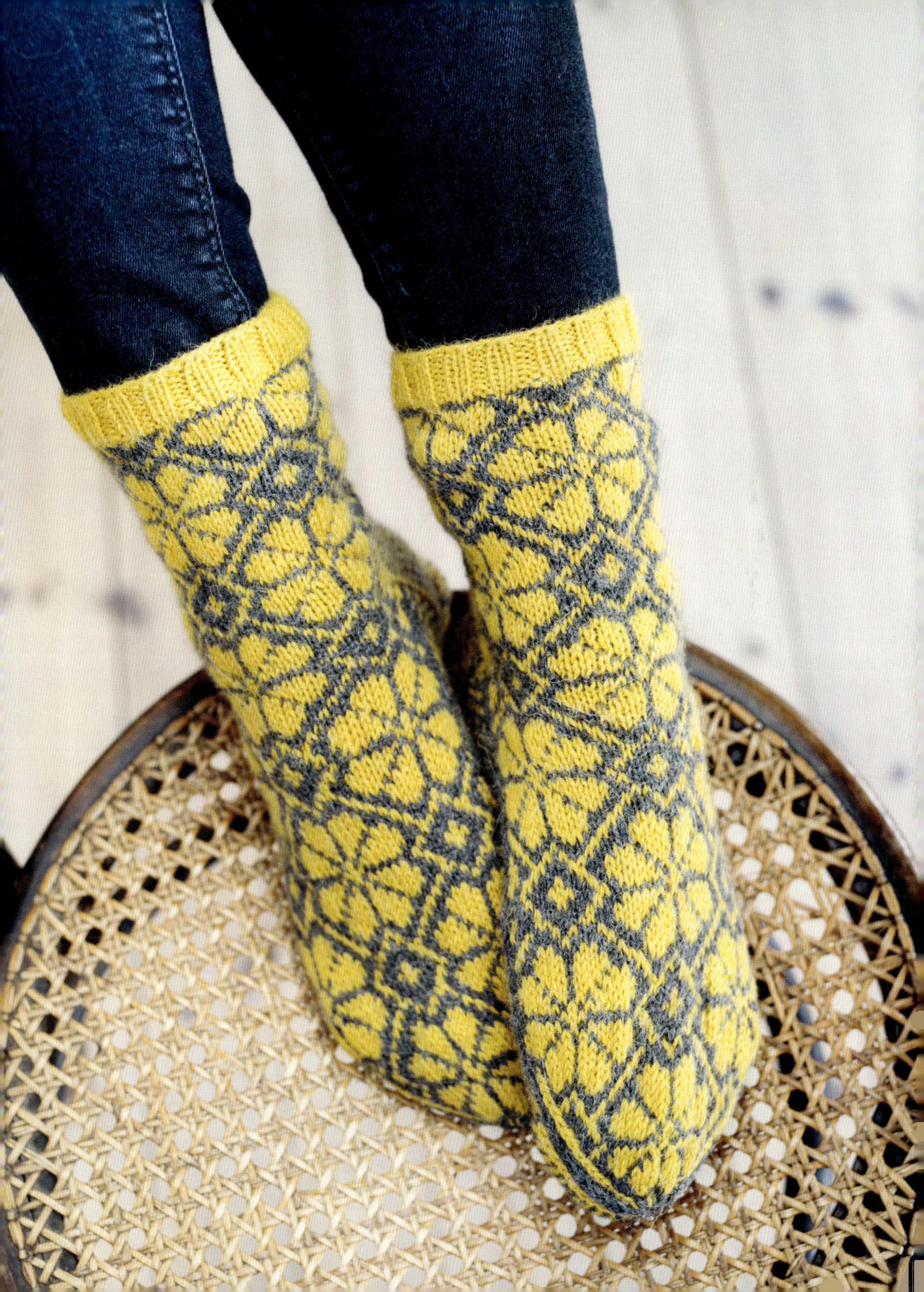

FOOT

↑ CO an extra st   ↑ CO an extra st

LEG

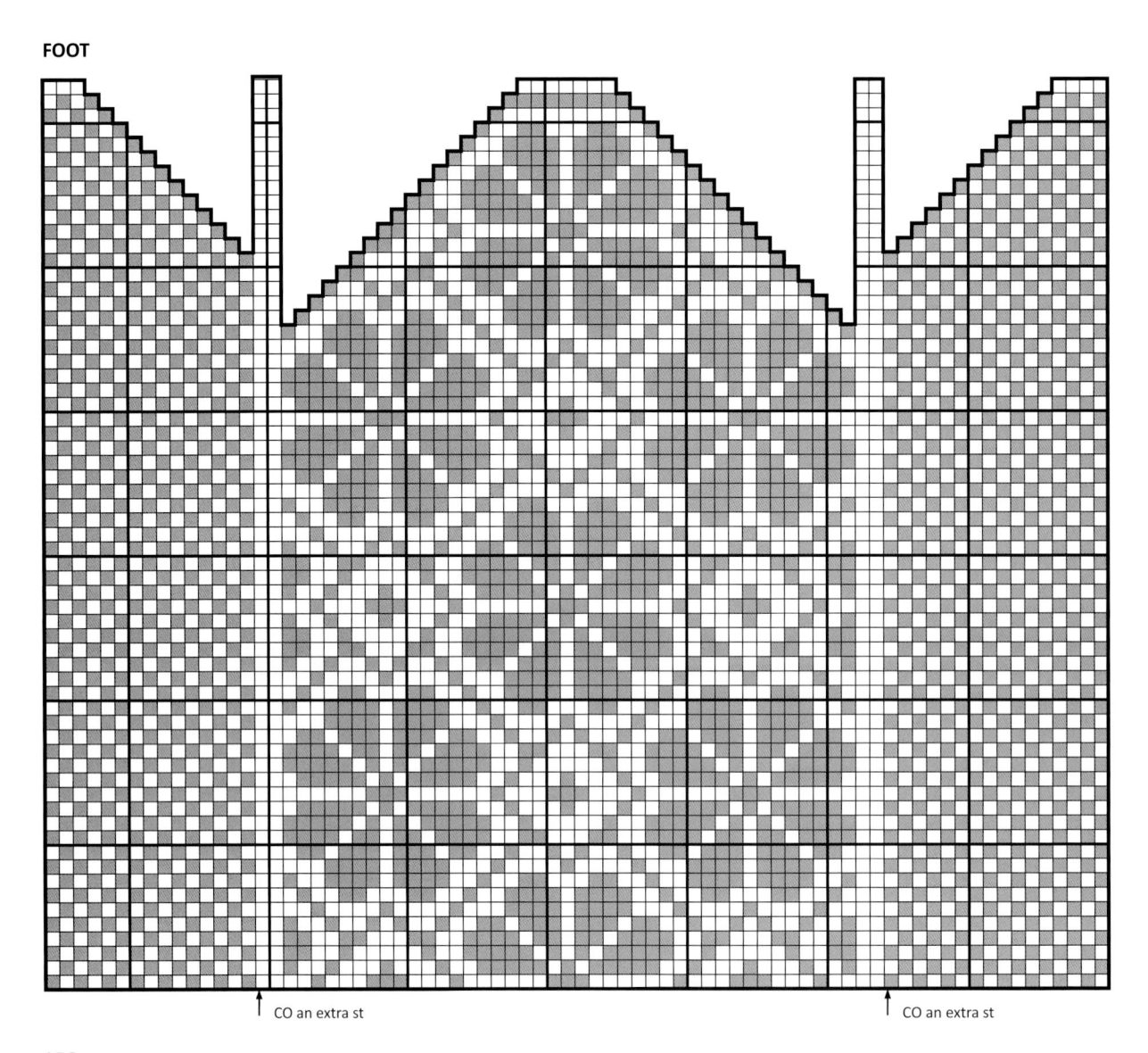

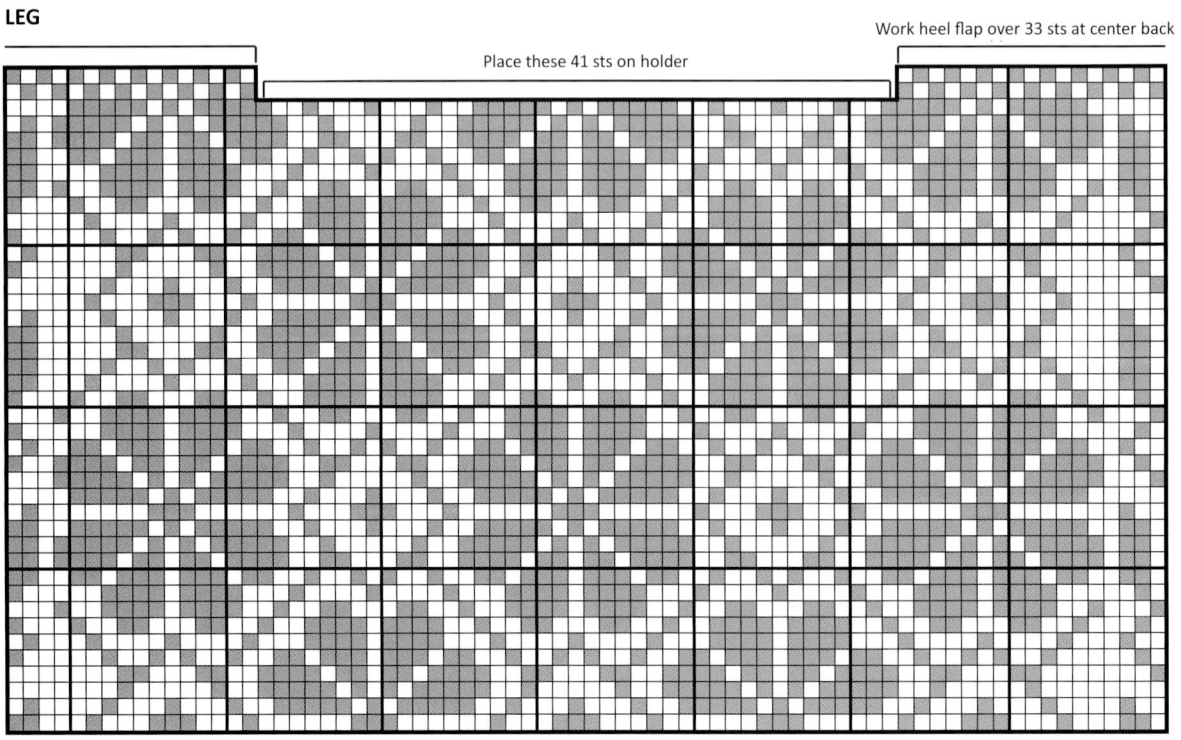

Work heel flap over 33 sts at center back

Place these 41 sts on holder

■ Charcoal Gray 807
□ Golden Yellow 835

CO 74 sts

INSTRUCTIONS

Skill Level: Experienced

Sizes: Women's (Men's)

MATERIALS
Yarn: CYCA #1 (fingering/2 ply), Mini Sterk from Du Store Alpakka (40% alpaca, 40% Merino wool, 20% polyamide, 182 yd/166 m / 50 g)

Yarn Colors and Amounts:
Charcoal Gray 807: 50 (100) g
Golden Yellow 835: 50 (100) g

Needles: U. S. size 1.5 (2.5) / 2.5 (3) mm: set of 5 dpn

Gauge: 34 (32) sts in pattern = 4 in / 10 cm. Adjust needle size to obtain correct gauge if necessary.

LEG
With Golden Yellow, CO 72 sts. Divide sts evenly onto 4 dpn. Join, being careful not to twist cast-on row. Pm for beginning of rnd. Work 8 rnds of k2, p2 ribbing. Knit 1 rnd, increasing 2 sts evenly spaced around = 74 sts. Now work following Leg chart.

After completing leg, place 41 sts on scrap yarn for the instep (see chart). These sts will "rest" until the heel is finished.

BAND HEEL
Place the rem 33 sts on one dpn and work the heel flap back and forth with two colors as shown on the chart.
Begin with WS facing you.
Row 1 (WS): Sl 1 purlwise wyf, purl to last st, end p1 with both colors.
Row 2: Sl 1 purlwise wyb, knit to last st, end k1 with both colors.
Rep these 2 rows until there are 12 chain sts at each side of flap.

Now decrease to shape the band:
Row 1: Sl 1, purl until 12 sts rem, p2tog with both colors; turn.
Row 2: Sl 1, knit until 12 sts rem, ssk with both colors; turn.
Row 3: Sl 1, purl until 1 st before gap, p2tog with both colors; turn.
Row 4: Sl 1, knit until 1 st before gap, ssk with both colors; turn.

Rep Rows 3-4 until all the side sts have been eliminated = 11 sts rem.

FOOT
Divide the instep sts onto 2 dpn and divide the rem heel sts onto 2 dpn so you have half of each section on a needle. Now work in the round with RS facing you. Begin rnd at center of heel. Work, alternating colors—see chart. Knit to flap. Pick up and knit 1 st in each chain st along side of heel flap. You can pick up the sts tbl or knit them tbl on next rnd. Work across instep following chart. Pick up and knit 1 st, alternating colors, in each chain st of opposite side of flap and then complete rnd as est = 76 sts total.

Work the foot following the chart.

TOE
Shape toe as shown on the chart. To decrease at right side: ssk with Golden Yellow. To decrease at left side: k2tog with Golden Yellow.

FINISHING
Cut yarn and draw end through rem sts; tighten. Weave in all ends neatly on WS. Make the second sock the same way.

Oslo Socks

The Norwegian Museum of Cultural History has five white cotton children's stockings in its collection. The socks are all different, but still similar enough to belong to the same "family." Small details indicate that they were most likely knitted by the same person—for example, the yarn, heel shaping, stitches, and seaming at center back of those socks which were knitted back and forth. Several of the socks have initials and numbers embroidered with small red cross stitches. These are somewhat hard to decipher, but G and 3 are obvious on one; AG and 15 on another; perhaps a J or G on a third; and G together with 18 or 78 on the fourth. The museum acquired the stockings in 1994 but estimates they were knitted in the 1890s.

Since there's only one stocking of each type and the stockings seem to have been numbered, I imagine these are stockings in a series made to help someone learn how to knit. The stockings have much in common with models we know were used for practice in school between 1850 and 1900. On the other hand, several of the stockings appear to have been worn. The heels show wear and tear and a couple have been darned.

As a starting point for my interpretation of the stockings, I took the stitch pattern from one of the stockings but made mine in fine wool yarn.

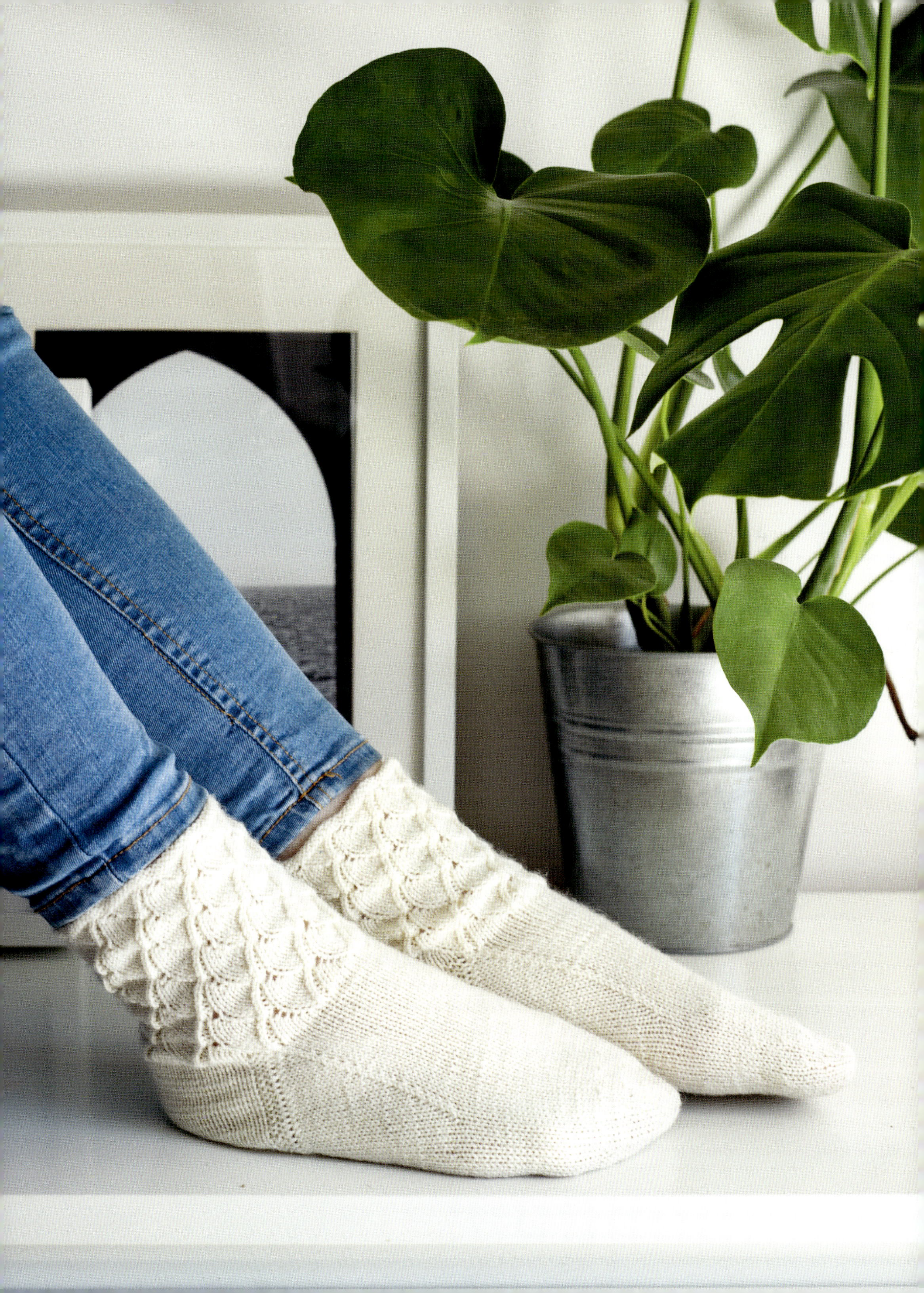

- Knit
- ☒ Purl
- ◯ Yarnover (yo)
- ╱ K2tog

Repeat

INSTRUCTIONS

Skill Level: Intermediate

Size: Women's

MATERIALS

Yarn: CYCA #1 (fingering/2 ply), Baby Panda from Rauma Ullvarefabrikk (100% Merino wool, 191 yd/175 m / 50 g), White 11: 100 g

Needles: U. S. size 0 / 2 mm: set of 5 dpn

Gauge: 32 sts in pattern = 4 in / 10 cm. Adjust needle size to obtain correct gauge if necessary.

LEG

CO 81 sts. Divide sts as evenly as possible onto 4 dpn. Join, being careful not to twist cast-on row. Pm for beginning of rnd—the pattern shifts to the right, so it's important to maintain the beginning of rnd marker. Knit 4 rnds. Turn work so WS faces you and continue, following the chart or the description below until piece measures approx. 4¾ in / 12 cm.

Pattern Repeat (multiple of 9 sts)

Rnd 1: *P1, yo, k6, k2tog*; rep * to * around.
Rnd 2: *P1, k1, yo, k5, k2tog*; rep * to * around.
Rnd 3: *P1, k2, yo, k4, k2tog*; rep * to * around.
Rnd 4: *P1, k3, yo, k3, k2tog*; rep * to * around.
Rnd 5: *P1, k4, yo, k2, k2tog*; rep * to * around.
Rnd 6: *P1, k5, yo, k1, k2tog*; rep * to * around.
Rnd 7: *P1, k6, yo, k2tog*; rep * to * around.

HEEL

After completing sock leg, place 41 sts on scrap yarn for instep. These sts will "rest" until the heel is finished.

Heel Flap

Place the rem 40 sts on one dpn and work the heel flap back and forth.
Begin with WS facing you.
Row 1 (WS): Sl 1 purlwise wyf, k2, p34, k3.
Row 2: Sl 1 purlwise wyb, knit across.
Rep these 2 rows until there are 20 chain sts at each side of flap.

Shaping Heel Gusset

Row 1: Sl 1, purl until 14 sts rem, p2tog, p1; turn.
Row 2: Sl 1, knit until 14 sts rem, ssk, k1; turn.
Row 3: Sl 1, purl until 1 st before gap, p2tog, p1; turn.
Row 4: Sl 1, knit until 1 st before gap, ssk, k1; turn.
Rep Rows 3-4 until all the side sts have been eliminated.

Gusset

Divide the instep sts onto 2 dpn and divide the rem heel sts onto 2 dpn so you have half of each section on a needle. Now work in the round with RS facing you. Begin rnd at center of heel. Knit to flap. Pick up and knit 1 st in each chain st along side of heel flap. You can pick up the sts tbl or knit them tbl on next rnd. Work across instep, rep (k2tog, k6) 4 times and ending with k2tog, and, *at the same time*, slip all yarnovers from last pattern rnd off needle (total of 5 sts) = 31 sts rem on instep. Pick up and knit 1 st in each chain st of opposite side of flap and knit to beginning of rnd at center of sole.

On the next rnd, begin shaping the gusset:
Knit until 2 sts rem on Ndl 1, k2tog. Knit across Ndls 2-3. At beginning of Ndl 4, ssk and knit to end of rnd.
Knit 1 rnd without decreasing. Rep these 2 rnds until 64 sts rem. Continue in st st without decreasing until foot measures 7 in / 18 cm or desired length to toe shaping.

STAR TOE

Begin at the center of the sole.
Rnd 1: (K5, k2tog) around. The 1 st rem on Ndl 4 will be decreased in subsequent rnds.
Rnds 2-6: Knit.
Rnd 7: (K4, k2tog) around.
Rnds 8-11: Knit.
Rnd 12: (K3, k2tog) around.
Rnds 13-15: Knit
Rnd 16: (K2, k2tog) around.
Rnds 17-18: Knit.
Rnd 19: (K1, k2tog) around.
Rnd 20: Knit.
Rnd 21: (K2tog) around.

FINISHING

Cut yarn and draw end through rem sts; tighten. Weave in all ends neatly on WS. Make the second sock the same way.

OSLO

Stockings from 1868

In 1916, the Norwegian Museum of Cultural History acquired a pair of small children's stockings with red motifs on a white background. The records reveal only sparse details: "period of 1868-70." The stockings were knitted with very fine wool and marked with the initials K. F. H.

The Folk Museum was founded in 1894 after an initiative by the librarian and museum curator Hans Aall. His model was the Nordic Museum in Stockholm, which had already been established in 1873. Aall's vision was for a Norwegian parallel to collect and exhibit "everything that illustrated Norwegian Folk Cultural Life."

The museum opened in an apartment on Christian IV Street in 1896 and, two years later, a plot of land was purchased on Bygdøy for the planned open-air museum.

When Aall and his staff began to collect items for the museum, it was the items themselves that were the point, not information about the use or user, so we know very little about the oldest items in these collections.

The red motifs on the stockings have a characteristic shape and can be interpreted as pinwheeling flowers.

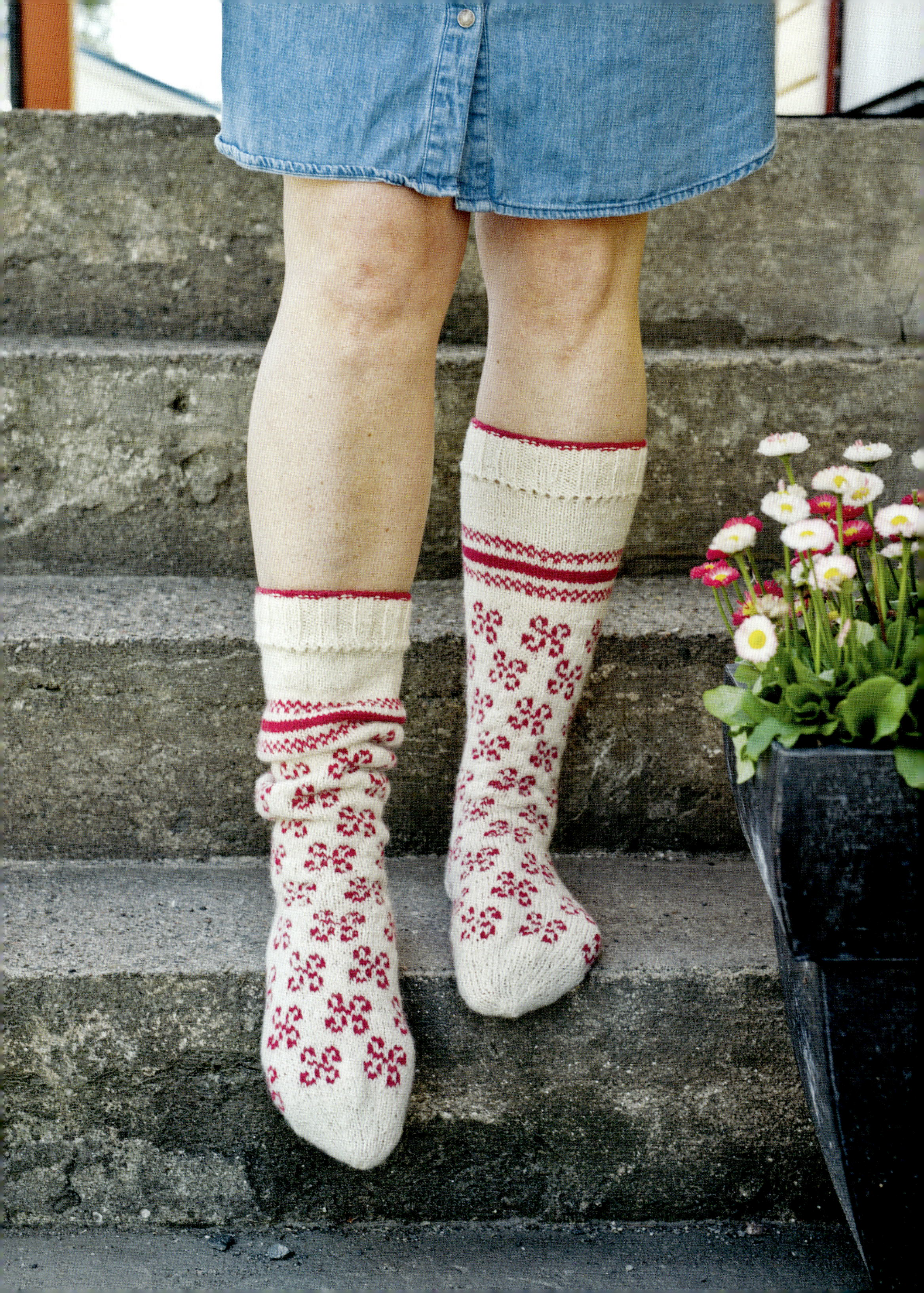

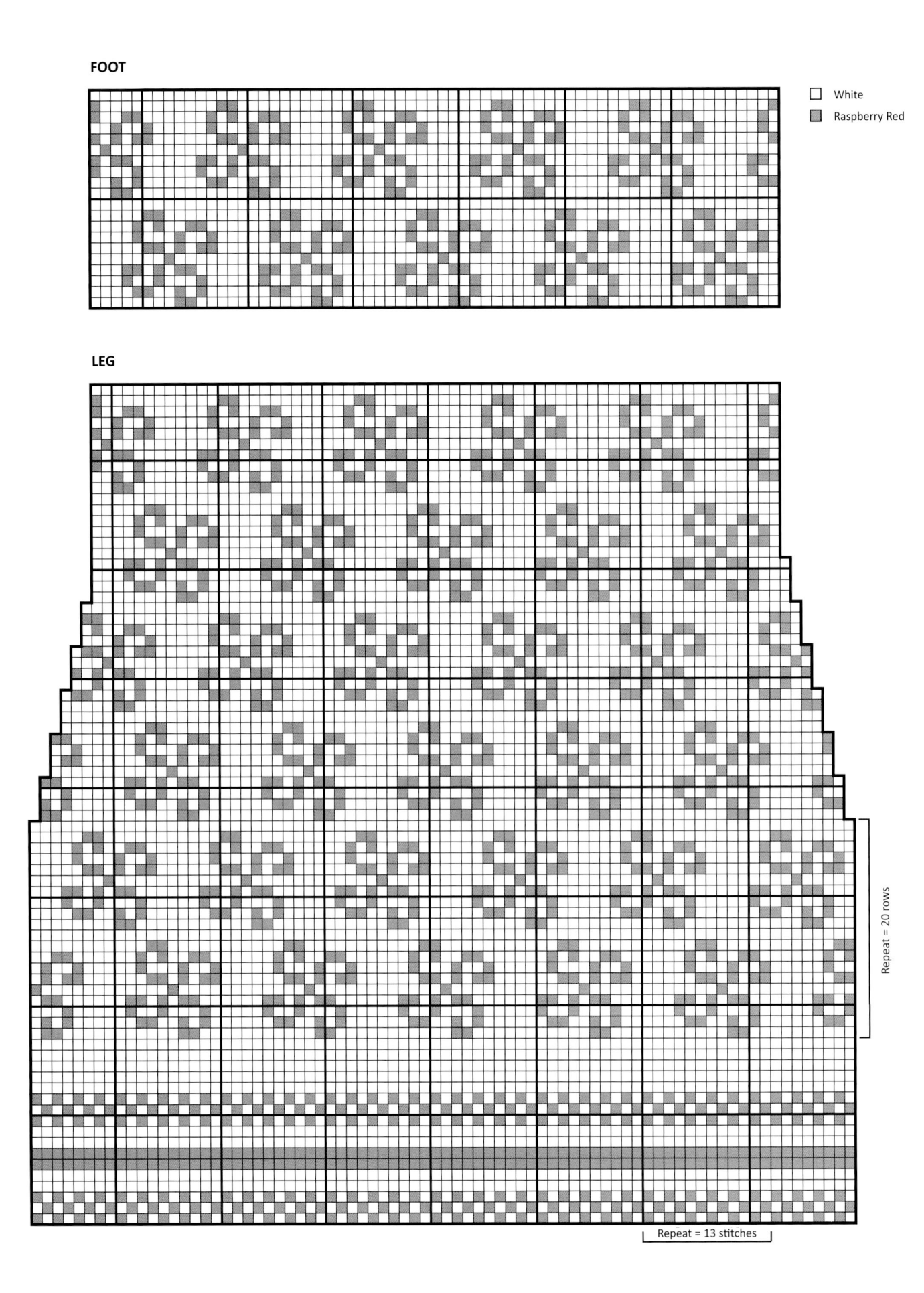

FOOT

LEG

White
Raspberry Red

Repeat = 20 rows

Repeat = 13 stitches

INSTRUCTIONS

Skill Level: Experienced

Size: Women's

MATERIALS
Yarn:
CYCA #1 (fingering/2 ply), 2-ply Gammelserie from Rauma (100% wool, 175 yd/160 m / 50 g), White 401: 100 g

CYCA #1 (fingering/2 ply), Finullgarn from Rauma (100% wool, 191 yd/175 m / 50 g), Raspberry Red 456: 100 g

Needles:
U. S. size 1.5 / 2.5 mm: set of 5 dpn

Gauge: 28 sts in pattern = 4 in / 10 cm. Adjust needle size to obtain correct gauge if necessary.

LEG
With Red, CO 78 sts. Divide sts as evenly as possible onto 4 dpn. Join, being careful not to twist cast-on row; pm for beginning of rnd. Knit 1 rnd. Change to White and work in k3, p3 ribbing for 15 rnds.
Purl 1 rnd.
Next, work an eyelet rnd: (k2tog, yo) around. Now work 15 rnds in st st and then work 1 repeat following chart. As shown on chart, decrease 2 sts at center back on every 4th rnd, but on the last rnd, decrease only 1 st = a total of 13 sts decreased and 65 sts rem. Continue following the chart through last chart row = a total of 3 pattern repeats have been worked.

HOURGLASS HEEL
After completing sock leg, divide sts, placing 32 sts on scrap yarn for instep. These sts will "rest" until the heel is finished.

Place rem 33 sts on one dpn and work back and forth with White.
Row 1 (RS): Sl 1 purlwise wyb, knit 32; turn.
Row 2: Sl 1 purlwise wyf, purl until 1 st rem; turn.
Row 3: Sl 1, knit until 1 st rem; turn.
Row 4: Sl 1, purl until 2 sts rem; turn.
Row 5: Sl 1, knit until 2 sts rem; turn.
Continue as est until 12 sts rem at center of heel. The last row is worked on RS.

Sl 1, work as many purl sts as last knitted (12 sts). Pick up the strand between the last st and next, twist it and purl it tog with the next st; turn.
Sl 1, knit as many sts as last worked (12 sts). Pick up strand between last st and next, twist it and knit it tog with next st; turn.
Rep these two rows, always with 1 more st before turning.
NOTE: Tighten the yarn a bit each time you turn to prevent holes.
Continue as est, with 1 st more on each row until, on the last row, you work all the sts across heel.
Now work in the round over all the sock sts. *At the same time*, work in pattern following the chart for the foot for 2 rep of charted rows. Cut Red and continue with White only.

STAR TOE
Begin at the center of the sole.
Rnd 1: (K5, k2tog) around.
The 2 sts rem on Ndl 4 will be decreased in subsequent rnds.
Rnds 2-6: Knit.
Rnd 7: (K4, k2tog) around.
Rnds 8-11: Knit.
Rnd 12: (K3, k2tog) around.
Rnds 13-15: Knit
Rnd 16: (K2, k2tog) around.
Rnds 17-18: Knit.
Rnd 19: (K1, k2tog) around.
Rnd 20: Knit.
Rnd 21: (K2tog) around.

FINISHING
Cut yarn and draw end through rem sts; tighten. Weave in all ends neatly on WS. Make the second sock the same way.

OSLO

Rose Ankle Socks

The Norwegian Museum of Cultural History has a pair of long men's stockings with a simple stripe pattern and large, characteristic eight-petal roses at the ankles. The stockings were knitted with very fine wool yarn. The eight-petal roses at the ankles are usually called *okleroser* or "ankle roses".

The technique of knitting is relatively young. Knitted stockings became common among the upper classes in Europe during the 1600s and more and more gained access to them in the 16th and 17th centuries. Before that, people sewed stockings from woven fabric. Ågot Noss has documented that sewn stockings were worn in certain parishes in Telemark all the way up to the 1950s and early 1960s in Norway.

The problem with sewn stockings was that they weren't elastic and didn't fit the feet closely. Another disadvantage was they had an inward-facing seam. The seam could both tear and chafe when one moved.

At the ankles, on both the inside and outside of the foot, sewn stockings might be decorated with pretty embroidery. In English, this type of embroidery was called "quirks and clocks." In Danish, the embellishments at the gussets were called *svikler*, and in Norwegian we just used the word *klokker*—"clocks".

Once people started knitting stockings, they copied elements from sewn stockings. So early knitted stockings—which were one color at the beginning—were made with a false "seam" of purl stitches at the center back of the leg and decorations at the ankles. Various motifs were worked in, with eight-petal roses, crowns, and motifs called *kirkespir* or "church spires" appearing most often. On single-color stockings, these were worked with purl stitches. We seldom see ankle roses on two-color stockings. That shows how old the stockings in the Norwegian Museum of Cultural History are.

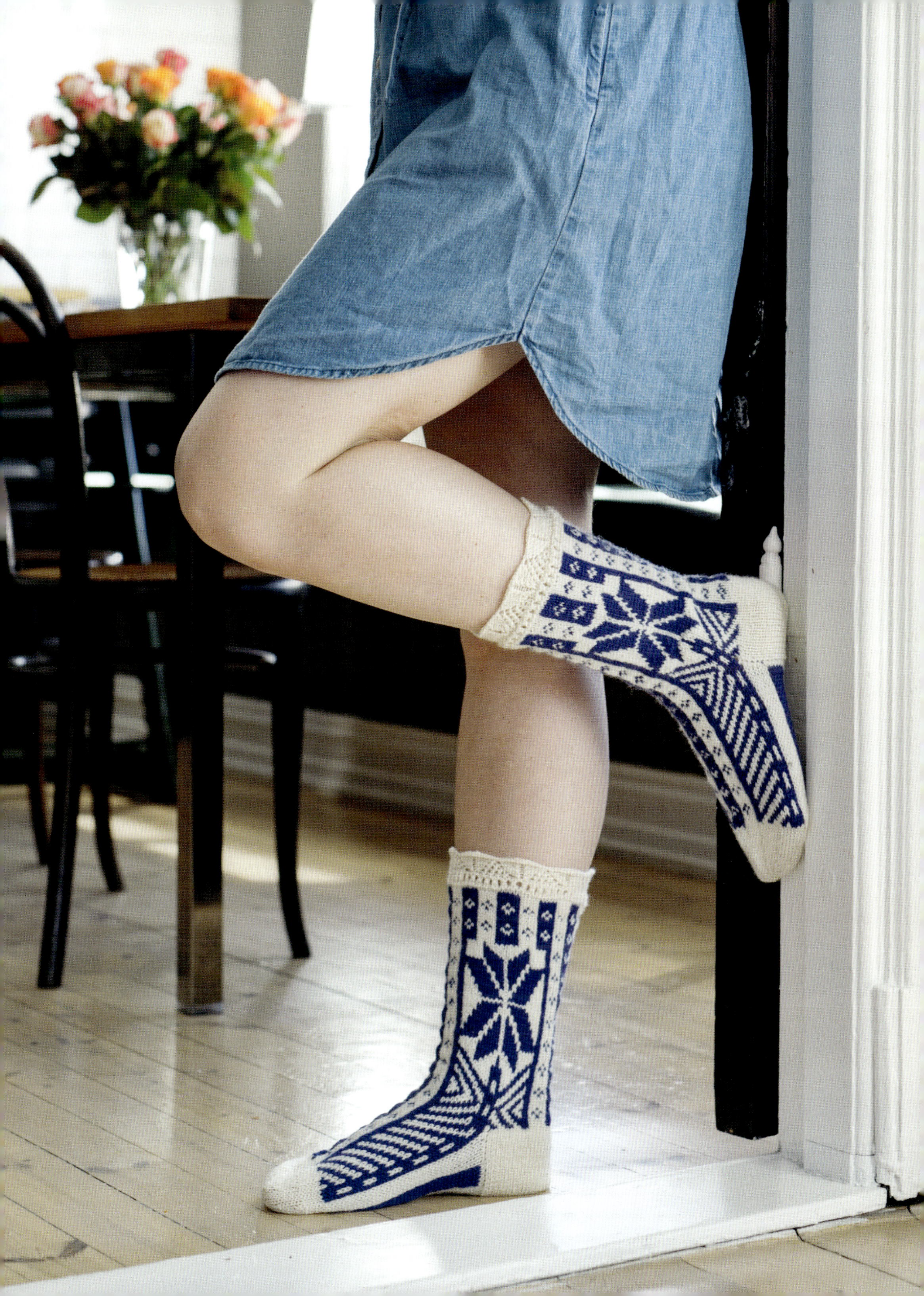

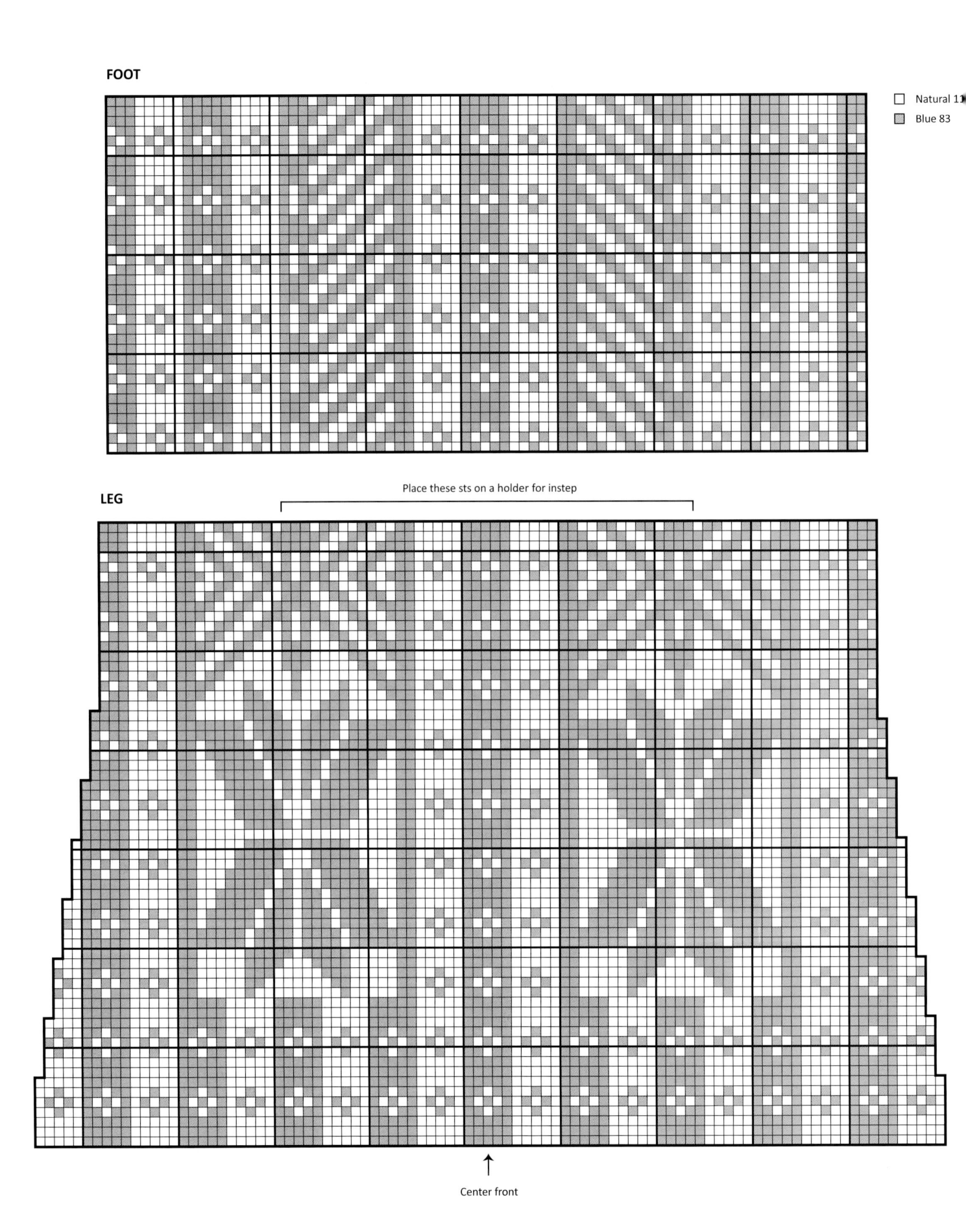

FOOT

LEG

Place these sts on a holder for instep

↑
Center front

Natural 11
Blue 83

INSTRUCTIONS

Skill Level: Experienced

Sizes: Women's (Men's)

MATERIALS
Yarn: CYCA #1 (fingering/2 ply), Baby Panda from Rauma Ullvarefabrikk (100% Merino wool, 191 yd/175 m / 50 g)

Yarn Colors and Amounts:
Natural White 11: 100 (100) g
Blue 38: 100 (100) g

Needles: U. S. size 1.5 (2.5) / 2.5 (3) mm: set of 5 dpn

Gauge: 30 (28) sts in pattern = 4 in / 10 cm.
Adjust needle size to obtain correct gauge if necessary.

LEG
Lace Edging for Women's Stockings
With Natural White, CO 96 sts. Divide sts evenly onto 4 dpn. Join, being careful not to twist cast-on row. Pm for beginning of rnd and work lace pattern as follows:
Rnd 1: *K2tog, k4, yo, k4, ssk*; rep * to * around.
Rnd 2: Knit.
Rnd 3: *K2tog, k3, yo, k1, yo, k3, ssk*; rep * to * around.
Rnd 4: K4, *ssk, k9*; rep * to * around, ending with ssk, k5.
Rnd 5: *K2tog, k2, yo, k1, yo, k1, yo, k2, ssk*; rep * to * around.
Rnd 6: K3, *ssk, ssk, k7*; rep * to * around, ending with ssk, ssk, k4.
Rnd 7: *K2tog, (k1, yo) 4 times, k1, ssk*; rep * to * around.
Rnd 8: K2, *ssk, ssk, ssk, k5*; rep * to * around, ending with ssk, ssk, ssk, k3.
Rnd 9: *K2tog, (yo, k1) 4 times, yo, ssk*; rep * to * around.
Rnd 10: K1, *ssk, ssk, ssk, ssk, k3*; rep * to * around, ending with ssk, ssk, ssk, ssk, k2.
There are now 56 sts around.
Rnd 11: Knit, increasing around as evenly spaced as possible to 95 sts.
Rnd 12: Purl.
Rnd 13: *K2tog, yo*; rep * to * around
Rnd 14: Knit.
Rnd 15: Purl.
Rnd 16: Knit.
Continue to leg.

Men's Stocking
With Natural White, CO 96 sts. Divide sts evenly onto 4 dpn. Join, being careful not to twist cast-on row. Pm for beginning of rnd and work around in k2, p2 ribbing for 1½ in / 4 cm. Decrease 1 st at center back.

LEG, BOTH SIZES
Work following the Leg Chart = 81 sts rem at completion of chart.

COMMON HEEL
After completing sock leg, place 43 sts on scrap yarn (see chart) for instep. These sts will "rest" until the heel is finished.

Heel Flap
Divide the remaining 38 stitches onto two dpn (Ndls A and B) and work back and forth with Natural White. Begin with the RS facing you. **NOTE:** On the first row only, decrease 1 st at the center of each needle = 18 sts rem on each dpn.
Row 1 (RS): Sl 1 purlwise wyb, knit all sts on Ndls A and B.
Row 2: Sl 1 purlwise wyf, purl all sts on Ndls A and B.
Repeat these 2 rows until there are 13 chain sts at each side of the flap.

Shaping the Heel
Now you will shape the back by decreasing as follows:
Row 1: Sl 1, knit until 5 sts rem on Ndl A, k2tog, k3. On Ndl B, k3, ssk, knit to end of needle.
Row 2: Sl 1, purl to end of row.
Row 3: Sl 1, knit until 4 sts rem on Ndl A, k2tog, k2. On Ndl B, k2, ssk, knit to end of needle.
Row 4: Sl 1, purl to end of row.
Row 5: Sl 1, knit until 3 sts rem on Ndl A, k2tog, k1. On Ndl B, k1, ssk, knit to end of needle.
Row 6: Sl 1, purl to end of row.
Row 7: Sl 1, knit until 2 sts rem on Ndl A, k2tog. On Ndl B, ssk, knit to end of needle.
Row 8: Sl 1, purl to end of Ndl B. Yarn is now at center of heel flap.
Hold the two dpn with RS facing in (so WS faces out on each side). Join the sets of sts with 3-needle BO: K2tog with 1 st from each needle, *k2tog with next st from each needle, pass first st over the second*. Repeat from * to * until 1 st loop rem.

Divide the instep sts onto 2 dpn. With RS facing, Natural White (carrying Blue), and Ndl 1, beginning at the center of the sole, pick up and knit 1 st in each chain st on the side of the flap. You can pick up the chain sts through back loops or knit them tbl on the next rnd. Work the instep sts on Ndls 2-3, in pattern following the chart. With Ndl 4, pick up and knit sts on opposite side of heel flap = 78 sts total.

FOOT
Work foot following the foot chart to desired length before toe.

STAR TOE
Begin at the center of the sole.
Rnd 1: (K5, k2tog) around. The 1 st rem on Ndl 4 will be decreased in subsequent rnds.
Rnds 2-6: Knit.
Rnd 7: (K4, k2tog) around.
Rnds 8-11: Knit.
Rnd 12: (K3, k2tog) around.
Rnds 13-15: Knit
Rnd 16: (K2, k2tog) around.
Rnds 17-18: Knit.
Rnd 19: (K1, k2tog) around.
Rnd 20: Knit.
Rnd 21: (K2tog) around.

FINISHING
Cut yarn and draw end through rem sts; tighten. Weave in all ends neatly on WS. Make the second sock the same way.

HEDMARK

Striped Stockings from Glåmdalen

Dyeing yarn so it produces a pattern when woven is a skill that's been known and practiced around the world for several centuries. Dyeing yarn in sections to make striped knitting is also nothing new. Several stockings preserved from Elverum were artisanally dyed using the ikat technique. The ikat method of dyeing involves covering sections of the yarn to prevent dye penetration and create patterning.

In some cultures, ikat dyeing has been developed to an extremely precise technique where every single millimeter of yarn is controlled—nothing is left to chance. Most of those who dye yarns for knitting today are less strict. Colors which go well together are blended to see what happens. Some old stockings from the Glomdal Museum show that we must have had a well-developed dyeing tradition in this country—even if it wasn't as precise as in Indonesia and Japan, for example. The stockings that inspired me have relatively similar stripes in natural sheep's white and indigo blue, but within the light stripes there are very dark, small dashes of lice. It's likely these were knitted with two skeins of yarn. One yarn was ikat style with blue and white stripes, and the other yarn was bound to create the small black oblong lice. To get the darkest color possible, the yarn must have been dipped in multiple dye baths.

The stockings most likely belonged to Ole Bjølset Skavhaugen, born in 1846 in Elverum—or maybe one of his brothers, Olav or Otto. They might have been knitted by Ole's wife, Karen (born in 1847) or maybe the boys' mother made them? The Glomdal Museum obtained the stockings from Ole's daughter Anna (1888-1985). She studied art and handcrafts in Oslo, and was especially interested in cultural history, handwork, and home customs. Many of the items in the museum's collection came from her.

Perhaps you have been inspired to dye yarn? Dyeing produces unbelievably lively patterns. My design for these stockings is knitted with three different single-color yarns, though, instead of one or two multi-color strands.

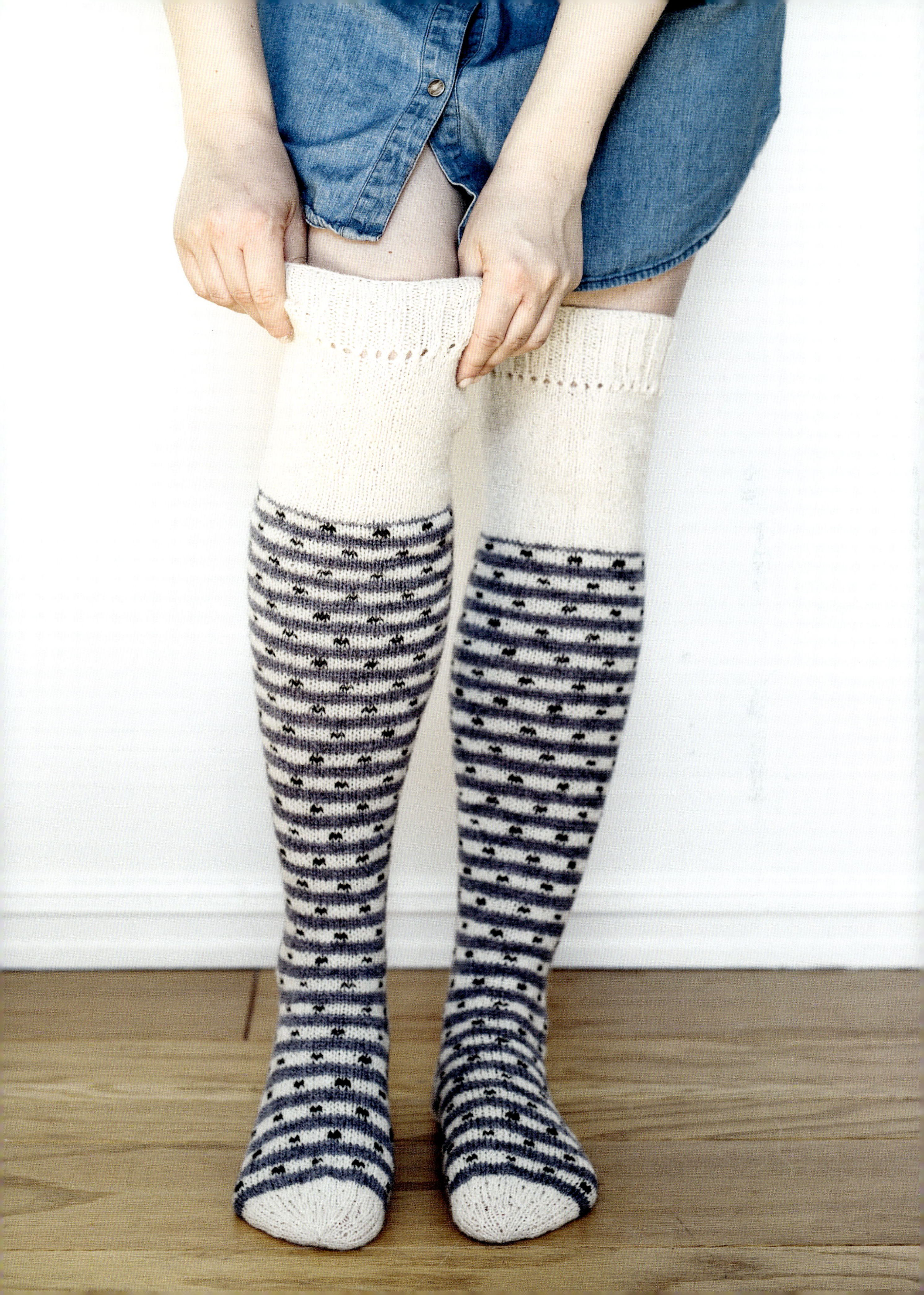

LEG AND FOOT

Repeat

Repeat

HEEL FLAP

☐ White—knit
▨ Blue—knit
■ Charcoal Gray—knit

INSTRUCTIONS

Skill Level: Experienced

Size: Women's

MATERIALS
Yarn:
CYCA #2 (sport/4 ply), Ask Hifa 2 from Hillesvåg Ullvarefabrikk (100% Norwegian wool, 344 yd/315 m / 100 g)

Yarn Colors and Amounts:
Natural White 316057: 100 g
Light Country Blue 316037: 100 g
Charcoal Gray 316056: 50 g

Needles: U. S. size 1.5 / 2.5 mm: set of 5 dpn

Gauge: 25 sts in pattern = 4 in / 10 cm.
Adjust needle size to obtain correct gauge if necessary.

LEG
With Natural White, CO 85 sts. Divide sts evenly onto 4 dpn. Join, being careful not to twist cast-on row; pm for beginning of rnd. Work around in k3, p2 ribbing for 20 rnds or approx. 2 in / 5 cm. Next, work an eyelet rnd: (K2tog, yo) to last st, end p1.
NOTE: Always purl the last st of the rnd on the leg. Knit 6 rnds and then begin shaping on each side of center purl st as follows:
Ndl 1: Ssk and knit to end of Ndl 3.
Ndl 4: Knit until 3 sts rem, k2tog, p1.
Decrease the same way on every 7th rnd 5 times = 76 sts rem. Continue with White and st st until leg measures 6¾ in / 17 cm and then change to charted stripe pattern for leg.
When leg measures 13½ in / 34 cm or desired length, begin ankle shaping: Decrease as before on every 3rd rnd 8 times = 60 sts rem. Continue in pattern until leg measures 21¼ in / 54 cm or desired length.

BAND HEEL
After completing leg, place 30 sts on scrap yarn for the instep (to "rest" while you work the heel flap).
Place rem 30 sts on one dpn and work heel flap back and forth in charted stripe pattern for heel flap.

Begin with WS facing you.
Row 1 (WS): Sl 1 purlwise wyf, purl to end of row.

Row 2: Sl 1 purlwise wyb, knit to end of row.
Rep these 2 rows until there are 14 chain sts at each side of flap.

Now decrease to shape the band (with Blue):
Row 1: Sl 1, purl until 11 sts rem, p2tog; turn.
Row 2: Sl 1, knit until 11 sts rem, ssk; turn.
Row 3: Sl 1, purl until 1 st before gap, p2tog; turn.
Row 4: Sl 1, knit until 1 st before gap, ssk; turn.
Rep Rows 3-4 until all the side sts have been eliminated.

FOOT
Divide the instep sts onto 2 dpn and divide the rem heel sts onto 2 dpn so you have half of each section on a needle. Now, continuing in stripe pattern, work in the round with RS facing you. Begin rnd at center of sole with White. Pick up and knit 1 st in each chain st along side of heel flap. You can pick up the sts tbl or knit them tbl on next rnd. Knit across instep following chart. Pick up and knit 1 st in each chain st of opposite side of flap and then complete rnd as est.

Gusset
Knit until 2 sts rem on Ndl 1, k2tog. Knit across instep (Ndls 2-3) in charted pattern. Ndl 4: Ssk, knit to end of rnd. Knit the next rnd without decreasing. Following the chart, repeat these 2 rnds until 60 sts rem. Work rest of foot in pattern without decreasing. When foot measures 7 in / 18 cm or desired length before toe, work star toe.

STAR TOE
Begin at the center of the sole and work only with Natural White.
Rnd 1: (K5, k2tog) around. The 4 sts rem on Ndl 4 will be decreased in subsequent rnds.
Rnds 2-6: Knit.
Rnd 7: (K4, k2tog) around.
Rnds 8-11: Knit.
Rnd 12: (K3, k2tog) around.
Rnds 13-15: Knit
Rnd 16: (K2, k2tog) around.
Rnds 17-18: Knit.
Rnd 19: (K1, k2tog) around.
Rnd 20: Knit.
Rnd 21: (K2tog) around.

FINISHING
Cut yarn and draw end through rem sts; tighten. Weave in all ends neatly on WS. Make the second sock the same way.

Color Party

Hulleborg Smidt (1771-1847) came from a well-established bourgeois family in Stavanger. Her father was a goldsmith. In 1792, she married Hans Christopher Langballe from Nedstrand in Tysvær where they ran a farm, guest house, and country shop.

The state archives in Stavanger have a book by Hulleborg that contains both food and and dye recipes: *Women's Cakes and Dye Book*. The book measures 4 x 6 in / 10 x 15 cm and includes 177 closely written pages. On the title page her son wrote: "Transcribed for My Mother." The instructions are written in somewhat random order, and it's likely that Hulleborg had collected both her own and others' recipes in the notebook.

Main dishes, soups, desserts, small cakes, and tarts—likely prepared for social entertainment—are found among the food recipes. Instructions for distilling liquors and blueberry wine are also included. The last part of the book consists of 82 "recipes" for dyeing yarn and wool fabric, silk, cotton canvas, and a little linen. Most of the recipes are for red or blue dyestuff, but other colors are included, such as black, yellow, green, and purple. Still other descriptions include instructions on how to wash dyed silk stockings and fine fabrics.

Dyeing was hardly something every housewife had mastery of, even if many of dyestuffs grew wild in nature. It was an aspect of handcraft requiring knowledge. So most people knitted with natural-colored yarn until commercially spun yarn became more common. If one didn't have enough money for that, one could take yarn or finished garments to a professional dyer in town.

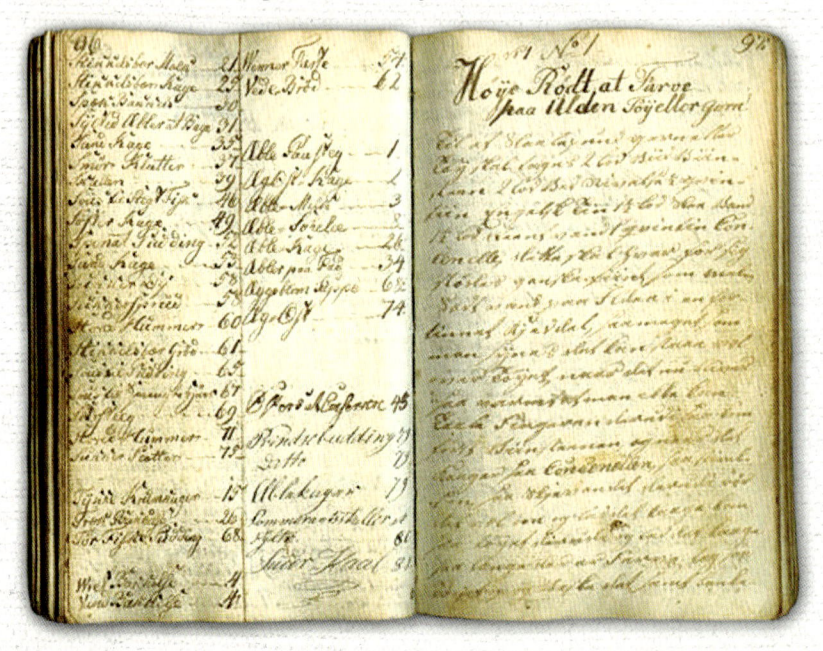

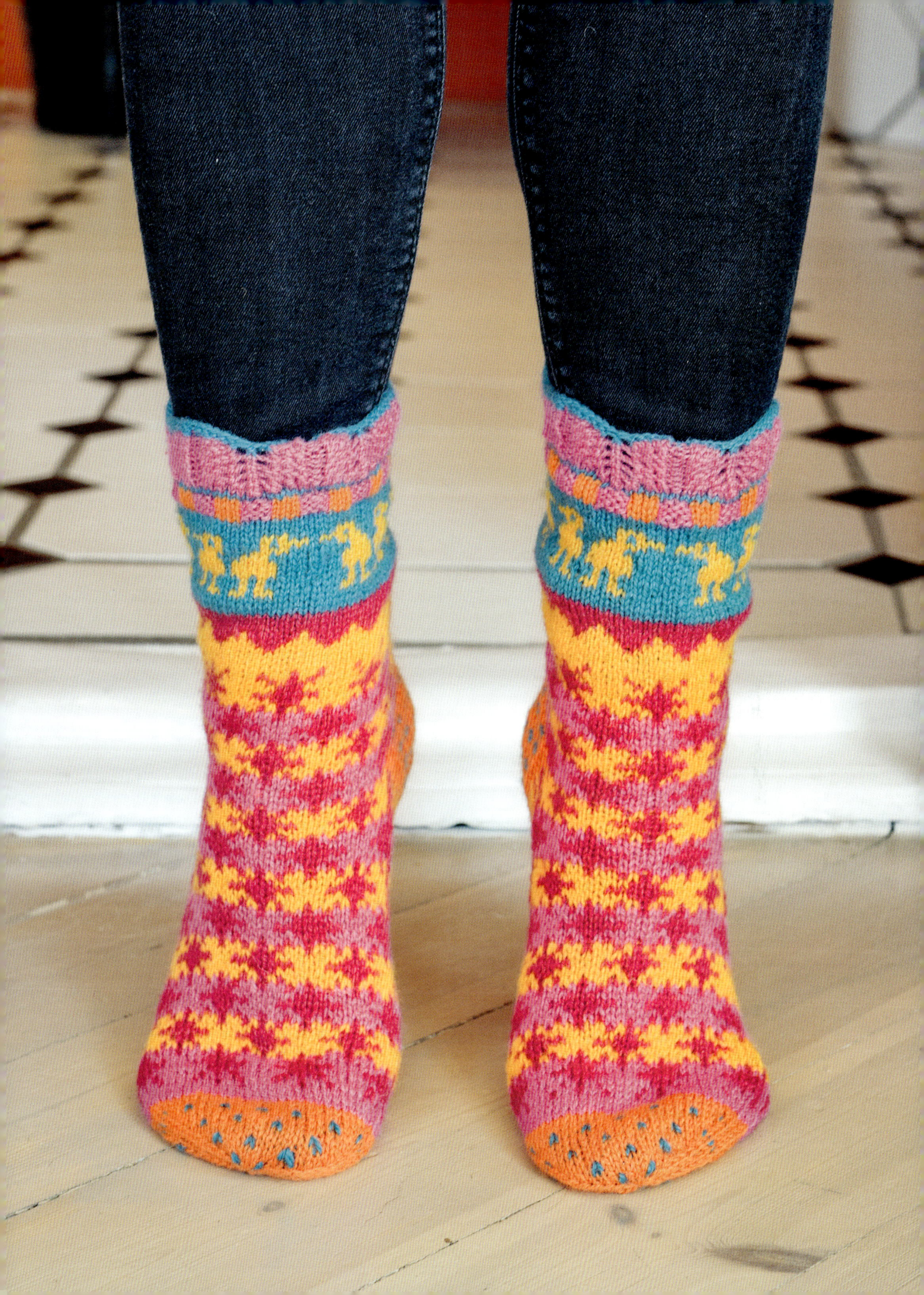

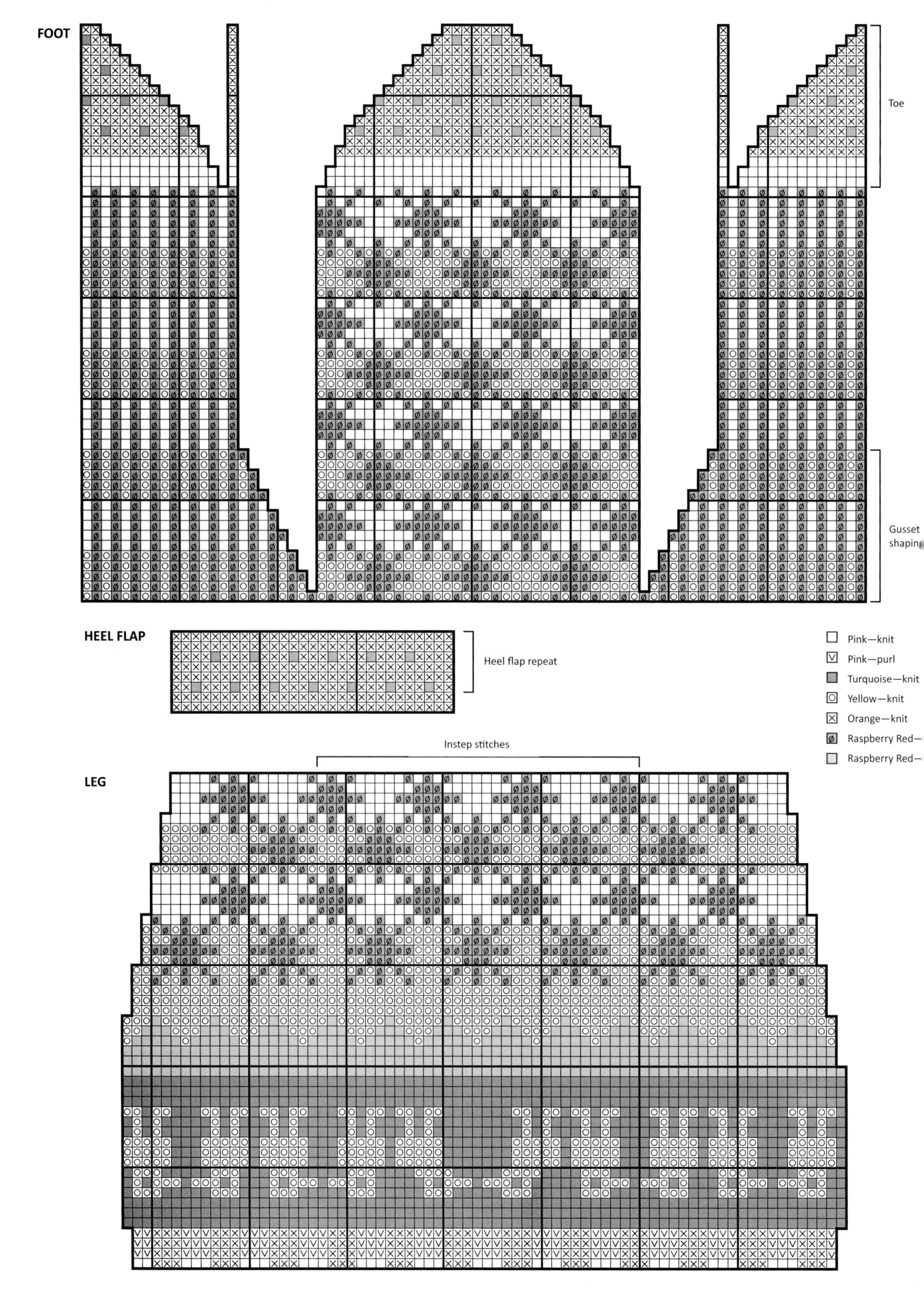

FOOT

Toe

Gusset shaping

HEEL FLAP

Heel flap repeat

Instep stitches

LEG

☐ Pink—knit
☑ Pink—purl
▨ Turquoise—knit
◯ Yellow—knit
☒ Orange—knit
⦰ Raspberry Red—
▥ Raspberry Red—

INSTRUCTIONS

Skill Level: Experienced

Size: Women's

MATERIALS
Yarn:
CYCA #1 (fingering/2 ply), Finullgarn from Rauma Ullvarefabrikk (100% wool, 191 yd/175 m / 50 g)

Yarn Colors and Amounts:
50 g each:
Turquoise 483
Raspberry Red 456
Pink 4686
Orange 4205
Yellow 4305

Needles: U. S. 1.5 / 2.5 mm: set of 5 dpn

Gauge: 28 sts in pattern = 4 in / 10 cm.
Adjust needle size to obtain correct gauge if necessary.

LEG
With Turquoise, CO 72 sts. Divide sts evenly onto 4 dpn. Join, being careful not to twist cast-on row; pm for beginning of rnd. Purl 1 rnd. Change to Pink and work lace edging as follows:
Rnd 1: *K2tog, k3, yo, k1, yo, k3, ssk, p1*; rep * to * around.
Rnd 2: *K11, p1*; rep * to * around.
Rnd 3: *K2tog, k2tog, (yo, k1), 3 times, yo, ssk, ssk, p1*; rep * to * around.
Rnd 4: *K11, p1*; rep * to * around.
Rep Rnds 3-4 a total of 4 times.
Change to Turquoise and knit 1 rnd. Continue as shown on the Leg chart.
NOTE: As shown on chart, at the beginning of the bird panel, increase 2 sts at center back. After completing panel, decrease 2 sts at center back. Continue following chart, decreasing as shown until 63 sts rem.

HEEL
After completing leg, divide the sts, placing 34 sts (see chart) on scrap yarn for instep. These sts will "rest" until the heel is complete.
Place the rem 29 sts on 1 dpn and work the heel flap back and forth in pattern following the chart. Begin with WS facing you.
Row 1 (WS): Sl 1 purlwise wyf, purl to end of row.
Row 2: Sl 1 purlwise wyb, knit to end of row.
Rep these 2 rows until there are 14 chain sts on each side of heel flap.

Heel Gusset
Row 1: Sl 1, purl until 10 sts rem, p2tog, p1; turn.
Row 2: Sl 1, knit until 10 sts rem, ssk, k1; turn.
Row 3: Sl 1, purl until 1 st before gap, p2tog, p1; turn.
Row 4: Sl 1, knit until 1 st before gap, ssk, k1; turn.
Rep Rows 3-4 until all the side sts have been eliminated—19 sts rem.

FOOT
Gusset
Divide the instep sts onto 2 dpn and divide the rem heel sts onto 2 dpn so you have half of each section on a needle. Now work in the round with RS facing you. Begin rnd at center of sole. Alternate knitting with Raspberry Red and Yellow as shown on the chart.
Pick up and knit 1 st in each chain st along side of heel flap. You can pick up the sts tbl or knit them tbl on next rnd. Work across instep following chart. Pick up and knit 1 st in each chain st of opposite side of flap and then knit as charted to last 2 sts; end k2tog = 80 sts rem.

On the next rnd, decrease for the gusset as shown on the chart:
Knit until 2 sts rem on Ndl 1, k2tog with Raspberry, knit across instep (Ndls 2-3). Ndl 4: Ssk with Raspberry, knit to end of rnd. Knit the next rnd without decreasing. Following the chart, repeat these 2 rnds until 64 sts rem. Work rest of foot in pattern without decreasing. When foot is desired length before toe, work wedge toe.

WEDGE TOE
Begin at the center of the sole and work pattern following the chart.
Rnd 1:
Ndl 1: Knit until 3 sts rem on needle, k2tog, k1.
Ndl 2: Ssk, knit to end of needle.
Ndl 3: Work as for Ndl 1.
Ndl 4: Work as for Ndl 2.
Rnd 2: Knit without decreasing.

Repeat Rnds 1-2 4 times and then decrease on every rnd until 12 sts rem.

FINISHING
Cut yarn and draw end through rem sts; tighten. Weave in all ends neatly on WS. Make the second sock the same way.

OPPLAND

Stockings from Valdres

A collection from the parish of Bagn includes a pair of bride's stockings worn by Sigrid Hansdatter Islandsmoen from Søndre Aurdal. They were knitted with white cotton yarn and feature a wide panel of pink-red patterning on the legs.

Sigrid first appears in the census of 1865. At that time, she was unmarried, 26 years old, and working as a servant girl at the Østre Bagn Rectory of farmer, parish priest, and dean Heyerdahl. It was a large farm with 12 in the household. The farm animals included 3 horses, 11 cows, 10 sheep, and 4 pigs.

Sigrid herself came from one of the large farms in the parish and was the daughter of farmer and proprietor Hans Pedersen Islandsmoen and Marit Throndsdatter.

By the time of the 1910 census, Sigrid was recorded as a merchant's wife born on 2 August 1841. She was married to Knut Knutsen, a telephone central supervisor and storekeeper. They lived in a place called Liffengren. They shared the house with a teacher at the vocational school and a teacher at the continuing education school.

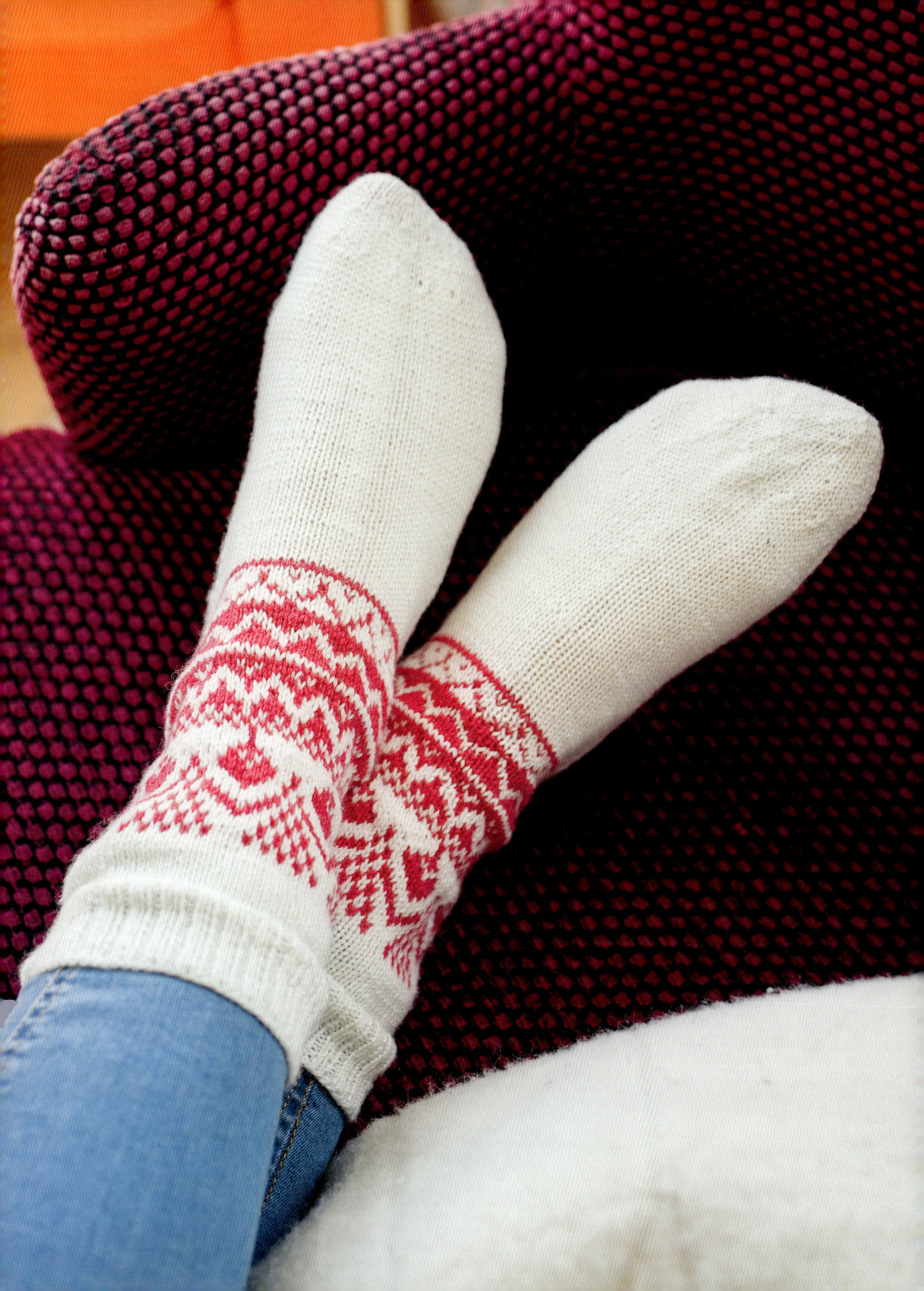

The Bagn collection also has a full-length photograph of her, identifying her as Sigrid Hansdatter Islandsmoen, married to the merchant Knut Haugen. It's difficult to tell how old she is from the photo. Her face looks young, without any wrinkles. Her hair is impressive, falling freely all the way down to her knees. The waves in her hair indicate that it had been braided, which was standard at the time. A later portrait shows her with braids in a wreath at the back of her head. The records show that Sigrid worked as a seamstress with her daughter, Ragnhild.

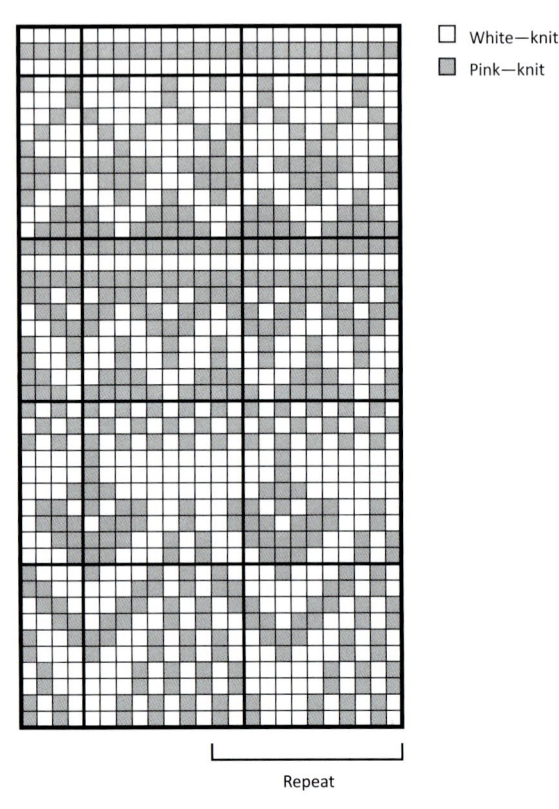

☐ White—knit
■ Pink—knit

Repeat

INSTRUCTIONS

Skill Level: Experienced

Sizes: Women's (Men's)

MATERIALS
Yarn:
CYCA #1 (fingering/2 ply), Sisu from Sandnes Garn (80% wool, 20% nylon), 191 yd/175 m / 50 g)

Yarn Colors and Amounts:
White 1012: 100 (100) g
Pink 4627: 50 (50) g

Needles: U. S. size 1.5 (2.5) / 2.5 (3) mm: set of 5 dpn

Gauge: 32 (30) sts in pattern = 4 in / 10 cm. Adjust needle size to obtain correct gauge if necessary.

LEG
With White, CO 76 sts. Divide sts evenly onto 4 dpn. Join, being careful not to twist cast-on row; pm for beginning of rnd. Work around in k2, p1 ribbing for 2 in / 5 cm. Change to st st, and, on the first rnd, decrease 2 sts at the center back. Work in st st for ¾ in / 2 cm. Decrease another 2 sts at center back and knit another ⅜ in / 1 cm = 72 sts rem. Work remainder of leg in charted pattern.

BAND HEEL
After completing leg, place 36 sts on scrap yarn for the instep (to "rest" while you work the heel flap).

Heel Flap
Place rem 36 sts on one dpn and, with White, work heel flap back and forth.

Begin with WS facing you.
Row 1 (WS): Sl 1 purlwise wyf, purl to end of row.
Row 2: Sl 1 purlwise wyb, knit to end of row.
Rep these 2 rows until there are 18 chain sts at each side of flap.

Now decrease to shape the band:

Row 1: Sl 1, purl until 12 sts rem, p2tog; turn.
Row 2: Sl 1, knit until 12 sts rem, ssk; turn.
Row 3: Sl 1, purl until 1 st before gap, p2tog; turn.
Row 4: Sl 1, knit until 1 st before gap, ssk; turn.
Rep Rows 3-4 until all the side sts have been eliminated.

FOOT
Divide the instep sts onto 2 dpn and divide the rem heel sts onto 2 dpn so you have half of each section on a needle. Work in the round with RS facing you. Begin rnd at center of sole. Pick up and knit 1 st in each chain st along side of heel flap. You can pick up the sts tbl or knit them tbl on next rnd. Knit across instep. Pick up and knit 1 st in each chain st of opposite side of flap and knit to end of rnd.

Gusset
Knit until 2 sts rem on Ndl 1, k2tog. Knit across instep (Ndls 2-3).
Ndl 4: Ssk, knit to end of rnd. Knit the next rnd without decreasing. Rep these 2 rnds until 72 sts rem. Work rest of foot in st st without shaping until 7½ in / 19 cm or desired length before toe.

STAR TOE
Begin at the center of the sole and work only with Natural White.
Rnd 1: (K5, k2tog) around. The 2 sts rem on Ndl 4 will be decreased in subsequent rnds.
Rnds 2-6: Knit.
Rnd 7: (K4, k2tog) around.
Rnds 8-11: Knit.
Rnd 12: (K3, k2tog) around.
Rnds 13-15: Knit.
Rnd 16: (K2, k2tog) around.
Rnds 17-18: Knit.
Rnd 19: (K1, k2tog) around.
Rnd 20: Knit.
Rnd 21: (K2tog) around.

FINISHING
Cut yarn and draw end through rem sts; tighten. Weave in all ends neatly on WS. Make the second sock the same way.

OPPLAND

Stockings from Gausdal

When the Norwegian Handcraft Association registered knitted work in connection with a traveling exhibition, "Knitting Then and Now", in 1983-84, a pair of children's stockings from Gausdal popped up. The stockings, distinguished with bold stripes, were knitted with natural white and blue-red yarn. In between the stripes are sections of the "medallion" (in Norwegian, *hullbragd*) technique.

Hullbragd is a technique borrowed from weaving. In knitting, one can form a similar texture by framing knit sections with purl stitches.

These stockings had been worn by Asta Melbø, who was born in 1888 in Benna.

ROGALAND

Bridegroom's Socks from Vindafjord

When Bertine Oline Thorsnes was preparing to marry in 1883, she knitted a lovely pair of stockings for her intended, Bård Olesen Dørheim (born about 1850). Bertine was from Ilsvåg in Vindafjord—northeast of Haugesund. Bård was a farmer at Dørhaim in Ølen, a few miles away. She moved in and they lived there until about 1900. The farm was then sold and they moved to Eide—also in Ølen.

The stockings were knitted with very, very fine handspun natural white yarn and a red and blue flame yarn. The initials B.O.S.D. and the year 83 were embroidered on.

By the ninth century, woad (*Isatis tinctoria*) was used to dye yarn. Woad dyed yarn blue, as does indigo. Woad seeds have been found in Osebergskipet. The Vikings also used lichen dyes. Perhaps it was the Irish who taught us this art? By the 1700s, people had begun sharing knowledge about plants and how they could be used. At the same time, handworkers began taking yarn and garments to the towns for dyeing. Also at that time, new dyestuffs came into use and yielded the possibility for many new shades of color. Dyeing with plants dominated completely, until it became possible to buy imported aniline dyes in the latter half of the 19th century.

Flame yarn was very popular all over the country. It was produced by tying off sections of yarn to prevent the dye from being absorbed. The result was spotted yarn with two colors. Most common was natural white combined with blue. One could also dip the yarn into red dye if one wanted a flame yarn that was partly red and partly dark blue-violet—as shown here.

INSTRUCTIONS

Skill Level: Experienced

Sizes: Women's (Men's)

MATERIALS
Yarn:
CYCA #1 (fingering/2 ply), Finullgarn from Rauma (100% wool, 191 yd/175 m / 50 g)

CYCA #1 (fingering/2 ply), 2-ply Gammelserie from Rauma (100% wool, 175 yd/160 m / 50 g)

Yarn Colors and Amounts:
Finullgarn
Color 1: Green 455: 50 (50) g—you need the most of this color
Color 2: Raspberry Red 456: 50 (50) g
Color 3: Turquoise 4705: 50 (50) g
Color 4: Pink 479: 50 (50) g
Color 5: Yellow 4103: 50 (50) g
Color 6: Orange 4205: 50 (50) g
2-ply Gammelserie
Color 7: Natural White 401: 50 (50) g

Reinforcing Thread:
Mettler extra strong sewing thread, Blue 0350: 33 (66) yd / 30 (60) m

Needles: U. S. size 1.5 (2.5) / 2.5 (3) mm

Gauge: 24 (22) sts in pattern = 4 in / 10 cm. Adjust needle size to obtain correct gauge if necessary.

LEG
With Raspberry Red, CO 60 sts. Divide sts evenly onto 4 dpn. Join, being careful not to twist cast-on row; pm for beginning of rnd. Work around in k2, p2 rib for 3 rnds.
Next rnd: (K1 Raspberry Rd, k1 Natural) around. Work two-end braid following instructions on page 9; work from X to X.
Now work following Chart 1.
Next rnd: (K1 Raspberry Rd, k1 Natural) around. Work two-end braid following instructions on page 9; work from X to X.
Work following Chart 2.
NOTE: Yellow is knitted on the first rnd and then purled after that.

GUSSET HEEL
After completing the leg, divide the stitches and place the 31 instep stitches onto scrap yarn. These instep stitches will "rest" until the heel is complete. Make sure the pattern is divided symmetrically.

Place the remaining 29 stitches onto one needle and work back and forth with Turquoise and reinforcing thread held together. Begin with the WS facing you.
Row 1 (WS): Sl 1 purlwise wyf, p28.
Row 2: Sl 1 purlwise wyb, k28.
Repeat these 2 rows until there are 14 chain sts at each side of the flap.

Shaping the Heel
Row 1: Sl 1, purl until 10 sts rem on the needle, p2tog, p1; turn.
Row 2: Sl 1, knit until 10 sts rem on needle, ssk, k1; turn.
Row 3: Sl 1, purl until 1 st before gap, p2tog, p1; turn.
Row 4: Sl 1, knit until 1 st rem before gap, ssk, k1; turn.
Repeat Rows 3-4 until all the side sts have been eliminated.
Cut reinforcing thread.

Gusset Shaping
Divide the instep sts from the holder onto 2 dpn; divide the sole sts onto 2 dpn with half of the sts on each. With RS facing, begin working in the round. Begin rnd at center of sole with Green. With Ndl 1, knit to flap; pick up and knit 1 st in each chain up side of flap. You can pick up the chain sts through back loops, or knit them through back loops on the next rnd. With Ndls 2-3, knit across the instep. Next, with Ndl 4, pick up and knit sts down opposite side of flap as for the first side. Knit to center of sole.

On the next rnd, begin decreasing to shape gusset: Knit until 2 sts rem on Ndl 1, k2tog. Knit across instep sts on Ndls 2-3. With Ndl 4, ssk and then knit to end of rnd.
Work the next rnd without decreasing.
Repeat these 2 rnds until 60 sts rem. Continue without further shaping, with instep and sole in st st until foot measures 6¼ (8) in / 16 (20) cm or desired length to toe shaping + Chart 3 rows. Work following Chart 3 and then begin toe shaping.

STAR TOE
Begin at the center of the sole with Turquoise.
Rnd 1: (K5, k2tog) around. The 4 sts rem on Ndl 4 will be decreased in subsequent rnds.
Rnds 2-6: Knit.
Rnd 7: (K4, k2tog) around.
Rnds 8-11: Knit.
Rnd 12: (K3, k2tog) around.
Rnds 13-15: Knit
Rnd 16: (K2, k2tog) around.
Rnds 17-18: Knit.
Rnd 19: (K1, k2tog) around.
Rnd 20: Knit.
Rnd 21: (K2tog) around.

FINISHING
Cut yarn and draw end through rem sts; tighten. Weave in all ends neatly on WS. Make the second sock the same way.

CHART 1 **CHART 2** **CHART 3**

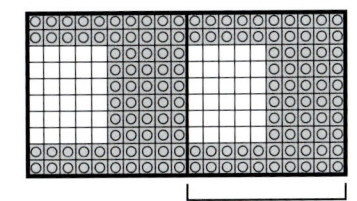

- ☒ Color 1, Green—knit
- ◉ Color 2, Raspberry Red—knit
- ⌀ Color 3, Turquoise—knit
- ■ Color 4, Pink—knit
- ⓒ Color 5, Yellow—knit
- ⱽ Color 5, Yellow—purl
- ▢ Color 6, Orange—knit
- ☐ Color 7, Natural White—knit

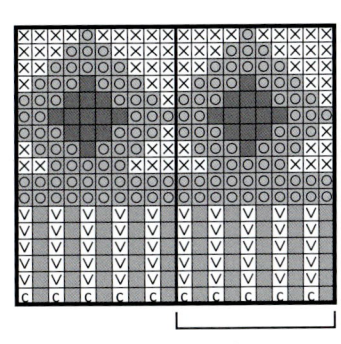

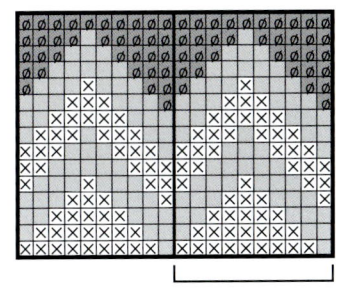

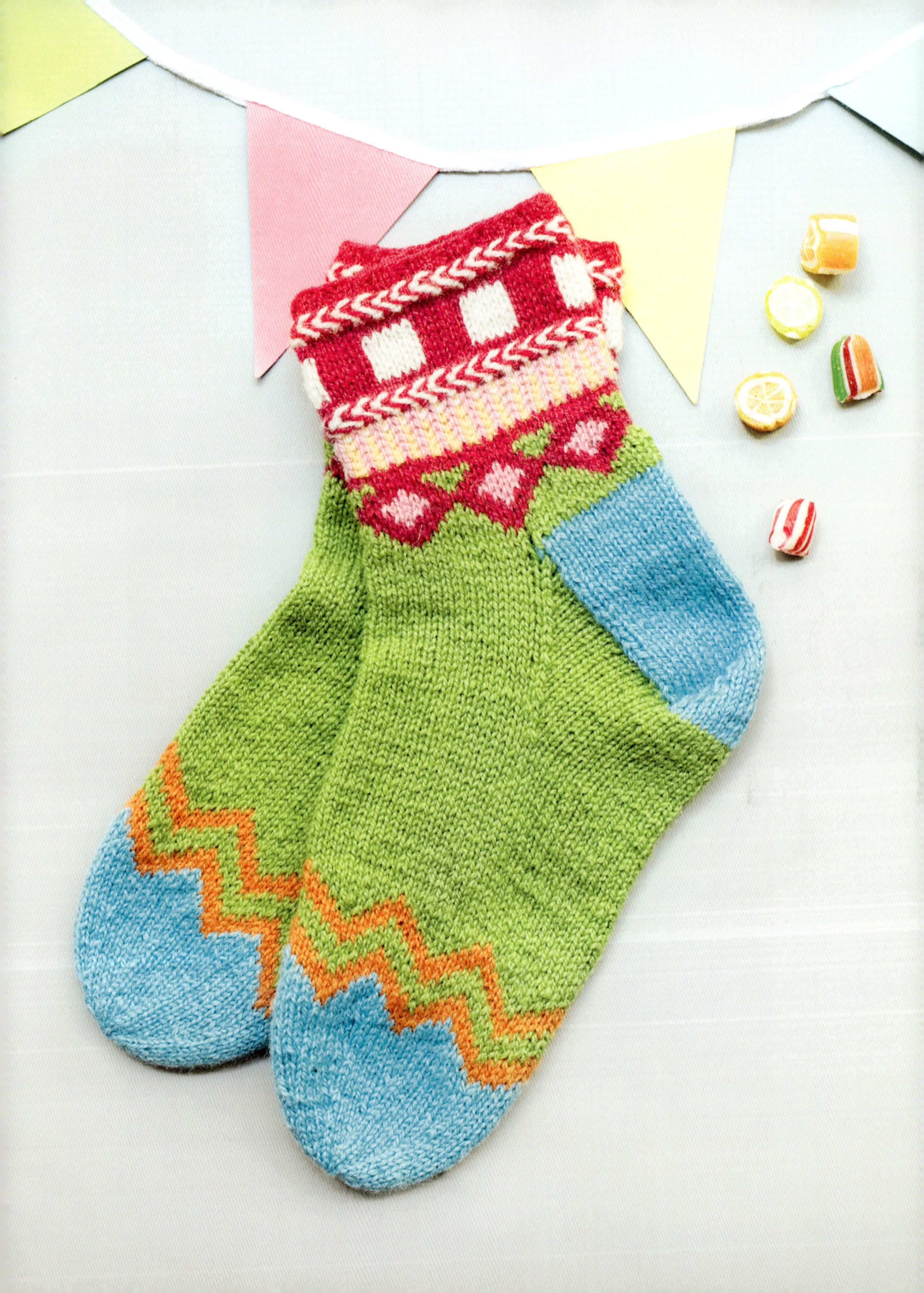

Leftover Party

Until mills began selling machine-spun yarn, people had to use handspun yarn. Spinning was a detailed and time-consuming process. Eventual access to commercially-spun yarn was a decisive factor in the large increase in the number of knitted garments after the war.

The first textile factories spun and wove cotton. Drammen's Cotton Mill (later Solberg), one of the first mills in Norway, was established in 1818.

From the end of the 1860s, a new industry developed based on Norwegian wool as the raw fiber rather than imported cotton. New inventions made it possible to mechanize production. At the same time, the American civil war created a crisis in the European cotton industry. Almost all exports of cotton from the American South were halted.

Ole Nielsen bought property at the waterfalls on Ålgård for 150 *speciedaler* from Svend Olsen Aalgard in 1870. He used the land to establish the Aalgaard Woolen Mill, which was run by water power. This was the first mill in Rogaland that specialized in custom spinning. Farmers brought in their wool and got yarn back. The women of Gjesdal could now weave large amounts of textiles to sell.

Commercial yarn for knitting was not common until a good while later—the early 20th century. The Dale mill was one of the early ones. It produced knitting yarn by 1912 and provided work for many women.

Most of us have yarn leftovers—some have more, some less. There's no reason not to use these extra yards/meters of yarn for smaller projects like socks! We've used 7 colors for these socks. You'll need about 50 grams of the main color and small amounts each of the other colors. Just make sure you have enough for both socks.

INSTRUCTIONS

Skill Level: Intermediate

Sizes: 2-4 (5-6, 7-10) years

MATERIALS
Yarn: CYCA #1 (fingering/2 ply), Baby Panda from Rauma Ullvarefabrikk (100% Merino wool, 191 yd/175 m / 50 g), Red 35: 100 (100, 100) g

Needles: U. S. size 0 (0, 1.5) / 2 (2, 2.5) mm: set of 5 dpn; cable needle

Gauge: 30 (30, 28) sts in pattern = 4 in / 10 cm. Adjust needle size to obtain correct gauge if necessary.

LEG
CO 63 (63, 63) sts. Divide sts as evenly as possible onto 4 dpn. Join, being careful not to twist cast-on row; pm for beginning of rnd. Work around in (k2, p1) ribbing for 1½ in / 4 cm. Increasing 1 st at center back on the first rnd (= 64 sts), work in charted cable pattern. The pattern is worked 8 times around. Work 4 repeats of the pattern lengthwise (or 6 as for the original stocking, if you prefer).
Change to (k2, p1) ribbing, decreasing 1 st at center back on the first rnd. When ribbing measures ¾ in / 2 cm, begin heel.

GUSSET HEEL
After completing the leg, divide the stitches, placing the 33 instep stitches onto scrap yarn. These instep stitches will "rest" until the heel is complete.

Place the remaining 30 stitches onto one needle and work back and forth. Begin with the WS facing you.
Row 1 (WS): Sl 1 purlwise wyf, p29.
Row 2: Sl 1 purlwise wyb, k29.
Repeat these 2 rows until there are 15 chain sts at each side of the flap.

Shaping the Heel
Row 1: Sl 1, purl until 10 sts rem on the needle, p2tog, p1; turn.
Row 2: Sl 1, knit until 10 sts rem on needle, ssk, k1; turn.
Row 3: Sl 1, purl until 1 st before gap, p2tog, p1; turn.
Row 4: Sl 1, knit until 1 st rem before gap, ssk, k1; turn.
Repeat Rows 3-4 until all the side sts have been eliminated.

Gusset Shaping
Divide the instep sts from the holder onto 2 dpn; divide the sole sts onto 2 dpn with half of the sts on each. With RS facing, begin working in the round. Begin rnd at center of sole. With Ndl 1, knit to flap; pick up and knit 1 st in each chain up side of flap (= total of 15 sts). You can pick up the chain sts through back loops, or knit them through back loops on the next rnd. With Ndls 2-3, work across the instep, decreasing every 3rd st: (p1, k2tog) across instep = 22 sts rem for instep. Next, with Ndl 4, pick up and knit 15 sts down opposite side of flap as for the first side. Knit to center of sole.

On the next rnd, begin decreasing to shape gusset: Knit until 2 sts rem on Ndl 1, k2tog. Knit across instep sts on Ndls 2-3. With Ndl 4, ssk and then knit to end of rnd.
Work the next rnd without decreasing.
Repeat these 2 rnds until 51 sts rem. Continue without further shaping, with instep and sole in st st until foot measures 3¾ (6¼, 7½) in / 9.5 (16, 19) cm or desired length to toe shaping.

STAR TOE
Begin at the center of the sole.
Rnd 1: (K5, k2tog) around. The 2 sts rem on Ndl 4 will be decreased in subsequent rnds.
Rnds 2-6: Knit.
Rnd 7: (K4, k2tog) around.
Rnds 8-11: Knit.
Rnd 12: (K3, k2tog) around.
Rnds 13-15: Knit
Rnd 16: (K2, k2tog) around.
Rnds 17-18: Knit.
Rnd 19: (K1, k2tog) around.
Rnd 20: Knit.
Rnd 21: (K2tog) around.

FINISHING
Cut yarn and draw end through rem sts; tighten. Weave in all ends neatly on WS. Make the second sock the same way.

☐ Knit
☒ Purl
▱ Place 3 sts on cable needle and hold in front of work, k3, k3 from cable needle

102

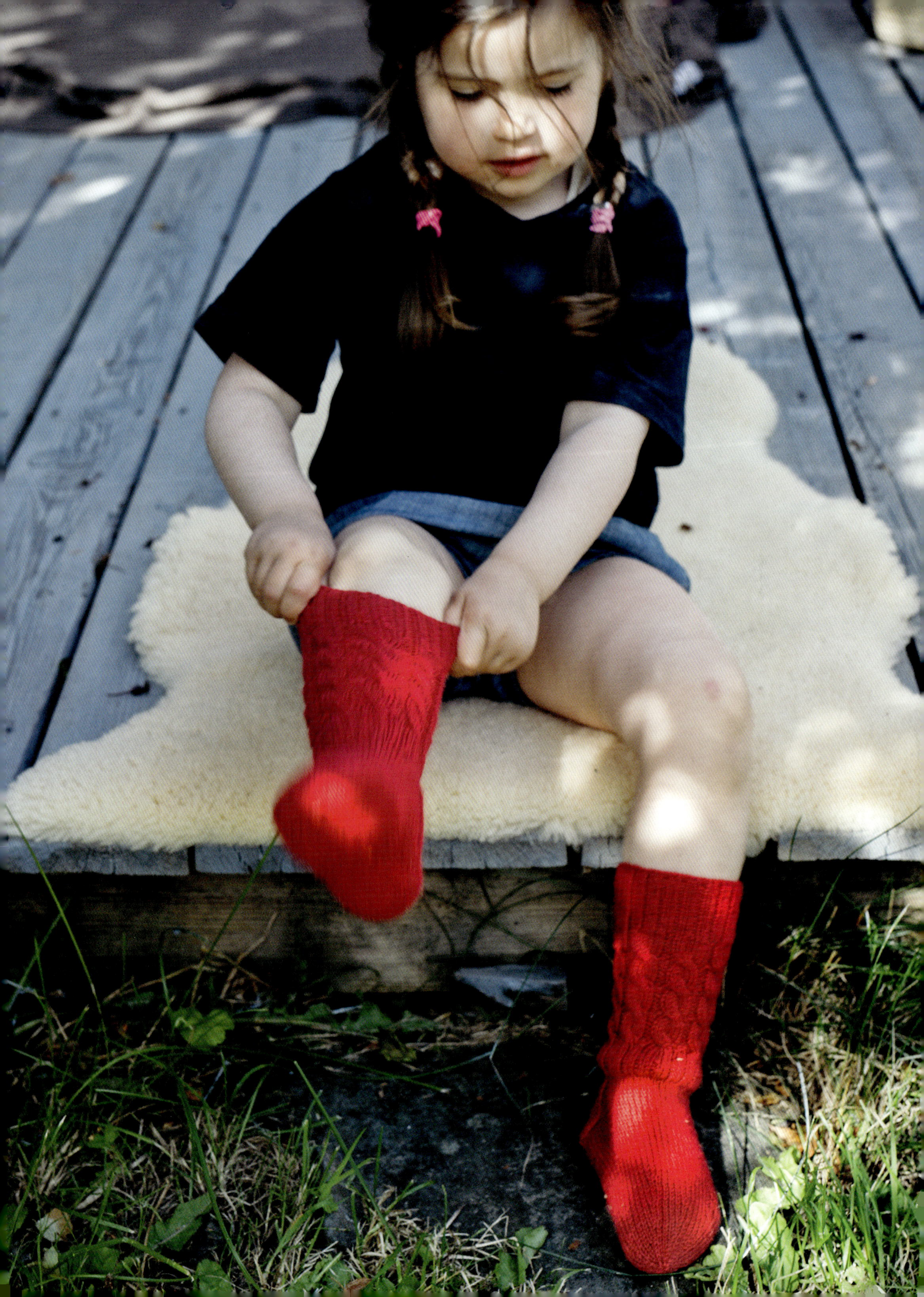

WEST AGDER

Cable Stockings from Marnardal

In 1983-84, the Norwegian Handcraft Association registered almost 3,000 items in conjunction with the traveling exhibit "Knitting Then and Now." The exhibit included several pairs of children's stockings from the Holmegaard Collection in Øyselbø that were photographed and described.

All the pairs belonged to Sofie Diesen from Heddeland. According to the census of 1910, Sørine Sofie was born on the 11th of July, 1880, in Øyselbø. She was the only daughter of Gunhild Sørine Heddeland and Colonel Gustav Fridtjov Diesen. In 1910, she was listed as unmarried with the address of East Strand Street 29 in Kristiansand. She lived with her father and a servant girl. The household income was 900 crowns a month.

Whether or not it was Sofie who wore the stockings, they must have been made in the 1880s. Perhaps her mother was the original knitter. Sofie might also have knitted as a way to earn some extra money. In that case, the stockings would have been newer. At that time, women, especially those from a middle-class family, didn't work outside the home. For them, knitting and other handcrafts became a valuable source of extra income.

The stockings were knitted with red wool yarn and obviously went up to the knees, as was common then.

INSTRUCTIONS

Skill Level: Intermediate

Size: Women's

MATERIALS
Yarn: CYCA #3 (DK, light worsted), Merino DK from Hedgehog Fibres (100% Merino wool, 219 yd/200 m / 115 g), Seaglass: 100 g

Needles: U. S. size 6 / 4 mm: set of 5 dpn

Gauge: 20 sts in st st = 4 in / 10 cm. Adjust needle size to obtain correct gauge if necessary.

LEG
CO 54 sts. Divide sts as evenly as possible onto 4 dpn. Join, being careful not to twist cast-on row; pm for beginning of rnd. Begin working in pattern as follows.
Rnd 1: *K2, p1*; rep * to * around.
Rnd 2: * Knit the 2nd st tbl in back of the 1st st without slipping st off needle, knit 1st st and slip both sts off needle, p1*; rep * to * round.
Rnd 3: *Knit the 2nd st in front of the 1st st without slipping it off needle, knit 1st st and slip both sts off needle, p1*; rep * to * around.
Rnds 2-3 form the zigzag pattern. Rep Rnds 2-3 until the leg is 4 in / 10 cm long.

GUSSET HEEL
After completing the leg, divide the stitches, placing the 29 instep sts onto scrap yarn. These instep stitches will "rest" until the heel is complete.

Heel Flap
Place the rem 25 sts (sts indicated on chart) onto one needle and work heel flap back and forth. Begin with the WS facing you.
Row 1 (WS): Sl 1 purlwise wyf, p24.
Row 2: Sl 1 purlwise wyb, k24.
Work the first and last st of each row with both yarn colors together—the white and the purple. Repeat these 2 rows until there are 12 chain sts at each side of the flap.

Shaping the Heel
Row 1: Sl 1, purl until 8 sts rem on needle, p2tog, p1; turn.
Row 2: Sl 1, knit until 8 sts rem on needle, ssk, k1; turn.
Row 3: Sl 1, purl until 1 st before gap, p2tog, p1; turn.
Row 4: Sl 1, knit until 1 st rem before gap, ssk, k1; turn.
Repeat Rows 3-4 until all the side sts have been eliminated.

Gusset Shaping
Divide the instep sts from the holder onto 2 dpn; divide the sole sts onto 2 dpn with half of the sts on each. With RS facing, begin working in the round. Begin rnd at center of sole. With Ndl 1, knit to heel flap. When at side of heel flap, pick up and knit 1 st in each chain up side of flap. You can pick up the chain sts through back loops, or knit them through back loops on the next rnd. Work across instep sts on Ndls 2-3 in pattern. With Ndl 4, pick up and knit sts in each chain st down opposite side of flap as for the first side. Knit to center of sole.

On the next rnd, begin decreasing to shape gusset: Knit until 2 sts rem on Ndl 1, k2tog. Work across instep sts on Ndls 2-3 in pattern. On Ndl 4, ssk and then knit to end of rnd.
Work the next rnd without decreasing. Repeat these 2 rnds until 54 sts rem. Continue as est without further shaping until foot measures 8 in / 20 cm or desired length before toe shaping.

WEDGE TOE
Knit the toe entirely in st st, decreasing as indicated below. Divide the sts so there are 14 sts on each instep needle and 13 sts on each sole needle. Begin at the center of the sole.
Rnd 1:
Ndl 1: Knit.
Ndl 2: K1, ssk, knit to end of needle.
Ndl 3: Knit until 3 sts rem on needle, k2tog, k1.
Ndl 4: Knit.
Now there are 13 sts on each needle. Knit 1 rnd without decreasing.
Continue as follows:
Rnd 1:
Ndl 1: Knit until 3 sts rem on needle, k2tog, k1.
Ndl 2: K1, ssk, knit to end of needle.
Ndl 3: Knit until 3 sts rem on needle, k2tog, k1.
Ndl 4: K1, ssk, knit to end of needle.
Rnd 2: Knit without decreasing.

Repeat these two rounds until 3 sts rem on each needle. Arrange the sts with 6 sole sts onto one needle and the 6 instep sts on a second needle. Turn the sock inside out, carefully bringing needles and yarn through.
Join the sets of sts with 3-needle BO: K2tog with 1 st from each needle, *k2tog with next st from each needle, pass first st over the second*. Repeat from * to * until 1 st loop rem.

FINISHING
Cut yarn and draw end through rem st loop; tighten. Weave in all ends neatly on WS. Make the second sock the same way.

	Heel flap				Instep						Heel flap		

□ Knit

☒ Purl

◺ Knit the 2nd st tbl in back of the 1st st without slipping st off needle, knit 1st st and slip both sts off needle

◸ Knit the 2nd st in front of the 1st st without slipping it off needle, knit 1st st and slip both sts off needle

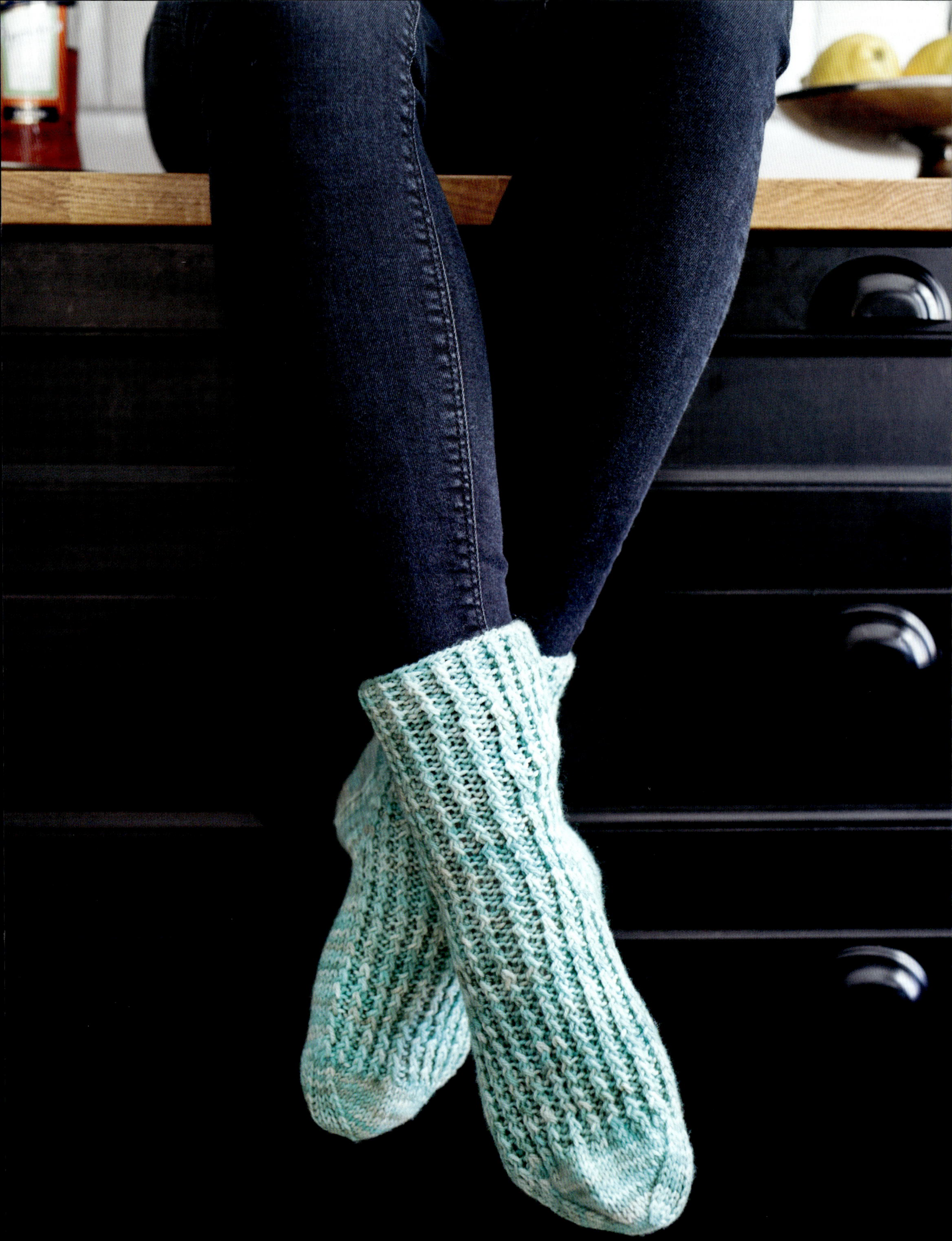

Zigzag Pattern Socks

We're reasonably certain that King Henry VIII was one of the first in Great Britain to wear knitted stockings. A few years later, his daughter, Elizabeth I, received a pair of luxurious silk stockings. They were most likely knitted in Spain or Italy. Elizabeth became very enamored of the exclusive silk stockings and ordered several more pairs.

Elizabeth I reigned for almost 40 years and during her reign a number of knitting schools were established. The queen would have been attentive to this because at the time, knitting provided a means of income for the poor. However, she'd also have wanted to ensure that they worked with wool—which Britain had a lot of—rather than silk.

On the continent, knitting was primarily the occupation of men who were organized in guilds. Similar guilds did not exist in England; therefore, there was nothing stopping the common man in the street from knitting. The queen was also anxious that women should learn this handcraft skill.

In the space of just a few years, knitting became a very important source of income in many places in the country. That gave England a great competitive advantage. At the beginning of the 15th century, it was the world's leading seller of stockings and knitted goods. It also exported knitted goods to the Nordic countries. There was an ample amount of wool and an enormous demand for it from all social classes. Dr. Joan Thirsk, who has researched British home industries, has said that 200,000 knitters produced over 20 million pairs of stockings annually.

It's possible that Denmark's King Christian IV was inspired by the English queen. There were no knitting guilds in united Denmark-Norway either. In Copenhagen, knitting was taught in both orphanages and prisons, which the king had had built in the early 1600s. Most of those who lived there were beggars and the poor. The 1639 charter for a house for women and servants in Trondheim required that they be taught knitting. This is one of the first traces of knitting in Norway.

INSTRUCTIONS

Skill Level: Intermediate

Size: Women's

MATERIALS
Yarn: CYCA #1 (fingering/2 ply), 2-ply Gammelserie from Rauma (100% wool, 175 yd/160 m / 50 g), Natural White 401: 100 g

Reinforcing thread: Sewing thread, 100% silk from AMANN Group, 1 spool, 55 yd/50 m

Needles: U. S. size 1.5 / 2.5 mm: set of 5 dpn; cable needle

Gauge: 24 sts in pattern = 4 in / 10 cm. Adjust needle size to obtain correct gauge if necessary.

LEG
CO 63 sts. Divide sts as evenly as possible onto 4 dpn. Join, being careful not to twist cast-on row; pm for beginning of rnd. Work in pattern following the Leg chart.

COMMON HEEL
After completing sock leg, divide the stitches, placing 27 sts on scrap yarn for instep. These sts will "rest" until the heel is finished.

Heel Flap
Divide the rem 36 sts (those marked on the chart) onto two dpn (= 18 sts per dpn) and work back and forth.
Begin with the RS facing you.
Row 1 (RS): Sl 1 purlwise wyb, k35.
Row 2: Sl 1 purlwise wyf, p35.
Repeat these 2 rows until there are 12 chain sts at each side of the flap.

Shaping the Heel
Now you will shape the back by decreasing as follows:
Row 1: Sl 1, knit until 5 sts rem on Ndl 1, k2tog, k3. On Ndl 2, k3, ssk, knit to end of needle.
Row 2: Sl 1, purl to end of row.
Row 3: Sl 1, knit until 4 sts rem on Ndl 1, k2tog, k2. On Ndl 2, k2, ssk, knit to end of needle.
Row 4: Sl 1, purl to end of row.
Row 5: Sl 1, knit until 3 sts rem on Ndl 1, k2tog, k1. On Ndl 2, k1, ssk, knit to end of needle.
Row 6: Sl 1, purl to end of row.
Row 7: Sl 1, knit until 2 sts rem on Ndl 1, k2tog. On Ndl 2, ssk, knit to end of needle.
Row 8: Sl 1, purl to end of Ndl 2. Yarn is now at center of heel flap.
Hold the two dpn with RS facing in (so WS faces out on each side). Join the sets of sts with 3-needle BO: K2tog with 1 st from each needle, *k2tog with next st from each needle, pass first st over the second*. Repeat from * to * until 1 st loop rem.

FOOT
Divide the instep sts onto 2 dpn. With RS facing and with Ndl 1, beginning at the center of the sole, knit to flap and then pick up and knit 1 st in each chain st on the side of the flap = total of 16 sts. You can pick up the chain sts through back loops or knit them tbl on the next rnd. Work the instep sts on Ndls 2-3 in pattern following the chart. With Ndl 4, pick up and knit sts on opposite side of heel flap = 59 sts total.

Move the last 4 sts on Ndl 1 to Ndl 2 and the first 4 sts on Ndl 4 to Ndl 3. Work sole sts in st st (Ndls 1 and 4) and instep sts (Ndls 2 and 3) in charted pattern. Work foot to end of foot chart or to desired length before toe.

STAR TOE
Begin at the center of the sole.
Rnd 1: (K5, k2tog) around. The 3 sts rem on Ndl 4 will be decreased in subsequent rnds.
Rnds 2-6: Knit.
Rnd 7: (K4, k2tog) around.
Rnds 8-11: Knit.
Rnd 12: (K3, k2tog) around.
Rnds 13-15: Knit
Rnd 16: (K2, k2tog) around.
Rnds 17-18: Knit.
Rnd 19: (K1, k2tog) around.
Rnd 20: Knit.
Rnd 21: (K2tog) around.

FINISHING
Cut yarn and draw end through rem sts; tighten. Weave in all ends neatly on WS. Make the second sock the same way.

FOOT

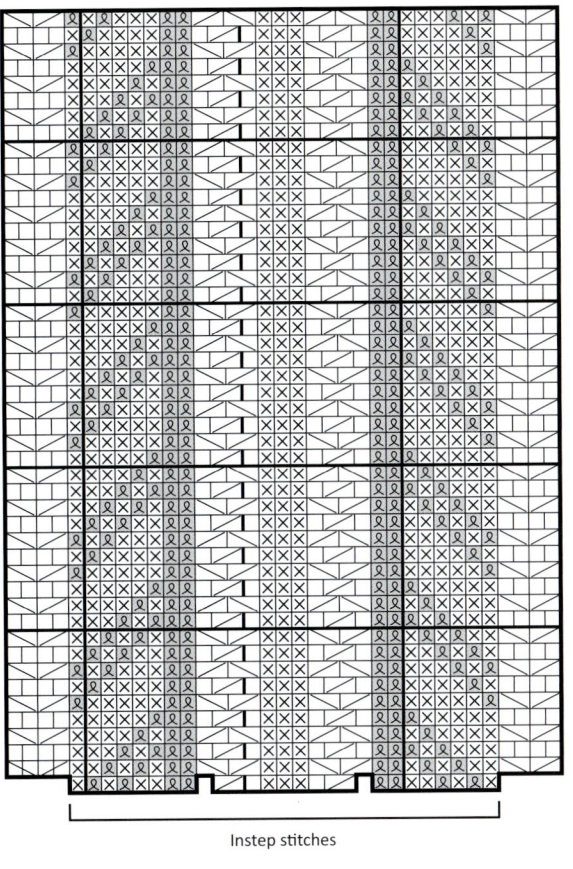

Instep stitches

LEG

Work heel flap over these stitches — Work heel flap over these stitches

☒	Purl
ȣ	Twisted knit (= k1tbl)
☐	Knit
◪	Place 1 st on cable needle and hold behind work, k1, k1 from cable needle
◩	Place 1 st on cable needle and hold in front of work, k1, k1 from cable needle

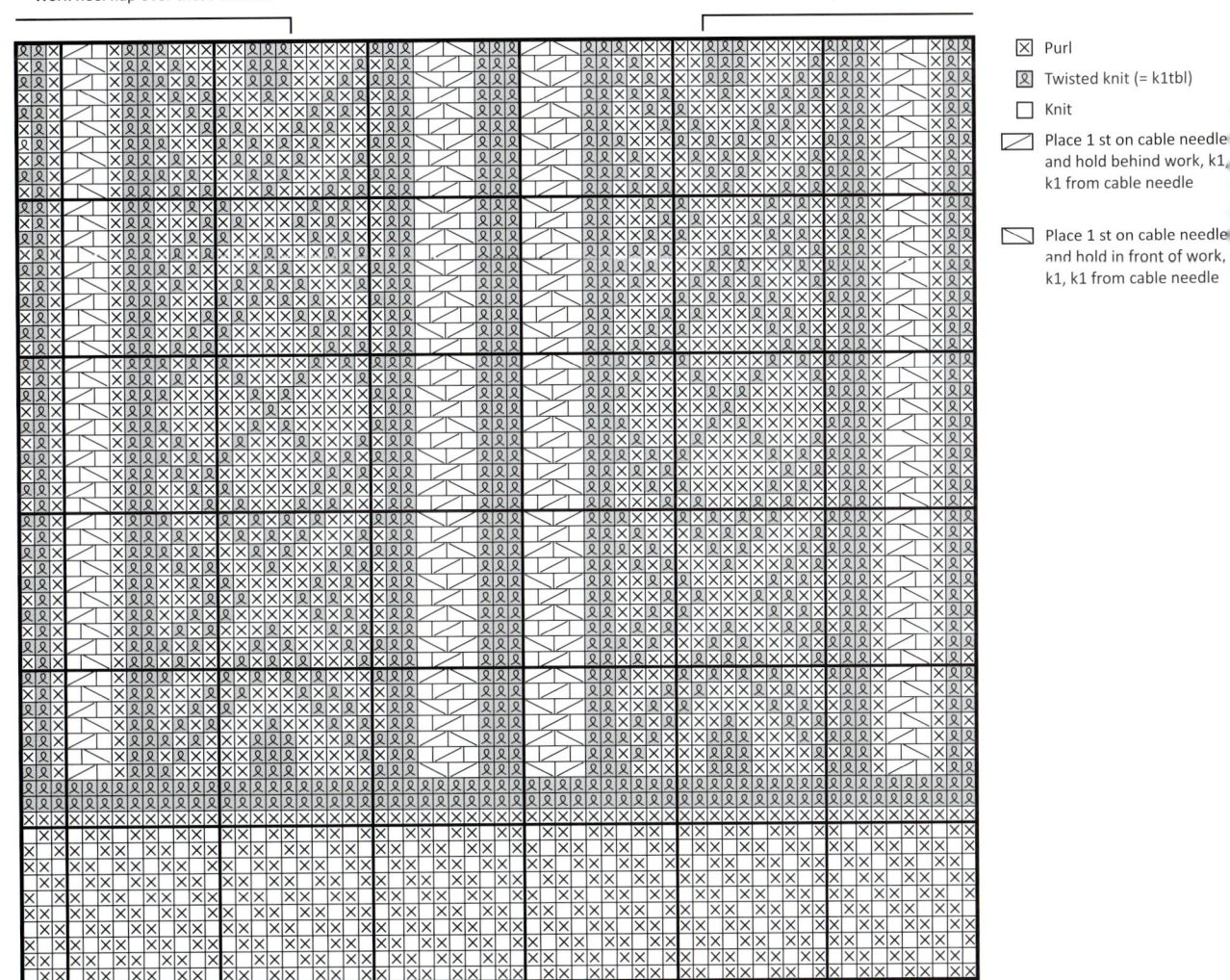

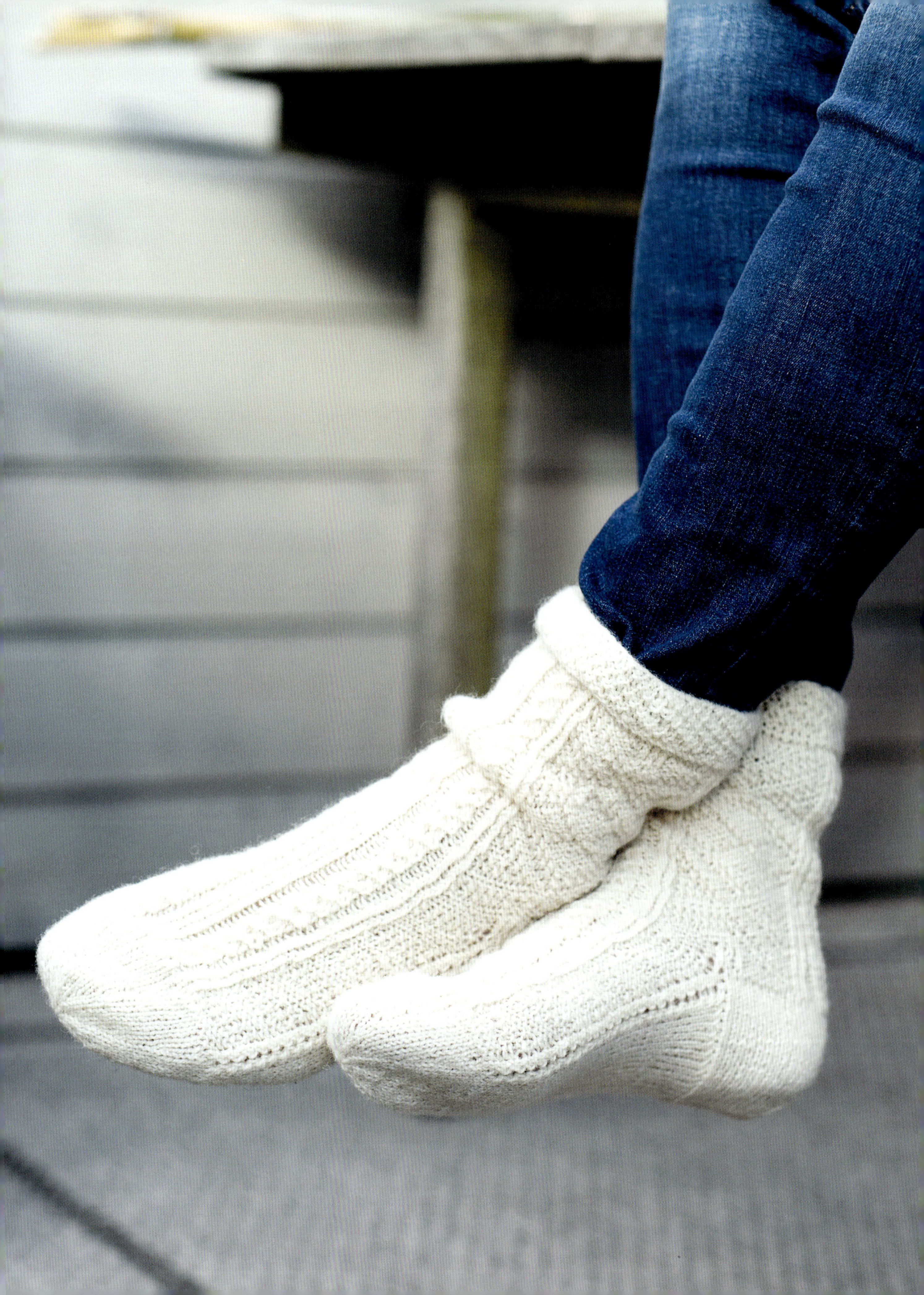

EAST AGDER

Setesdal *Krot* Socks

Even early on, the technique of knitting was well developed in Setesdal. Everyone recognizes the beautiful lice sweaters from this valley. Lots of these black and white sweaters are preserved, and there's also a wealth of photo material.

Stockings, distinctive and typical of the place, were also knitted in Setesdal. The stockings are single-color and the patterns are composed of knit, twisted, and purl stitches together with various cables. Men wore white stockings while women wore black ones. The stockings were dyed after having been knitted, since pattern knitting with dark yarn was almost impossible, particularly in bad light.

All the stockings have sections of cross and crown motifs on the top edging. We find the same patterns on both Setesdal cardigans and Marius sweaters. When the motifs are called "Marius patterns" today, it's only because the origins aren't recognized. These motifs were used in knitting for at least a century before the popular sweaters saw the light of day at the beginning of the 1950s.

Stockings from Setesdal all have a characteristic large bump on the back of the legs. That was because it was the highest fashion at the time to have strong legs—for both women and men. It has been said that people put in half potatoes or half apples at the back of the legs to further accentuate the shaping! Today's equivalent is buying a bra with extra padding—filling out a form for visual appeal is really nothing new.

All the stockings were knitted following the same shaping, but the patterning could vary from knitter to knitter. The local word for this style of stocking was *krot*, meaning "pattern".

The Telemark museum has a pair of women's stockings from Bykle, made between 1800 and 1850. The museum record from 1895 lists: "Women's costume from Setesdal, 1 pair of wool stockings in pattern knitting, natural white wool." The stockings look as if they had never been worn and they weren't dyed black.

INSTRUCTIONS

Skill Level: Intermediate

Sizes: Women's (Men's)

MATERIALS
Yarn:
CYCA #1 (light fingering/2 ply), Mari from Telespinn (80% mohair, 20% wool, 190 yd/174 m / 50 g), Medium Blue M301: 100 (100) g

Needles: U. S. size 0 / 2 mm: set of 5 dpn; cable needle

Gauge: 28 sts in pattern = 4 in / 10 cm. Adjust needle size to obtain correct gauge if necessary.

LEG
CO 105 (123) sts. Divide sts as evenly as possible onto 4 dpn. Join, being careful not to twist cast-on row; pm for beginning of rnd. Work in k2tbl, p1 ribbing for 14 rnds. On the last rnd, decrease 0 (1) st at center back = 105 (122) sts rem. Now work in charted pattern for the leg. After completing charted rows, 92 (109) sts rem.

HEEL
After completing the leg, divide the stitches, placing the 48 (65) instep stitches onto scrap yarn. These instep stitches will "rest" until the heel is complete. Make sure the cable pattern on the women's size or the block pattern on the men's is balanced from across the instep.

Heel Flap
Place the remaining 44 (44) stitches onto one needle and work back and forth in heel pattern as shown on the chart.
Begin with the WS facing you.
Row 1: Sl 1 purlwise wyf, purl to end of row.
Row 2: Sl 1 purlwise wyb, (k1, sl 1) until 1 st rem; end k1.
Repeat these 2 rows until there are 18 (20) chain sts at each side of the flap.

Shaping the Heel
Row 1: Sl 1, purl until 15 sts rem on the needle, p2tog; turn.
Row 2: Sl 1, knit until 15 sts rem on needle, ssk; turn.
Row 3: Sl 1, purl until 1 st before gap, p2tog; turn.
Row 4: Sl 1, knit until 1 st rem before gap, ssk; turn.
Repeat Rows 3-4 until all the side sts have been eliminated.

Gusset Shaping
Divide the instep sts from the holder onto 2 dpn; divide the sole sts onto 2 dpn with half of the sts on each. With RS facing, begin working in the round. Begin rnd at center of sole. With Ndl 1, to heel flap. When at side of heel flap, pick up and knit 1 st in each chain up side of flap. You can pick up the chain sts through back loops, or knit them through back loops on the next rnd.
With Ndls 2-3, work across the instep in pattern as shown on chart. Next, with Ndl 4, pick up and knit sts in each chain st down opposite side of flap as for the first side. Knit to center of sole.

On the next rnd, begin decreasing to shape gusset: Knit until 2 sts rem on Ndl 1, k2tog. Work across instep sts on Ndls 2-3 as shown on chart. On Ndl 4, ssk and then knit to end of rnd.
Work the next rnd without decreasing.
Repeat these 2 rnds until there are 32 knit sts on the sole and a total of 80 (97) sts. Continue without further shaping, following charted pattern, until foot measures 7½ (9) in / 19 (23) cm or desired length before toe.

STAR TOE
Begin at the center of the sole.
Rnd 1: (K5, k2tog) around. The 3 (6) sts left on Ndl 4 will be decreased on subsequent rnds.
Rnds 2-6: Knit.
Rnd 7: (K4, k2tog) around.
Rnds 8-11: Knit.
Rnd 12: (K3, k2tog) around.
Rnds 13-15: Knit
Rnd 16: (K2, k2tog) around.
Rnds 17-18: Knit.
Rnd 19: (K1, k2tog) around.
Rnd 20: Knit.
Rnd 21: (K2tog) around.

FINISHING
Cut yarn and draw end through rem sts; tighten. Weave in all ends neatly on WS. Make the second sock the same way.

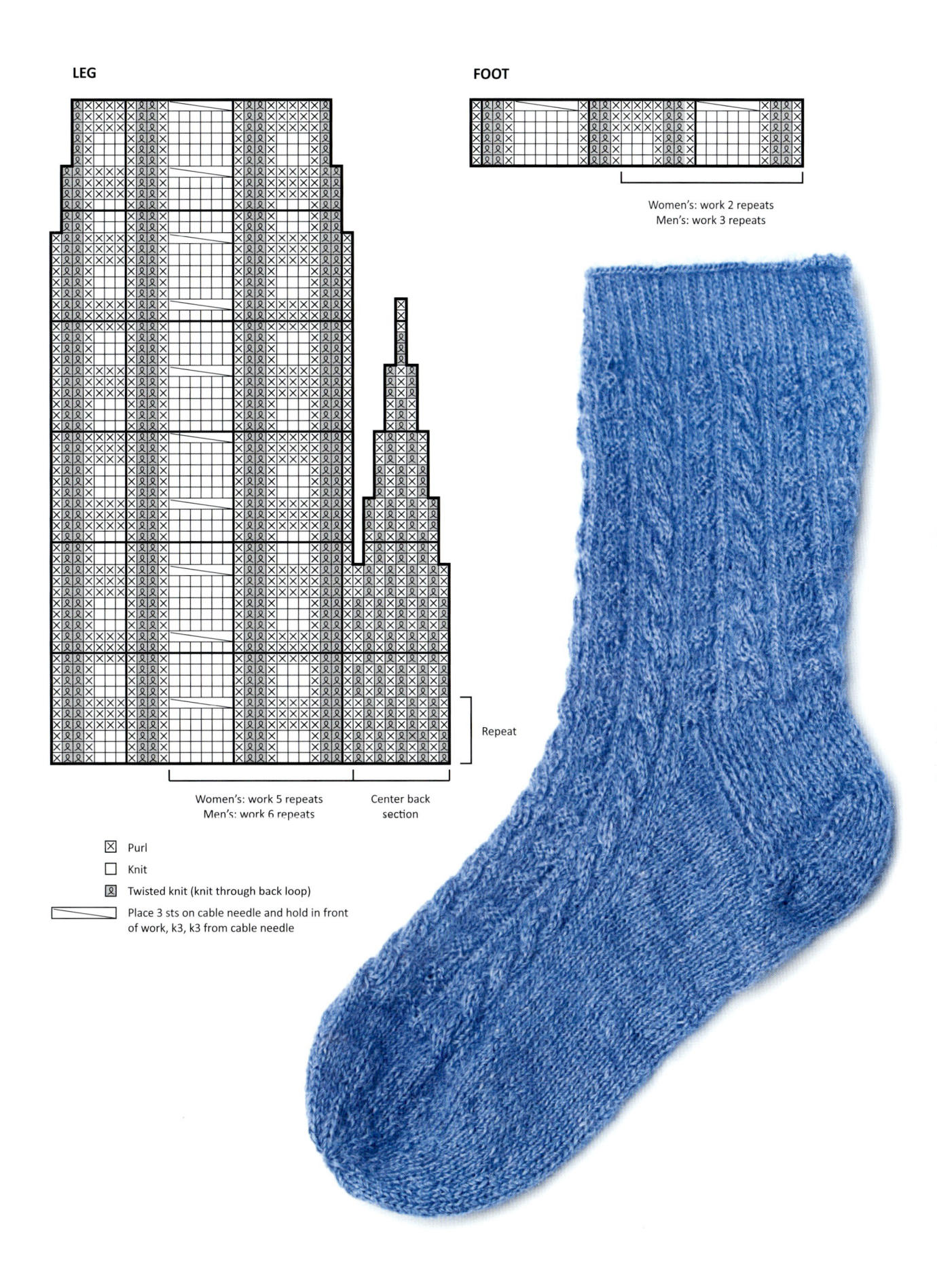

LEG

FOOT

Women's: work 2 repeats
Men's: work 3 repeats

Repeat

Women's: work 5 repeats
Men's: work 6 repeats

Center back section

☒ Purl
☐ Knit
🯄 Twisted knit (knit through back loop)
▱ Place 3 sts on cable needle and hold in front of work, k3, k3 from cable needle

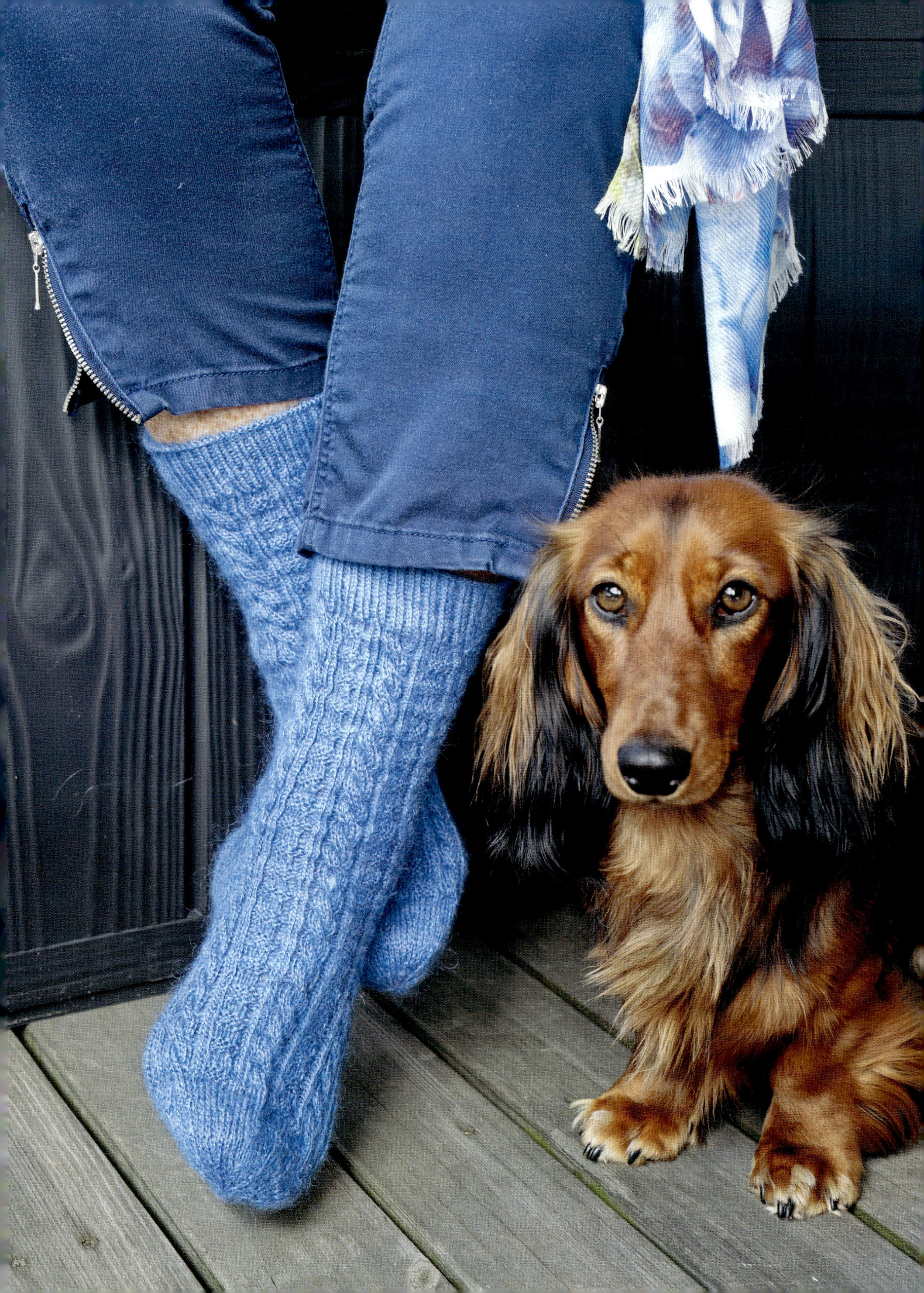

TELEMARK

Cable Socks from Tinn

You'll find many traces of cabled stockings in Agder and Telemark. The stockings were knitted with extremely fine wool yarn and the cable patterns were most often very complex. We seldom throw ourselves into this type of work today. Even finding the appropriate yarn and needles is difficult.

A pair of pretty stockings from Tinn is registered at The Norwegian Institute for Bunad and Folk Costume in Fagernes. They were knitted by Ole Nilsen Besager from Marumsrud in Attrå. He was born in 1790 in Besaker within the Bjørnøer Parish in Fosen, South Trøndelag.

Aagot Noss writes about a possible source for this story, named Mogens Nilsen. He is listed as a 13-year-old servant boy in the 1801 census for Bjørnøer. Perhaps this is the same person?

In the folk census of 1865, Ole Nilsen Besager was listed as a pensioner. He lived with his wife Torbjør Gjermundsdatter (70) and daughter Birgit Olsdatter (22) and his son Hans (16) and his family. The pair had three children. Earlier we find Ole recorded as a sexton and farmer. On 18 June 1838, he was selected as the first mayor in the Tinn municipality. He served for two years. There were stories about Ole walking and knitting.

The stockings are a dark indigo blue. The pattern consists of cables and vertical lines of purl stitches and knit blocks. Aagot Noss relates that the stockings of Mogens Nilsen had a pattern that was called *kjasehopp*. A *kjase* is a hare, and the pattern resembles a hare hopping. *Musevilsteg* ("mouse tracks") is the name of another pattern. Both stockings have holes and are torn on the heel. The tip of one stockings had been re-knitted on the edging and does not have the blue color.

According to Hans Jakob Willes in "Writings about Sillejords Parish" from 1786, it was common to use leggings and footless socks in Telemark. "In that area, their stockings were always without feet; instead, they had old wool bands called *skoklutar* that they wrapped around their feet." This tradition lasted longer in Tinn than in other villages—all the way up to the 1950s and 60s, according to Aagot Noss. For finery, they wore knitted stockings and the pattern-knitted ones were the most coveted.

INSTRUCTIONS

Skill Level: Experienced

Sizes: Women's (Men's)

MATERIALS
Yarn:
CYCA #1 (fingering/2 ply), 2-ply Gammelserie from Rauma (100% wool, 175 yd/160 m / 50 g, Natural White 401: 100 (100) g

CYCA #0 (lace/1 ply), Røros Embroidery yarn ("Brodergarn") from Rauma Ullevarefabrikk (100% Spelsau wool, 547 yd/500 m / 100 g), Purple 355, held double: 100 (100) g

Needles: U. S. size 0 (1.5) / 2 (2.5) mm: set of 5 dpn

Gauge: 34 (32) sts in pattern = 4 in / 10 cm. Adjust needle size to obtain correct gauge if necessary.

LEG
With Natural White, CO 84 sts. Divide sts evenly onto 4 dpn. Join, being careful not to twist cast-on row; pm for beginning of rnd. Work in k3, p3 ribbing for 1¼ in / 3 cm. Next, knit 6 rnds in st st and, on the last rnd, decrease 1 st at center back—83 sts rem. Now work charted Leg pattern until you've completed 4 block tiers. Hold the Purple embroidery yarn double throughout.

GUSSET HEEL
After completing the leg, divide the stitches, placing the 47 instep sts onto scrap yarn. These instep stitches will "rest" until the heel is complete.

Heel Flap
Place the rem 36 sts onto one needle and work back and forth in checkerboard pattern as shown at top of Leg chart.
Begin with the WS facing you.
Row 1 (WS): Sl 1 purlwise wyf, purl to end of row.
Row 2: Sl 1 purlwise wyb, knit to end of row. Work the first and last st of each row with both yarn colors together—the White and the Purple. Repeat these 2 rows until there are 12 chain sts at each side of the flap.

Shaping the Heel
With Natural White only:
Row 1: Sl 1, purl until 12 sts rem on the needle, p2tog, p1; turn.
Row 2: Sl 1, knit until 12 sts rem on needle, ssk, k1; turn.
Row 3: Sl 1, purl until 1 st before gap, p2tog, p1; turn.
Row 4: Sl 1, knit until 1 st rem before gap, ssk, k1; turn.
Repeat Rows 3-4 until all the side sts have been eliminated.

Gusset Shaping
Divide the instep sts from the holder onto 2 dpn; divide the sole sts onto 2 dpn with half of the sts on each. With RS facing, begin working in the round. Begin rnd at center of sole. With Ndl 1, k3 in Natural White as shown on chart. Continue with k3 Purple. When at side of heel flap, pick up and knit 1 st in each chain up side of flap. You can pick up the chain sts through back loops, or knit them through back loops on the next rnd.
NOTE: You need to carry both yarns here.
With Ndls 2-3, work across the instep in pattern as shown on chart. Next, with Ndl 4, pick up and knit sts in each chain st down opposite side of flap as for the first side. Knit to center of sole, increasing 1 st with M1 at end of rnd. Make sure the patterns match as you work around. You've now completed the first row of the foot chart and have 96 sts total.

On the next rnd, begin decreasing to shape gusset: Knit until 2 sts rem on Ndl 1, k2tog. Work across instep sts on Ndls 2-3 as shown on chart. On Ndl 4, ssk and then knit to end of rnd. Work the next rnd without decreasing. Repeat these 2 rnds until 82 sts rem. Continue without further shaping, following charted pattern. Make sure the foot ends with a complete pattern repeat.

STAR TOE
Begin at the center of the sole with Natural White.
Rnd 1: (K5, k2tog) around. The 5 sts rem at end of Ndl 4 will be decreased on subsequent rnds.
Rnds 2-6: Knit.
Rnd 7: (K4, k2tog) around.
Rnds 8-11: Knit.
Rnd 12: (K3, k2tog) around.
Rnds 13-15: Knit
Rnd 16: (K2, k2tog) around.
Rnds 17-18: Knit.
Rnd 19: (K1, k2tog) around.
Rnd 20: Knit.
Rnd 21: (K2tog) around.

FINISHING
Cut yarn and draw end through rem sts; tighten. Weave in all ends neatly on WS. Make the second sock the same way.

FOOT

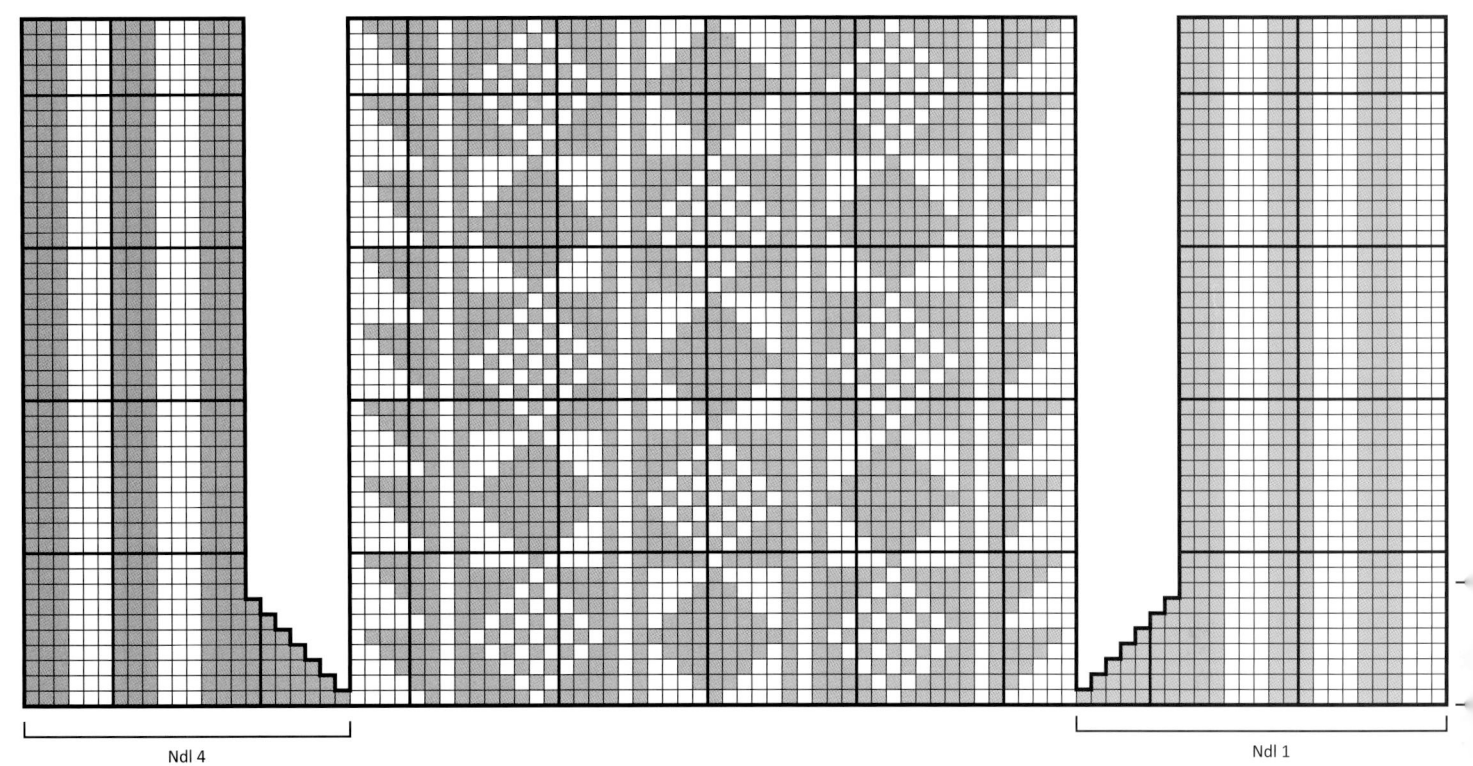

Ndl 4

Ndl 1

LEG

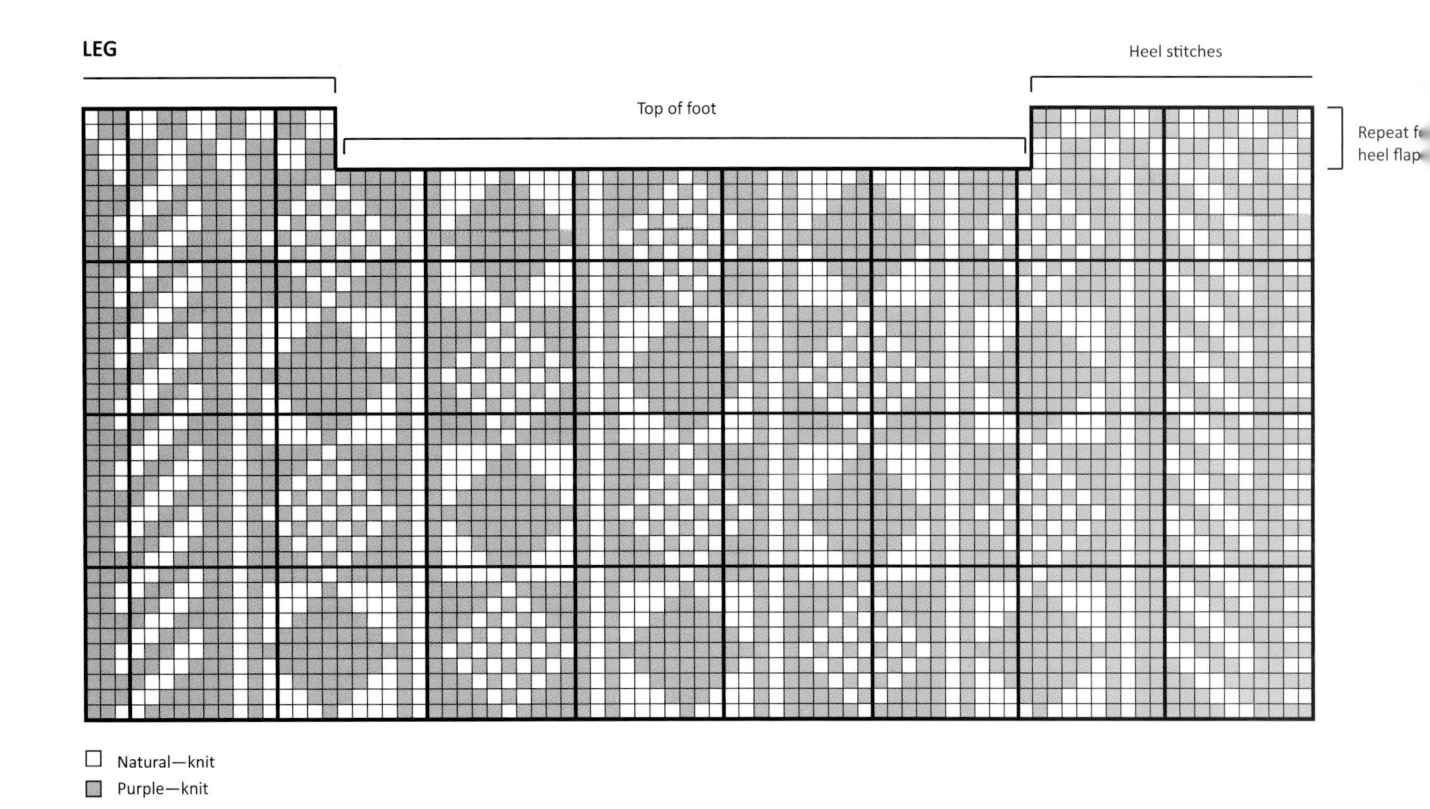

Heel stitches

Top of foot

Repeat for heel flap

☐ Natural—knit
■ Purple—knit

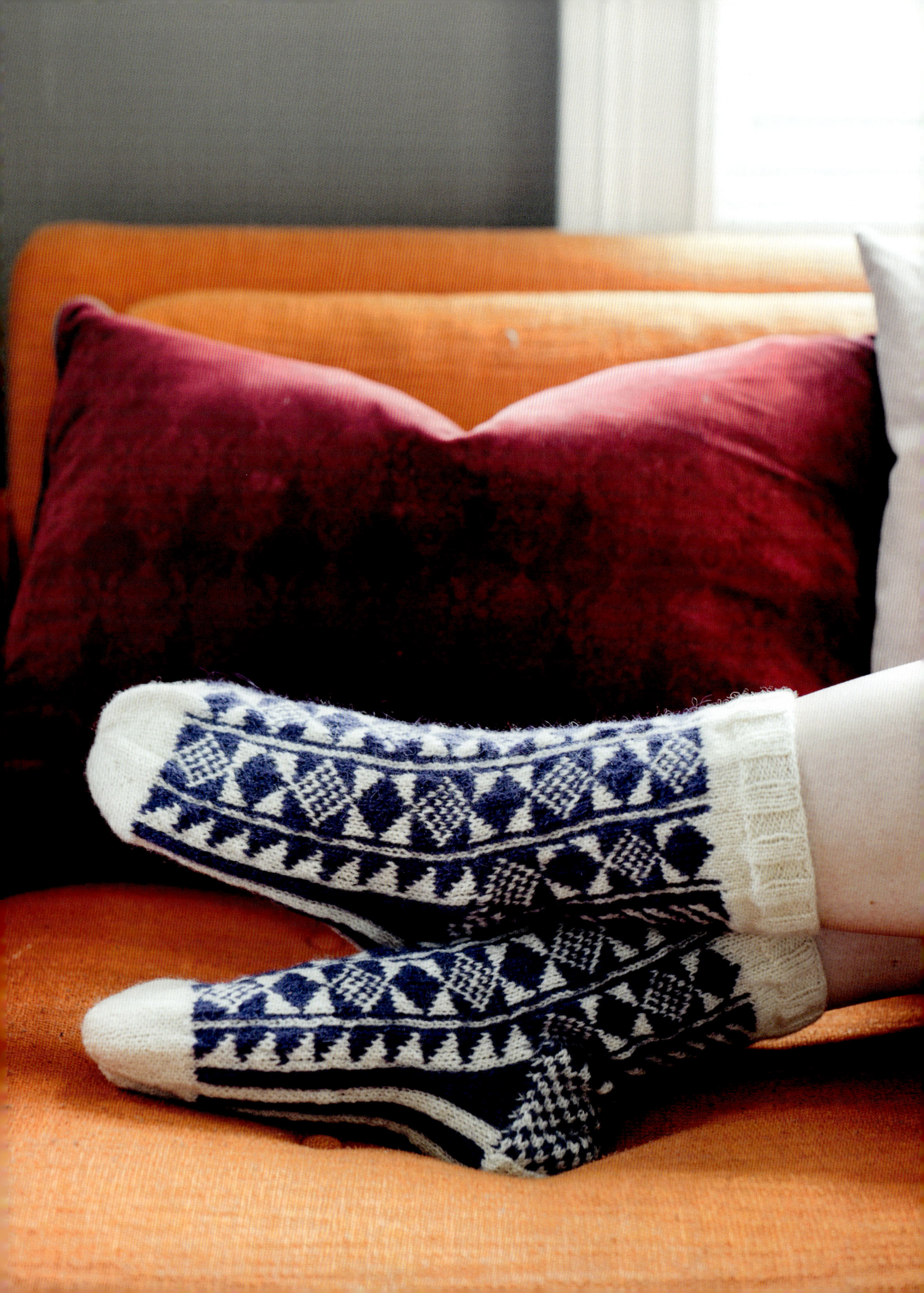

TELEMARK

Telemark Socks

We have several pairs of men's stockings from Telemark with characteristic block patterns in dark blue and sheep's natural white. The back of the calf features diagonally stylized stripes while the ankles sport decorative eight-petal roses. The feet are knitted somewhat differently on the various pairs.

One of these pairs was purchased by the Nordic Museum in Stockholm in 1880. Another pair came from the Heftyeske Collection. These stockings were later acquired by the Norwegian Museum of Cultural History in 1921. Thomas Heftye (1822-1886) owned one of the country's finest and most valuable antique collections of the nineteenth century. According to Aagot Noss, a previous conservator of the Nowegian Museum of Cultural History, the stockings from Heftye's collection had likely been in use between 1800 and 1880. A catalogue from 1890 lists "a pair of striped and block-pattern wool stockings for men, from Telemark." A third pair of the same type was purchased from P. Simonsen in Oslo in 1884. These had been in use in Drangedal.

In addition to these stockings, we can see more in two photographs taken by Axel Lindahl sometime between 1885 and 1890. In the picture below, we can see Master Sargeant Torkild Olsen Sem from Heddal, born in 1819, and his daughter Ingeborg, born in 1868. The daughter is stylishly dressed in what was at that time called a "farmer's skirt", "lampshade skirt", or "Heddal skirt", and what we would now call a belted skirt. She immigrated to the state of Washington in the U. S. and married a farmer named Sonstrud. The father is wearing a gray jacket and block-pattern stockings. It looks like there are as many as 16 silver buttons on the vest, 20 on the jacket, and 27 on the knee trousers of this elegant costume. "Master sergeant" was the highest ranking non-commissioned officer's title in Norway, and normally awarded after five years of service.

Since there are more stockings similar to these from the same period, we can be reasonably certain that this style of stocking was in production at one place or another in Telemark.

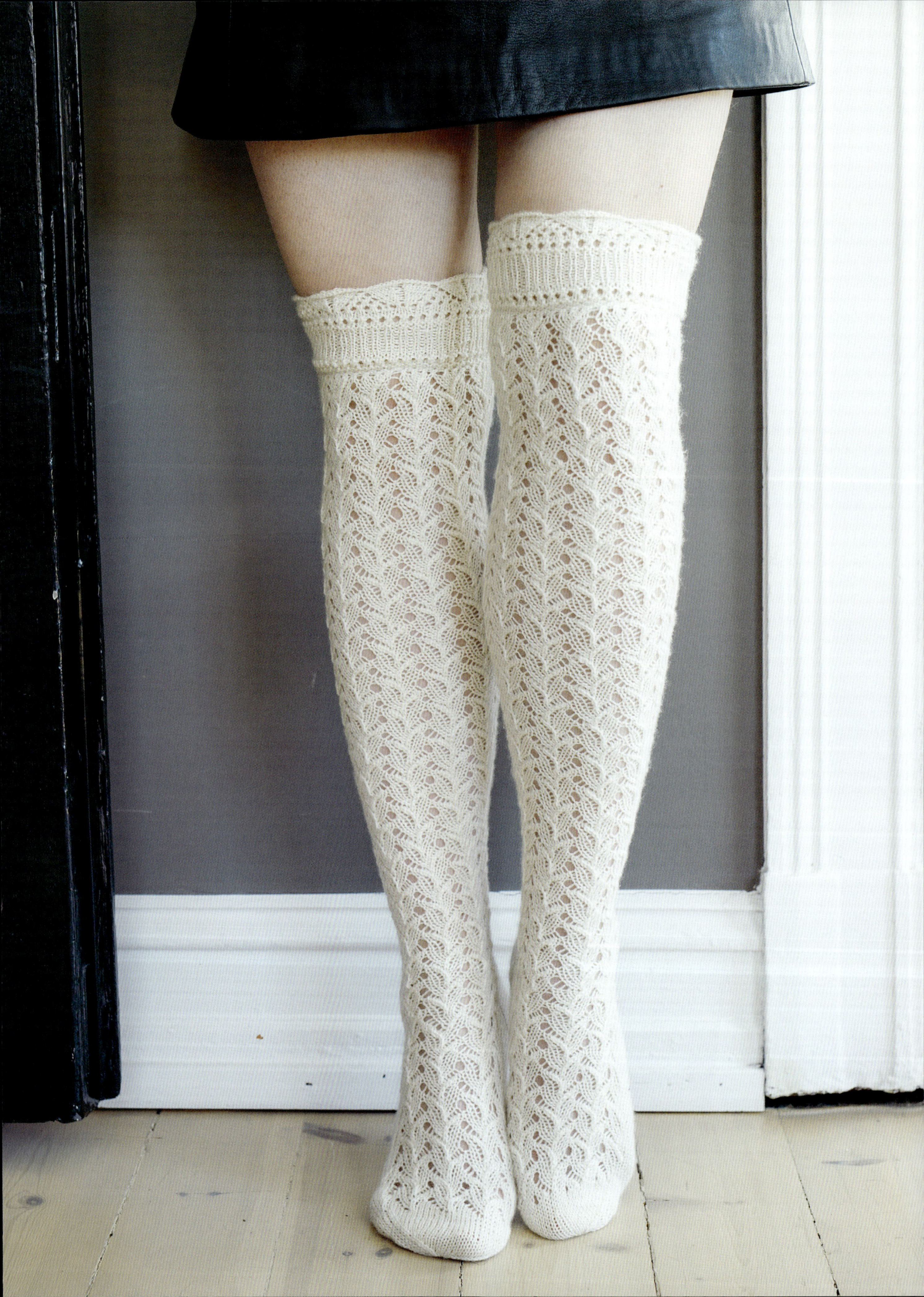

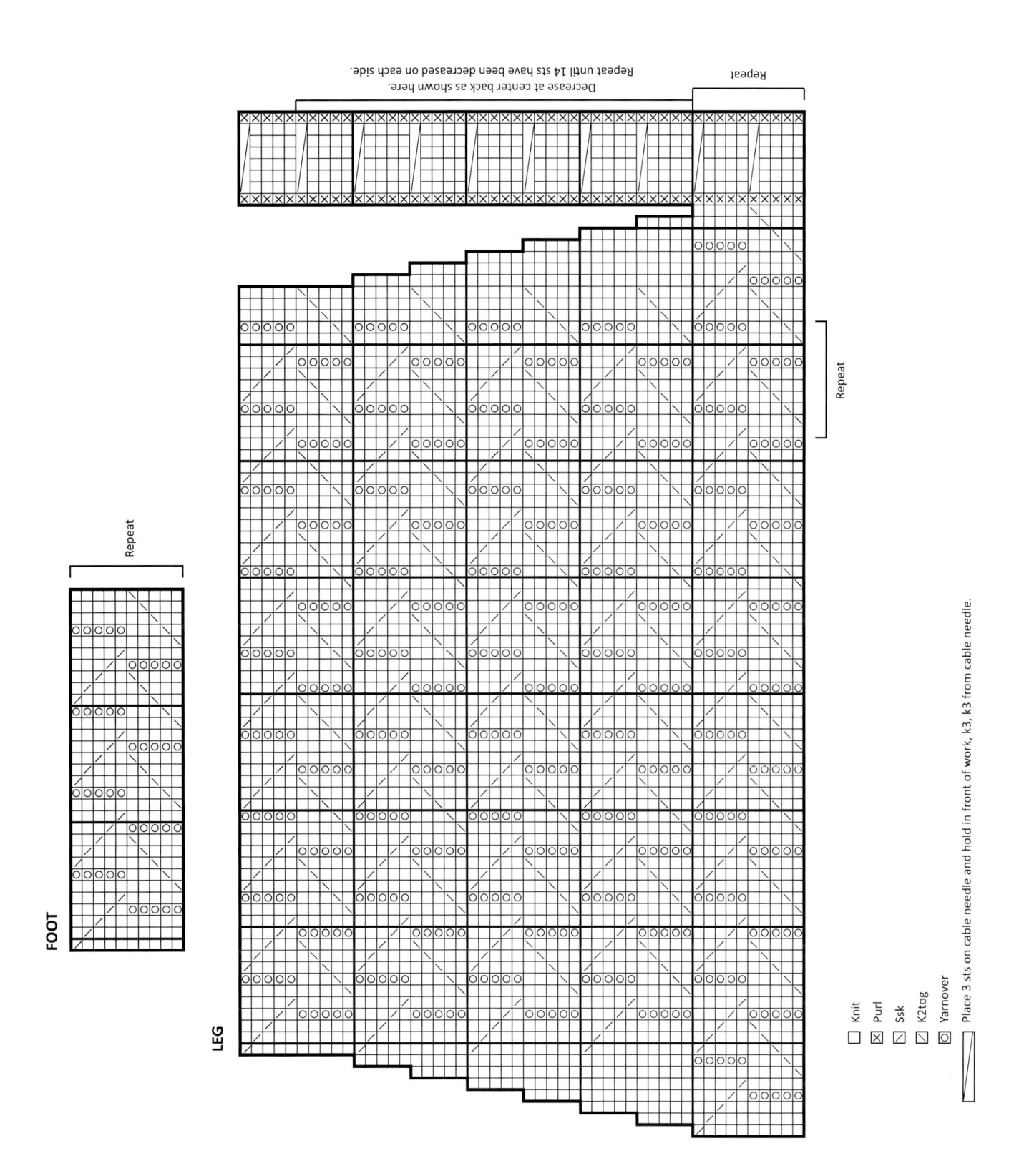

Decrease at center back as shown here.
Repeat until 14 sts have been decreased on each side.

Repeat

Repeat

FOOT

LEG

☐ Knit
☒ Purl
◪ Ssk
◪ K2tog
◉ Yarnover
◪ Place 3 sts on cable needle and hold in front of work, k3, k3 from cable needle.

Gusset Shaping
Divide the instep sts from the holder onto 2 dpn; divide the sole sts onto 2 dpn with half of the sts on each. With RS facing, begin working in the round. Begin rnd at center of sole. With Ndl 1, knit to flap; pick up and knit 1 st in each chain up side of flap. You can pick up the chain sts through back loops, or knit them through back loops on the next rnd. With Ndls 2-3, work across the instep in pattern as shown on chart. Next, with Ndl 4, pick up and knit sts down opposite side of flap as for the first side. Knit to center of sole.

On the next rnd, begin decreasing to shape gusset: Knit until 2 sts rem on Ndl 1, k2tog. Work across instep sts on Ndls 2-3 as shown on chart. With Ndl 4, ssk and then knit to end of rnd.
Work the next rnd without decreasing. Repeat these 2 rnds until 60 sts rem. Continue without further shaping, with instep in pattern and sole in st st until foot measures 7 (7½) in / 18 (19) cm or desired length to toe shaping. Make sure the foot ends with a complete pattern repeat.

WEDGE TOE
Divide sts evenly over 4 dpn.
Rnd 1:
Ndl 1: Knit until 3 sts rem on needle, k2tog, k1.
Ndl 2: K1, ssk, knit to end of needle.
Ndl 3: Work as for Ndl 1.
Ndl 4: Work as for Ndl 2.
Rnd 2: Knit without decreasing.

Repeat these two rounds 4 times and then decrease on every rnd until approx. 3 sts rem on each needle.

FINISHING
Cut yarn and draw end through rem sts; tighten. Weave in all ends neatly on WS. Make second sock the same way.

INSTRUCTIONS

Skill Level: Intermediate

Sizes: Women's shoe sizes: small—U. S. 4½-8 (large—8½-11½) / Euro small—35-38 (large—39-42)

MATERIALS
Yarn:
CYCA #1 (fingering), Baby Panda from Rauma Ullvarefabrikk (100% Merino wool, 191 yd/ 175 m / 50 g), Natural White 11: 200 (250) g

Reinforcing Thread: Natural White buttonhole thread

Needles: U. S. size 1.5 (2.5) / 2.5 (3) mm: set of 5 dpn; cable needle

Gauge: 34 (32) sts in pattern = 4 in / 10 cm. Adjust needle size to obtain correct gauge if necessary.

WAVY EDGING
CO 96 sts. Divide sts evenly onto 4 dpn (= 24 sts per needle) and join, being careful not to twist cast-on row. Pm for beginning of rnd.
Knit 1 rnd.

Wavy Lace Pattern
Rnd 1: *K2tog, k4, yo, k4, ssk*; rep from * to * around.
Rnd 2: Knit.
Rnd 3: *K2tog, k3, yo, k1, yo, k3, ssk*; rep * to * around.
Rnd 4: Knit.
Rnd 5: *K2tog, k2, yo, ssk, yo, k1, yo, k2, ssk*; rep * to * around.
Rnd 6: Knit.
Rnd 7: *K2tog, k1, yo, ssk, yo, ssk, yo, k1, yo, k1, ssk*; rep * to * around.
Rnd 8: Knit.
Rnd 9: *K2tog, yo, ssk, yo, ssk, yo, ssk, yo, k1, yo, ssk*; rep * to * around.
Rnds 10-11: Knit = 88 sts rem.

Garter, Rib, and Eyelet Cuff
Rnd 1: Purl.
Rnd 2: (K2tog, yo) around.
Rnd 3: Knit around.
Rnd 4: Purl 1 around.
Rnds 5-15: (K1, p1) around (= total of 11 rib rounds).
Rnd 16: Purl around.
Rnd 17: (K2tog, yo) around.
Rnd 18: Knit around.
Rnd 19: Purl around.

Basketweave Cable Pattern
Rnd 1: *From behind piece, k1tbl into 2nd st; knit 1st st and slip both sts from needle*; rep * to * to last st, end k1.
Rnd 2: *From front of piece, knit 2nd st and then knit 1st st and slip both sts from needle*; rep * to * around.
Repeat these 2 rnds.
Knit 1 rnd.

Continue in pattern as shown on the chart (see page 82). At the center back, work p1, k6, p1 for a cable which is turned every time a half pattern repeat is complete.
Continue as est until piece measures 11¾ in/ 30 cm and you have turned the cable 18 times. Now begin decreasing 1 st on each side of the cable *at the same time* as you turn it—as shown on chart.
As the stitch count decreases, it won't be possible to work a complete pattern. So the first and last st on the round must be worked in st st until you have decreased a total of 28 sts. Now 60 sts rem. Continue in pattern until stocking measures 22 in / 56 cm or there are 39 cable turns.

GUSSET HEEL
After completing the leg, divide the stitches, placing the 31 instep stitches onto scrap yarn. These instep stitches will "rest" until the heel is complete.

Place the remaining 29 stitches onto one needle and work back and forth. Begin with the WS facing you and attach reinforcing thread to hold together with working yarn.
Row 1 (WS): Sl 1 purlwise wyf, purl to end of row.
Row 2: Sl 1 purlwise wyb, knit to end of row.
Repeat these 2 rows until there are 16 chain sts at each side of the flap.

Shaping the Heel
Row 1: Sl 1, purl until 10 sts rem on the needle, p2tog, p1; turn.
Row 2: Sl 1, knit until 10 sts rem on needle, ssk, k1; turn.
Row 3: Sl 1, purl until 1 st before gap, p2tog, p1; turn.
Row 4: Sl 1, knit until 1 st rem before gap, ssk, k1; turn.
Repeat Rows 3-4 until all the side sts have been eliminated.
Cut reinforcing thread.

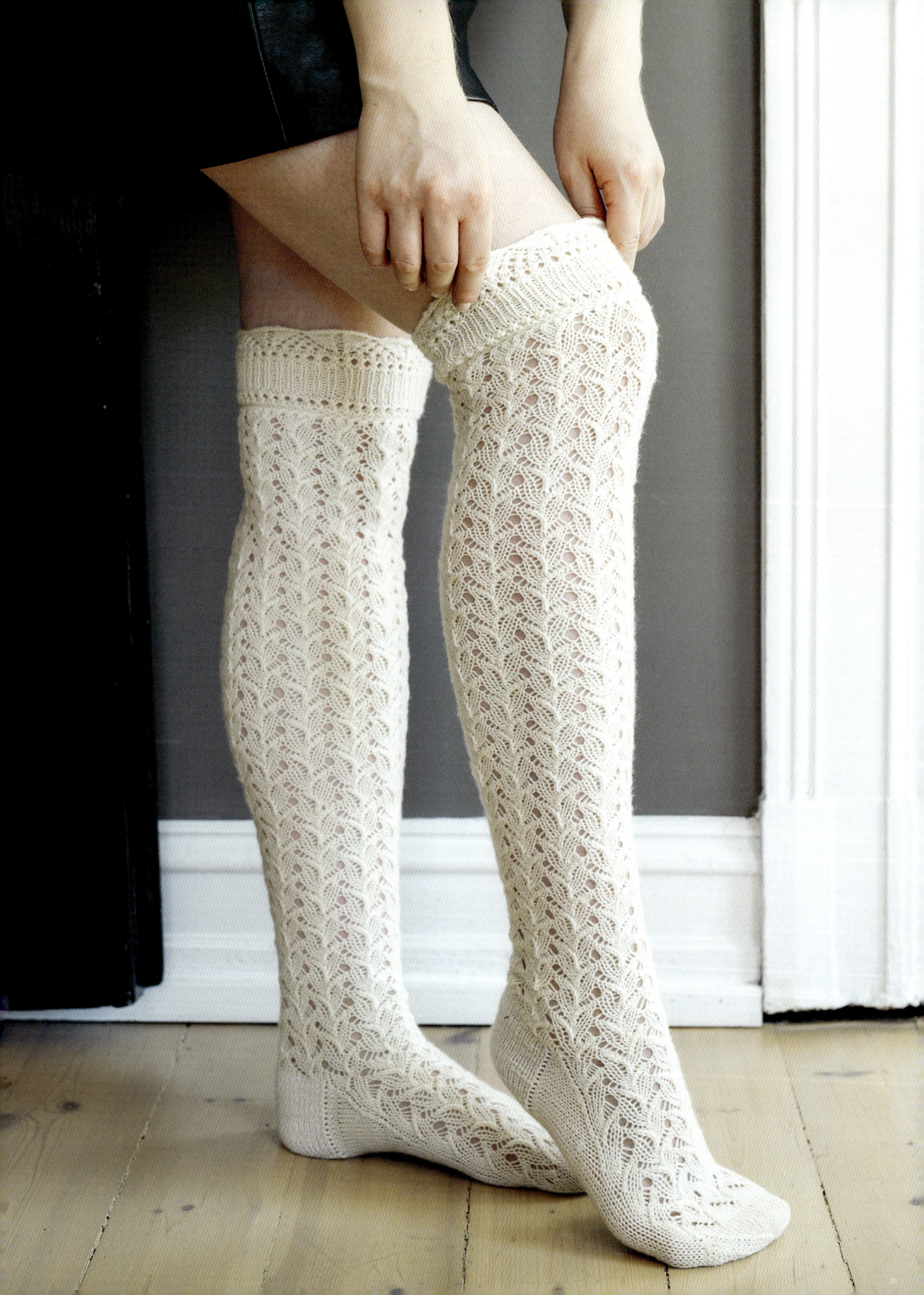

Long Lace Stockings

Knitting was an important part of handcraft education, and stocking knitting was a required course for small girls. One of Marie Rosing's lesson plans gives detailed information about how a stocking should be knitted.

The universal pattern, if one can call it that, consists of eight sections. The number of stitches in the ribbing for the cuff is the starting point, and that stitch count determines the rest of the numbers. The first decision is how long the ribbing should be: one-third of the stitch count. If, for example, 120 stitches are cast on (not an uncommon number), then the ribbing should be 40 rounds long.

The calf with the same stitch count would have two-thirds of the cast-on number or 80 rounds.

The next step was to decrease over a number of rounds equal to three-fourths of the stitch count = 90. Over these 90 rounds, one should decrease one-fourth the cast-on stitch count or 30 stitches. In this case, 2 stitches are decreased on each decrease round for a total of 15 decrease rounds. Decreases are, therefore, worked every 6th round. When this section is finished, 90 stitches remain.

The lower part of the leg is worked with one-third the count for the rounds = 40 rounds.

Now it's time for the heel. The height should be three-fourths of the width. It was normal to knit the heel over half of the total number of stitches remaining at this point—in this case, 45 stitches. This means knitting 33 or 34 rows back and forth before beginning to shape the heel turn. From the drawing, we can see that a gusset heel is recommended.

The foot is three-fourths rounds long: 90 rounds.

Finally, the toe is shaped over one-fourth of the stitches or 30 rounds.

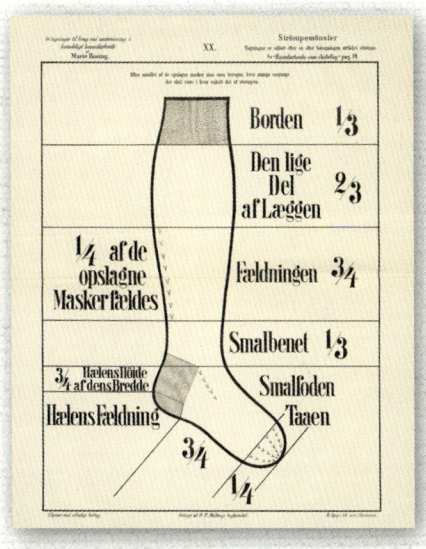

INSTRUCTIONS

Skill Level: Experienced

Sizes: Women's (Men's)

MATERIALS
Yarn:
CYCA #1 (fingering/2 ply), Mini Sterk from Du Store Alpakka (40% alpaca, 40% Merino wool, 20% polyamide, 182 yd/166 m / 50 g), Gray 822 (MC): 100 (100) g

CYCA #1 (fingering/2 ply), Superfine Merino/nylon Sock from The Happy Little Dye Pot (75% wool, 25% nylon, 437 yd / 400 m / 100 g), Hand-dyed (CC): 50 (50) g

Needles: U. S. 0 (1.5) / 2 (2.5) mm: set of 5 dpn

Gauge: 26 (28) sts in pattern = 4 in / 10 cm. Adjust needle size to obtain correct gauge if necessary.

LEG
With Gray, CO 72 sts. Divide sts evenly onto 4 dpn. Join, being careful not to twist cast-on row; pm for beginning of rnd. Work in k2, p2 ribbing for 8 rnds.
Now work in pattern as follows:
*With Gray, knit 5 rnds in st st and then work pattern stripe.
With CC, knit 1 rnd.
With CC, purl 1 rnd.*
Rep * to * a total of 5 times.
Knit 1 rnd with Gray.
On the next rnd, decrease at center back: K2tog, knit until 2 sts rem, ssk.
Knit 3 more rnds with Gray and then work the 2-round pattern stripe.
Work this sequence with decreases a total of 3 times = 66 sts rem. Work 1 more pattern rep without decreasing and end with 5 rnds Gray.

BAND HEEL WITH SHORT HEEL FLAP
After completing leg, place 34 sts on scrap yarn for the instep (to "rest" while you work the heel flap).

Heel Flap
Place rem 32 sts on one dpn and, with Gray, work reinforced heel flap back and forth. Begin with WS facing you.
Row 1 (WS): Sl 1 purlwise wyf, purl to end of row.
Row 2: Sl 1 purlwise wyb, k1, sl 1 to last st and end with k1.
Rep these 2 rows until there are 11 chain sts at each side of flap.

Heel Gusset:
Row 1: Sl 1, purl until 12 sts rem, p2tog; turn.
Row 2: Sl 1, knit until 12 sts rem, ssk; turn.
Row 3: Sl 1, purl until 1 st before gap, p2tog; turn.
Row 4: Sl 1, knit until 1 st before gap, ssk; turn.
Rep Rows 3-4 until all the side sts have been eliminated = 10 sts rem.

FOOT
Divide the instep sts onto 2 dpn and divide the rem heel sts onto 2 dpn so you have half of each section on a needle. Work in the round with RS facing you.

Begin rnd at center of sole. With CC, k5. Pick up and knit 11 sts in chain sts along left side of heel flap. You can pick up the sts tbl or knit them tbl on next rnd. Knit across instep. Pick up and knit 11 sts in chain sts of opposite side of flap and then knit to end of rnd = 66 sts total. Purl the next rnd.

Work 7 (8) rep with Gray and dyed yarn pattern as est or to desired length before toe. Continue the pattern sequence while shaping the toe.

STAR TOE
Begin at the center of the sole.
Rnd 1: (K5, k2tog) around. The 3 sts rem at end of Ndl 4 will be decreased on the last 2 rounds.
Rnds 2-6: Knit.
Rnd 7: (K4, k2tog) around.
Rnds 8-11: Knit.
Rnd 12: (K3, k2tog) around.
Rnds 13-15: Knit
Rnd 16: (K2, k2tog) around.
Rnds 17-18: Knit.
Rnd 19: (K1, k2tog) around.
Rnd 20: Knit.
Rnd 21: (K2tog) around.

FINISHING
Cut yarn and draw end through rem sts; tighten. Weave in all ends neatly on WS. Make the second sock the same way.

5
Holmestrand
MOSS
HORTEN
TØNSBERG
SANDE-
FJORD
LARVIK
Stavern
Nevlunghavn
Selvik
Svelvik
Drøbak
Vestby
Son
Spetalen

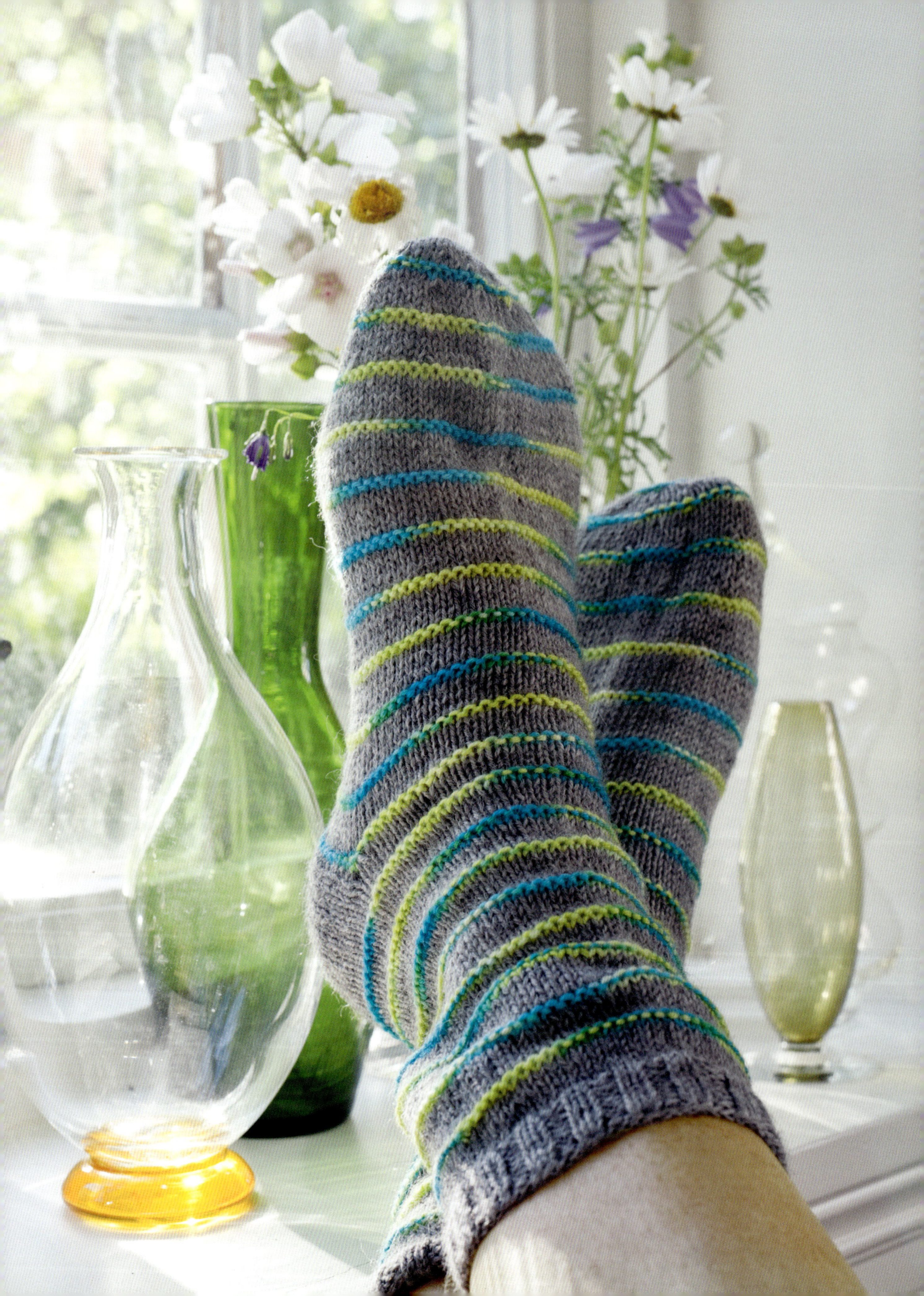

Larvik Socks

Larvik Museum has a pair of children's stockings knitted with gray and white wool yarn. The pattern striping is worked by first knitting a certain number of rounds in stockinette (stocking stitch) with one color and then knitting one round with a contrast color. The next round is purled with the contrast color. The technique is easy and a good choice for beginner knitters.

The museum's socks are patterned only on the legs and there is very little contrast between the background and pattern colors. I decided to use a hand-dyed flame yarn for the stripes and to extend the stripes down the feet. Another option would be to use a variety of leftover yarns for the striping.

All of the earliest European knitted textiles we know about were worked in stockinette. Texture patterns with knit and purl stitches likely did not appear until the end of the 13th century or beginning of the 14th century. The first knitted garments we have found with purl stitches on the right side are a pair of stockings that belonged to Eleanore of Toledo. She was a Spanish princess who married the Italian duke Cosimo I of Medici in Florence in 1539. He was one of the richest and most powerful men of that time.

When, at the age of 40, Eleanore died of malaria in 1562, she was buried with red knee-length silk stockings on her legs. They have been surprisingly well-preserved and can be seen today at the Pitti Palace near the Uffizi Gallery. Besides the knit and purl stitches, small details with lace knitting embellish the stockings.

Patterns with knit and purl stitches were universal for several centuries. It took a surprisingly long time before people began to knit patterns with several colors. Here in the Nordic countries, it wasn't common before the beginning of the 17th century.

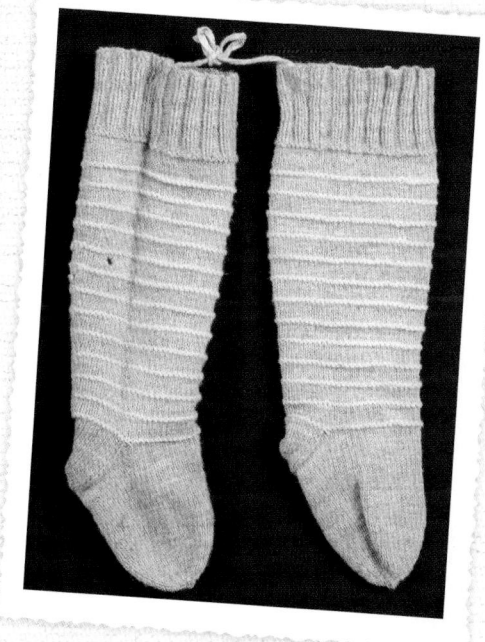

INSTRUCTIONS

Skill Level: Experienced

Sizes: Women's (Men's)

MATERIALS
Yarn: CYCA #1 (fingering/2 ply), Mini Sterk from Du Store Alpakka (40% alpaca, 40% Merino wool, 20% polyamide, 182 yd/166 m / 50 g)

Yarn Colors and Amounts:
Light Pink 850: 100 (100) g
Black 809: 50 (50) g

Needles: U. S. size 1.5 (2.5) / 2.5 (3) mm: set of 5 dpn

Gauge: 34 (32) sts in pattern = 4 in / 10 cm. Adjust needle size to obtain correct gauge if necessary.

LEG
With Pink, CO 76 sts. Divide sts evenly onto 4 dpn. Join, being careful not to twist cast-on row; pm for beginning of rnd. Work in k2, p2 ribbing for 1½ in / 4 cm. On the last rnd, increase 1 st at center back. Now work in pattern following Chart 1. Work the repeat 4 times in length.

BAND HEEL
After completing leg, place 40 sts on scrap yarn for the instep (to "rest" while you work the heel flap). Make sure the pattern is centered.

Heel Flap
Place rem 37 sts on one dpn and, with Pink, work heel flap back and forth.
Begin with WS facing you.
Row 1 (WS): Sl 1 purlwise wyf, purl to last st.
Row 2: Sl 1 purlwise wyb, (k1, sl 1) to last st and end with k1.
Rep these 2 rows until there are 18 chain sts at each side of flap.

Now decrease to shape the band:
Row 1: Sl 1, purl until 12 sts rem, p2tog; turn.
Row 2: Sl 1, knit until 12 sts rem, ssk; turn.
Row 3: Sl 1, purl until 1 st before gap, p2tog; turn.
Row 4: Sl 1, knit until 1 st before gap, ssk; turn.
Rep Rows 3-4 until all the side sts have been eliminated.

FOOT
Divide the instep sts onto 2 dpn and divide the rem heel sts onto 2 dpn so you have half of each section on a needle. Work in the round with RS facing you.

Begin rnd at center of sole. Alternating Black and Pink, knit to heel flap. Pick up and knit 1 st in each chain st along side of heel flap. You can pick up the sts tbl or knit them tbl on next rnd. The last st should be Pink so that you have 2 Pink sts next to each other. Knit across instep in pattern as est. Beginning with Pink and alternating Black and Pink, pick up and knit 1 st in each chain st of opposite side of flap and then knit to end of rnd.

Gusset
Work sole with Pink over Black and Black over Pink as shown on Chart 2. Ndl 1 always ends with Pink and Ndl 4 always begins with Pink. Continue pattern on instep as est.

Knit until 2 sts rem on Ndl 1, k2tog. Work across instep (Ndls 2-3) in pattern.
Ndl 4: Ssk, knit to end of rnd. Knit the next rnd without decreasing. Rep these 2 rnds until 77 sts rem. Work rest of foot in st st without shaping until 8 (9½) in / 20 (24) cm or desired length before toe.

STAR TOE
Begin at the center of the sole and work only with Pink.
Rnd 1: (K5, k2tog) around.
Rnds 2-6: Knit.
Rnd 7: (K4, k2tog) around.
Rnds 8-11: Knit.
Rnd 12: (K3, k2tog) around.
Rnds 13-15: Knit
Rnd 16: (K2, k2tog) around.
Rnds 17-18: Knit.
Rnd 19: (K1, k2tog) around.
Rnd 20: Knit.
Rnd 21: (K2tog) around.

FINISHING
Cut yarn and draw end through rem sts; tighten. Weave in all ends neatly on WS. Make the second sock the same way.

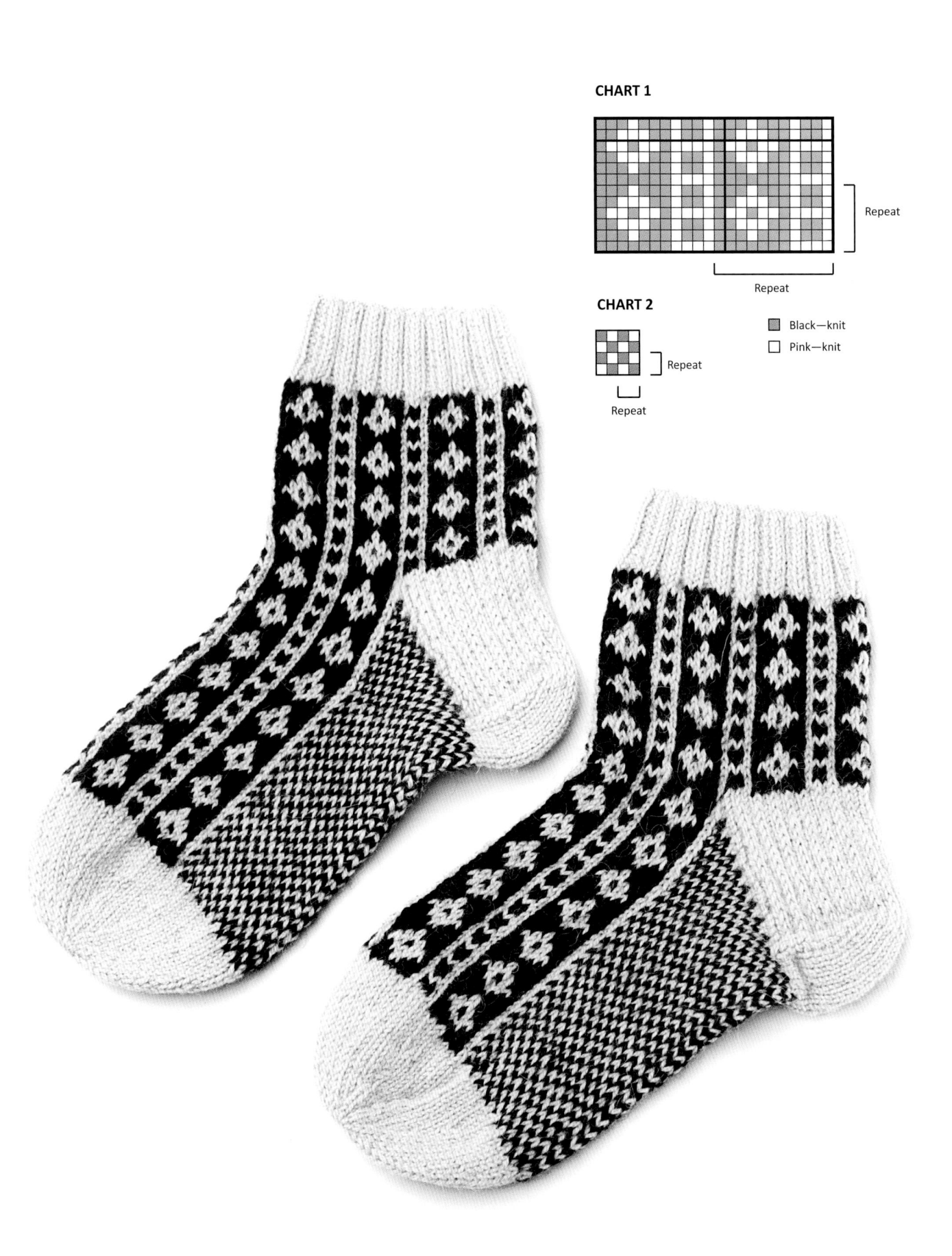

CHART 1

CHART 2

☐ Black—knit
☐ Pink—knit

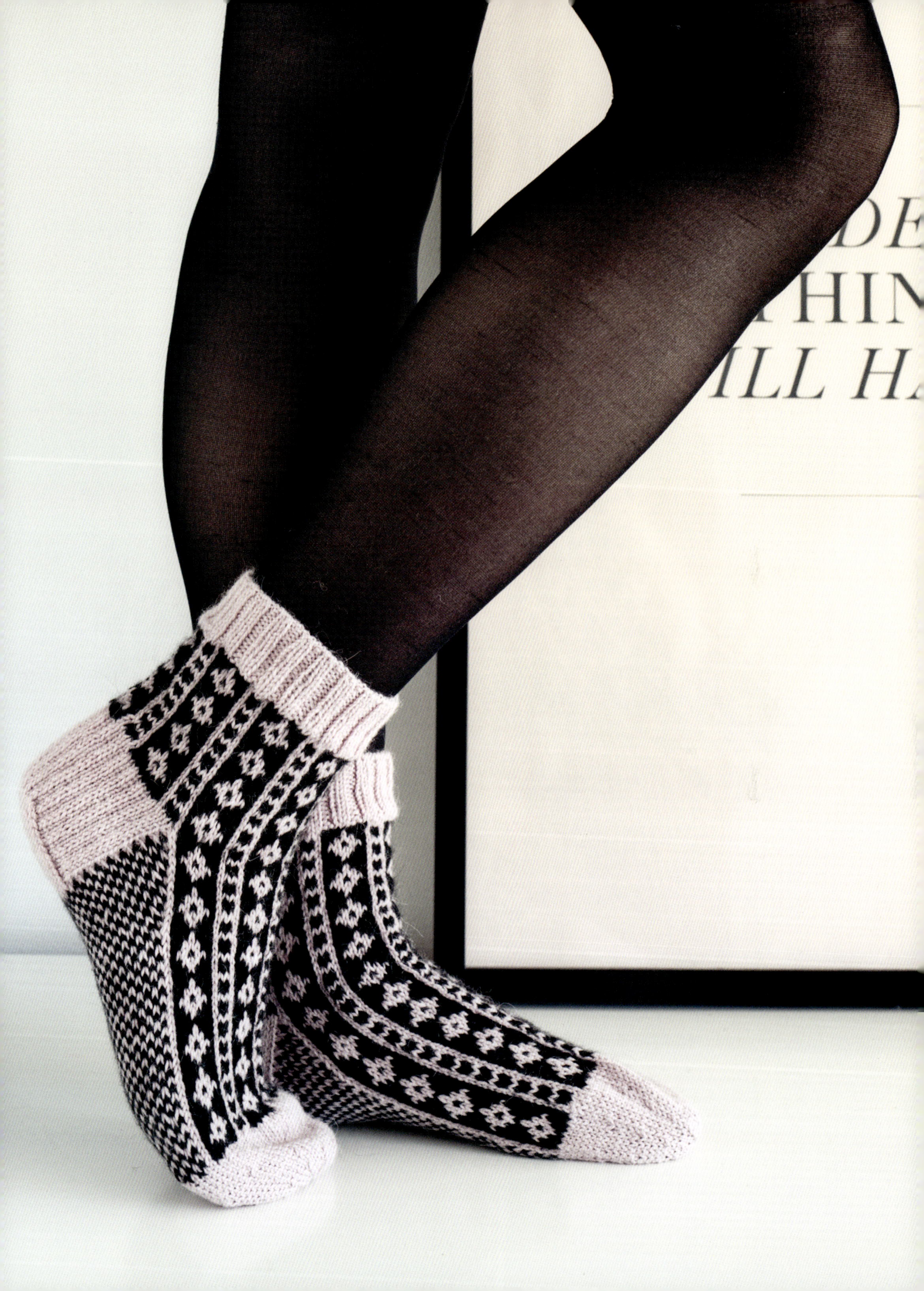
DE
HIN
ILL HA

BUSKERUD

Halling Socks

An elderly woman whom I met at a lecture told me that she had been so lucky as to acquire some yarn for a pair of extra-long stockings during the war. They went up to the thighs and were great to wear under a skirt when it was bitterly cold. There was only one disadvantage—they itched so much!

Norwegian wool has many good qualities. It's strong and has good elasticity. The disadvantage is that it's spun with relatively coarse fiber, and the coarser the fiber, the more it irritates the skin. This doesn't bother some people much at all, but others can be very sensitive to it. Most people today prefer Merino wool or alpaca right next to their skin. We're very lucky to have so many yarns to choose from when we want to knit a new garment.

Maybe these long stockings were also itchy? They were called *hosurpar* or two-strand *hosu* on Flå in Hallingdal. In both Telemark and Buskerud we find that "two-end knitting" refers to common pattern knitting with two strands (colorwork knitting), but in other parts of the country, it refers to the two-end knitting technique in which one holds both strands on the right side to form patterns (see page 9; also called "twined knitting" in English).

According to the registry of the Norwegian Handcraft Association in 1983-84, the yarn for these was spun by Margit Liabråten, a dairymaid on Gislerud in Flå. Margit Steingrimsdatter Liabråten was born on 10 March 1892. The stockings themselves were likely knitted by Elida Sæverud-moen from Nes during the last war, and they were worn by Gunhild Gislerud (1903-1976).

The long vertically striped pattern covers the legs. It's clear the stockings have had new feet knitted on. The new feet were worked with natural black and white sheep's wool in simple blocks with white over black and black over white. It was uncommon to end a pattern in this way, but quite common to re-knit sections of a sock's foot when darning no longer sufficed.

INSTRUCTIONS

Skill Level: Intermediate

Sizes: Women's (Men's)

MATERIALS
Yarn:
CYCA #1 (fingering/2 ply), 2-ply Gammelserie from Rauma (100% wool, 175 yd/160 m / 50 g), White 401: 150 g

Reinforcing Thread: Røros embroidery yarn, (Brodergarn) from Rauna Ullvarefabrikk (100% Spelsau wool), White 311: 50 g

Needles: U. S. 0 (0) / 2 (2) mm: set of 5 dpn

Gauge: 28 sts in pattern = 4 in / 10 cm. Adjust needle size to obtain correct gauge if necessary.

Knitting Tip: Use stitch markers to set off pattern repeats.

LEG
With White, CO 80 (86) sts. Divide sts evenly onto 4 dpn. Join, being careful not to twist cast-on row; pm for beginning of rnd. Work in pattern as shown on chart. After 2½ in / 6 cm, decrease 2 sts at center back. At 3¼ in / 8 cm, decrease another 2 sts at center back = 76 (82) sts rem. Continue following chart until leg is complete.

GUSSET HEEL
After completing leg, place 39 (41) sts on scrap yarn for instep. These sts will "rest" until the heel is complete.

Heel Flap
Place the rem 37 (41) sts on 1 dpn and work the heel flap back and forth, holding reinforcing thread with working yarn.
Begin with WS facing you.
Row 1 (WS): Sl 1 purlwise wyf, purl to end of row.
Row 2: Sl 1 purlwise wyb, knit to end of row.
Rep these 2 rows until there are 17 (18) chain sts on each side of heel flap.

Heel Gusset
Row 1: Sl 1, purl until 12 (13) sts rem, p2tog, p1; turn.
Row 2: Sl 1, knit until 12 (13) sts rem, ssk, k1; turn.
Row 3: Sl 1, purl until 1 st before gap, p2tog, p1; turn.
Row 4: Sl 1, knit until 1 st before gap, ssk, k1; turn.

Rep Rows 3-4 until all the side sts have been eliminated.
Cut reinforcing thread.

FOOT
Gusset
Divide the instep sts onto 2 dpn and divide the rem heel sts onto 2 dpn so you have half of each section on a needle. Now work in the round with RS facing you. Begin rnd at center of sole, knit to heel flap. Pick up and knit 1 st in each chain st along side of heel flap. You can pick up the sts tbl or knit them tbl on next rnd. Work across instep following chart. Pick up and knit 1 st in each chain st of opposite side of flap and then knit to end of rnd.

On the next rnd, decrease for the gusset: Knit until 2 sts rem on Ndl 1, k2tog, work in pattern across instep (Ndls 2-3). Ndl 4: Ssk, knit to end of rnd. Work the next rnd without decreasing. Following the chart for instep, repeat these 2 rnds until 74 (80) sts rem. Work rest of foot in pattern on instep and in st st on sole without decreasing. When foot measures 8 (9½) in / 20 (24) cm or desired length before toe, work star toe.

STAR TOE
Begin at the center of the sole.
Rnd 1: (K5, k2tog) around. The 4 (3) sts rem on Ndl 4 will be decreased in subsequent rnds.
Rnds 2-6: Knit.
Rnd 7: (K4, k2tog) around.
Rnds 8-11: Knit.
Rnd 12: (K3, k2tog) around.
Rnds 13-15: Knit.
Rnd 16: (K2, k2tog) around.
Rnds 17-18: Knit.
Rnd 19: (K1, k2tog) around.
Rnd 20: Knit.
Rnd 21: (K2tog) around.

FINISHING
Cut yarn and draw end through rem sts; tighten. Weave in all ends neatly on WS. Make the second sock the same way.

Repeat Foot

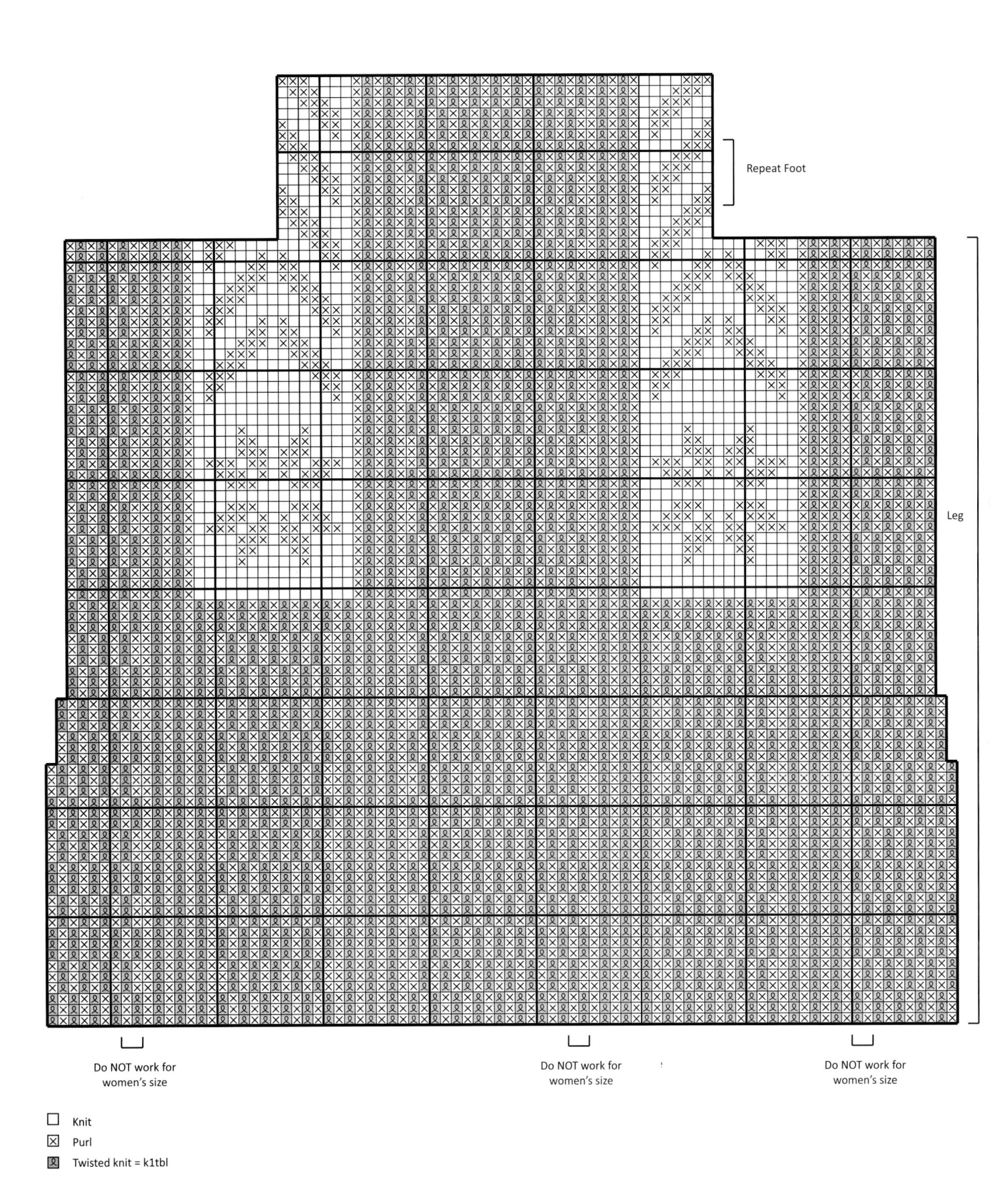

Leg

Do NOT work for women's size

Do NOT work for women's size

Do NOT work for women's size

☐ Knit
☒ Purl
⊠ Twisted knit = k1tbl

68

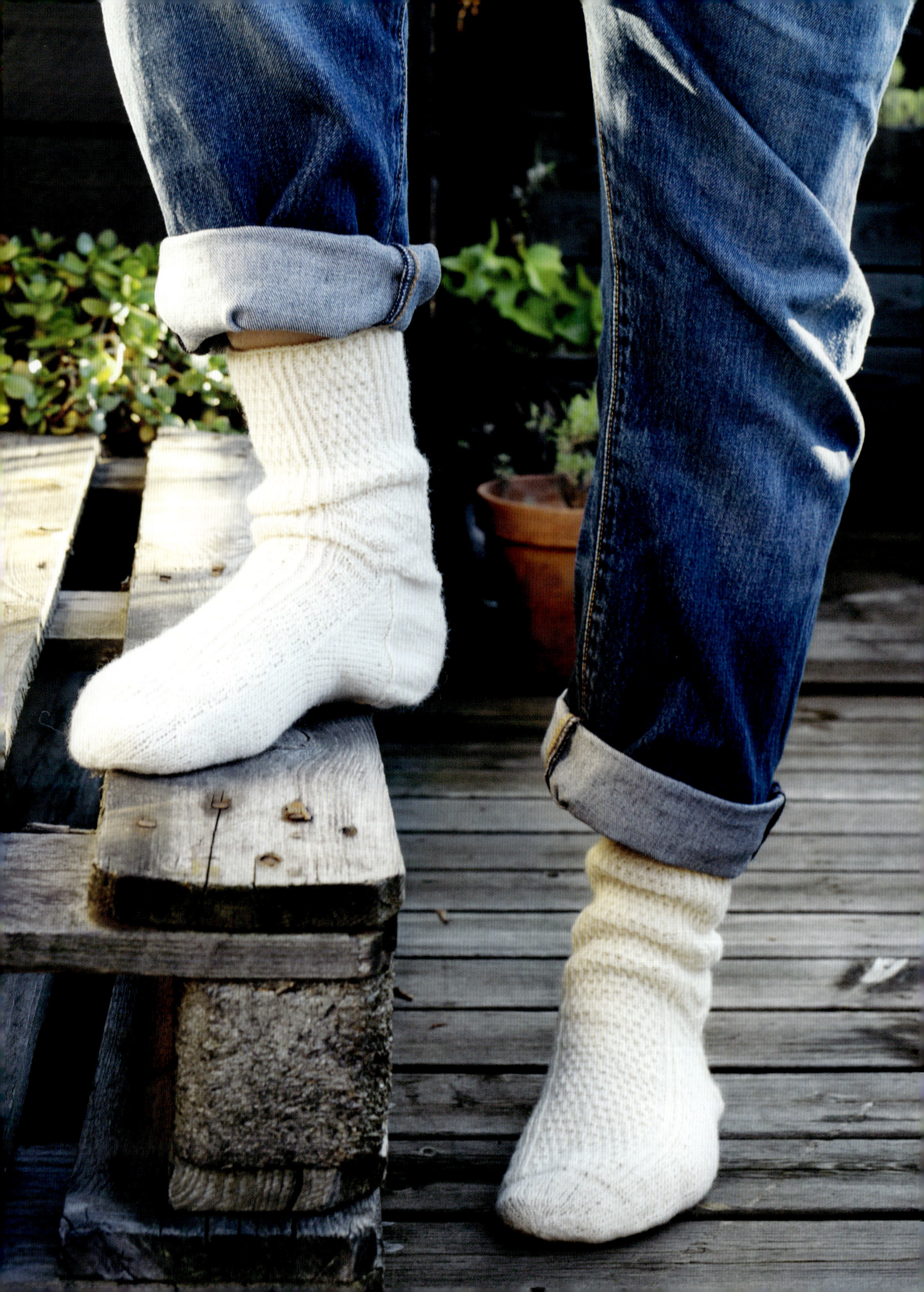

BUSKERUD

Barleycorn (*Byggkorn*) Socks from Numedal

Several pairs of stockings from Flesberg in Numedal have been preserved. They are knitted in a technique with a local name of *byggkorn*—"barleycorn". This special pattern forms when one switches between twisted knit and purl stitches. The appearance has much in common with the weaving pattern of the same name. The folk costume stockings from the district were designed based on a pair acquired by the Norwegian Museum of Cultural History in 1906. The pattern is arranged in sections so the stockings appear to have long stripes.

The Norwegian Institute of Bunad and Folk Costume has also registered a stocking of this type, knitted for Viel Landes' confirmation in 1917 by her mother, Turi Gudbrandsdatter. Viel Nirisdatter was born on 7 November 1903 and lived at the Bakli farm during the 1910 census.

The stockings are primarily knitted with blue wool, although the top part is brown and the toes are white. The ankles bear typical ankle roses.

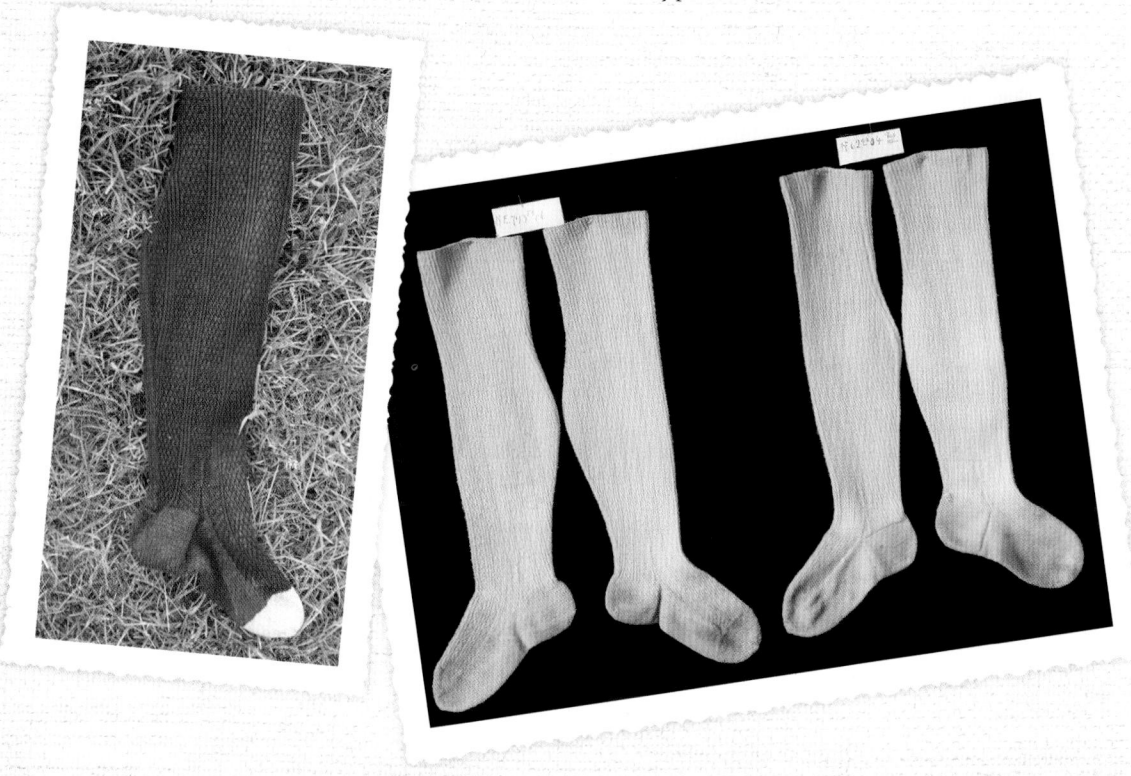

INSTRUCTIONS

Skill Level: Experienced

Size: Women's

MATERIALS
Yarn:
CYCA #3 (DK, light worsted), Sterk from Du Store Alpakka (40% Merino wool, 40% alpaca, 20% nylon, 150 yd/137 m / 50 g)

Yarn Colors and Amounts:
Natural White 806: 50 g
Red 828: 50 g
Dark Pink: 825: 100 g
Orange 836: 50 g

Needles: U. S. size 2.5 / 3 mm: set of 5 dpn

Gauge: 24 sts in pattern = 4 in / 10 cm.
Adjust needle size to obtain correct gauge if necessary.

LEG
With White, CO 84 sts. Divide sts evenly onto 4 dpn. Join, being careful not to twist cast-on row; pm for beginning of rnd. Work around in k2, p2 ribbing, working the stripe sequence *at the same time*:
2 rnds White, 2 rnds Red, 2 rnds White, 2 rnds Red, 2 rnds White.

Now work 1 rep of the medallion (*hullbragd*) pattern (a total of 18 rounds):
Rnd 1, with Pink: Knit.
Rnd 2, with Pink: Purl.
Rnds 3-4, with Orange: K2, *sl 2 sts purlwise wyb, k4*; rep * to * around, ending with k2.
Rnd 5, with Pink: K2, *sl 2 sts purlwise wyb, k4*; rep * to * around, ending with k2.
Rnd 6, with Pink: Purl.
Rnds 7-8, with Orange: Sl 1, *k4, sl 2 sts*; rep * to *, ending with sl 1.
Rnd 9, with Pink: Sl 1, *k4, sl 2*; rep * to *, ending with sl 1.
Rnd 10, with Pink: Purl.
Rep Rnds 3-10.

The next stripe sequence is worked in st st (see chart). *At the same time*, decrease 2 sts at center back on the 2nd, 5th, and 8th rnds of the repeat = 6 sts decreased per repeat. Rep the medallion and stripe sequences 4 times and then end with 1 medallion rep = 60 sts rem.

GUSSET HEEL WITH SHORT HEEL FLAP
After completing leg, divide the sts, placing 30 sts on a holder for instep. These sts will "rest" until the heel is complete.
Place the rem 30 sts on 1 dpn and work the heel flap back and forth in pattern as described below:
Begin with White and WS facing you.
Row 1 (WS): Sl 1 purlwise wyf, purl to end of row.
Row 2: Sl 1 purlwise wyb, knit to end of row.
Rep these 2 rows until there are 6 chain sts on each side of flap. *At the same time*, work in stripe sequence:
2 rows Red
2 rows White
2 rows Red
2 rows White
2 rows Red
1 row White

Now, with White only, shape the heel:
Row 1: Sl 1, purl until 11 sts rem, p2tog, p1; turn.
Row 2: Sl 1, knit until 11 sts rem, ssk, k1; turn.
Row 3: Sl 1, purl until 1 st before gap, p2tog, p1; turn.
Row 4: Sl 1, knit until 1 st before gap, ssk, k1; turn.
Rep Rows 3-4 until all the side sts have been eliminated.

FOOT
Divide the instep sts onto 2 dpn and divide the rem heel sts onto 2 dpn so you have half of each section on a needle. Work in the round with RS facing you. Begin rnd at center of sole with White. Pick up and knit 6 sts in chain sts along side of heel flap. You can pick up the sts tbl or knit them tbl on next rnd. Knit across instep. Pick up and knit 6 sts in chain sts of opposite side of flap and knit to end of rnd = 62 sts total.

Decrease Rnd: K9, k2tog. Knit until 11 sts rem on Ndl 4: ssk, knit to end of rnd = 60 sts rem.
Change to Red and work (1 stripe sequence, 1 medallion sequence) 2 times.

TOE
Continue the medallion sequence as before and, *at the same time*, decrease on the rounds with only purl sts:
1st Decrease Rnd: Decrease 6 sts evenly spaced around = (p8, p2tog) around = 54 sts rem.
2nd Decrease Rnd: Decrease 12 sts evenly spaced around = (p2, p2tog, p3, p2tog) around = 42 sts rem.
3rd Decrease Rnd: Decrease 12 sts evenly spaced around = (p1, p2tog, p2, p2tog) around = 30 sts rem.
4th Decrease Rnd: Decrease 12 sts evenly spaced around = (p1, p2tog, p2tog) around = 18 sts rem.
5th Decrease Rnd: Decrease 12 sts evenly spaced around = p3togaround = 6 sts rem.

FINISHING
Cut yarn and draw end through rem sts; tighten. Weave in all ends neatly on WS. Make the second sock the same way.

- Stripe repeat
- Medallion repeat
- Ribbing

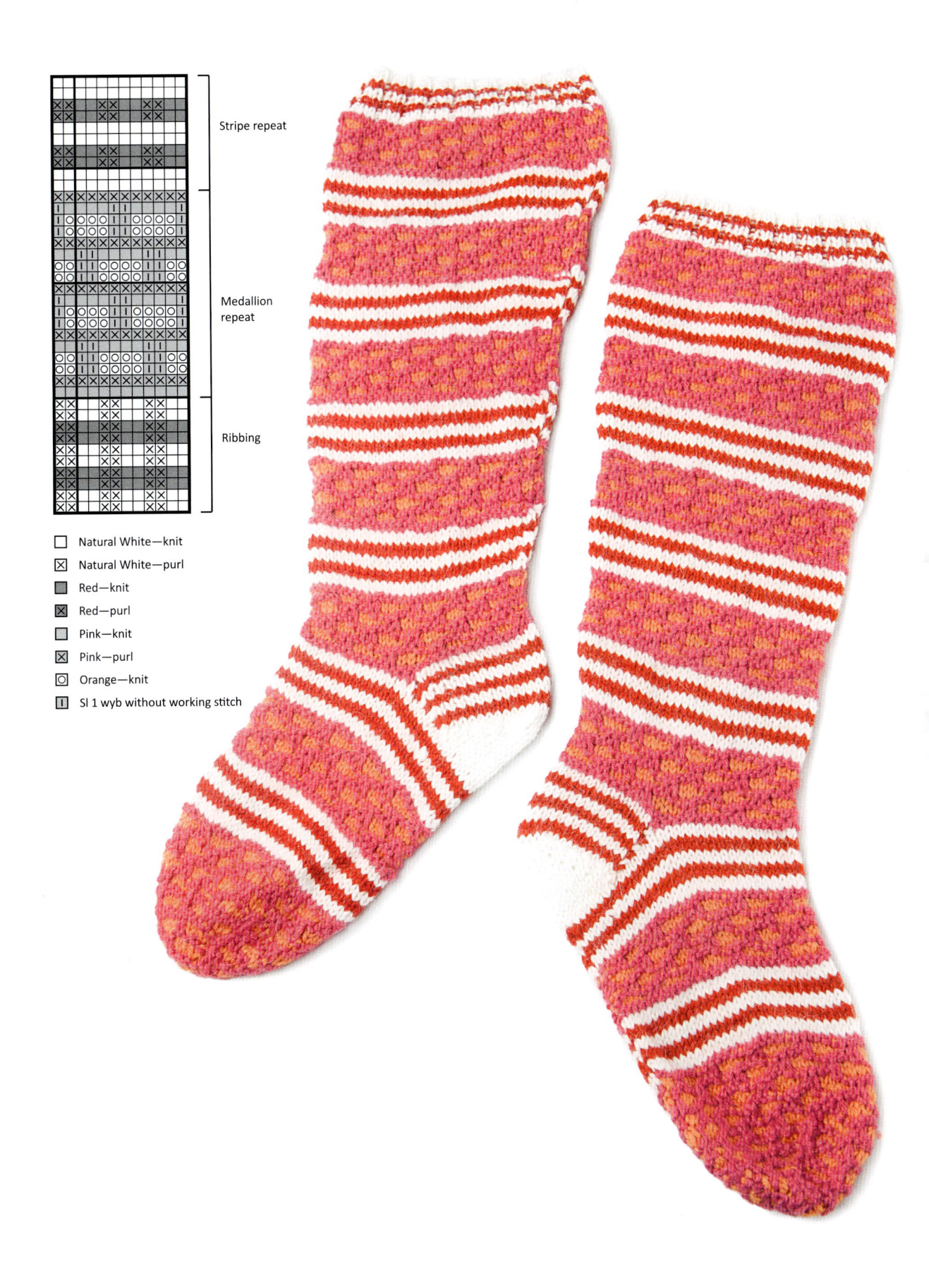

- ☐ Natural White—knit
- ☒ Natural White—purl
- ▦ Red—knit
- ▨ Red—purl
- ▢ Pink—knit
- ▩ Pink—purl
- ◯ Orange—knit
- | Sl 1 wyb without working stitch

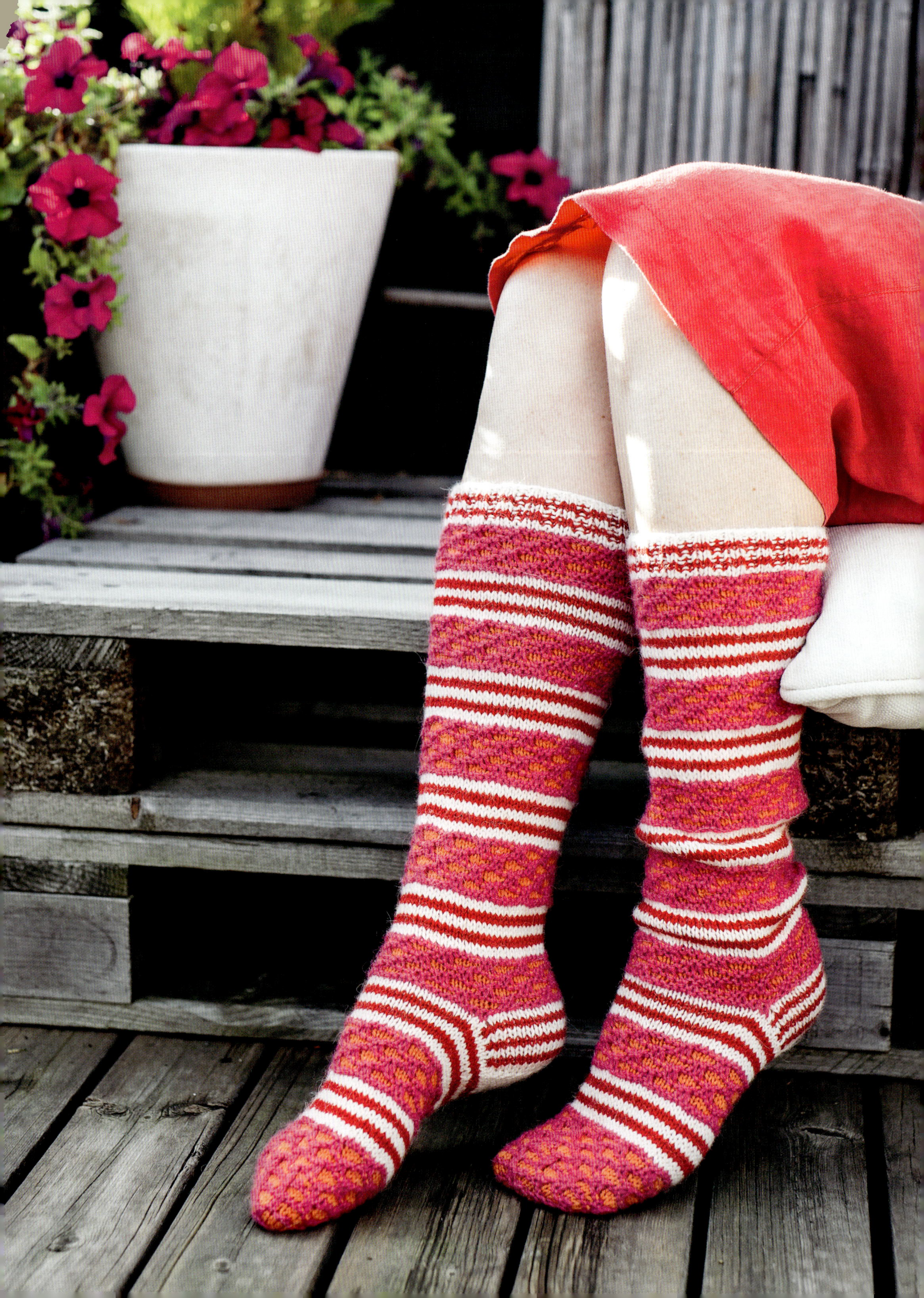

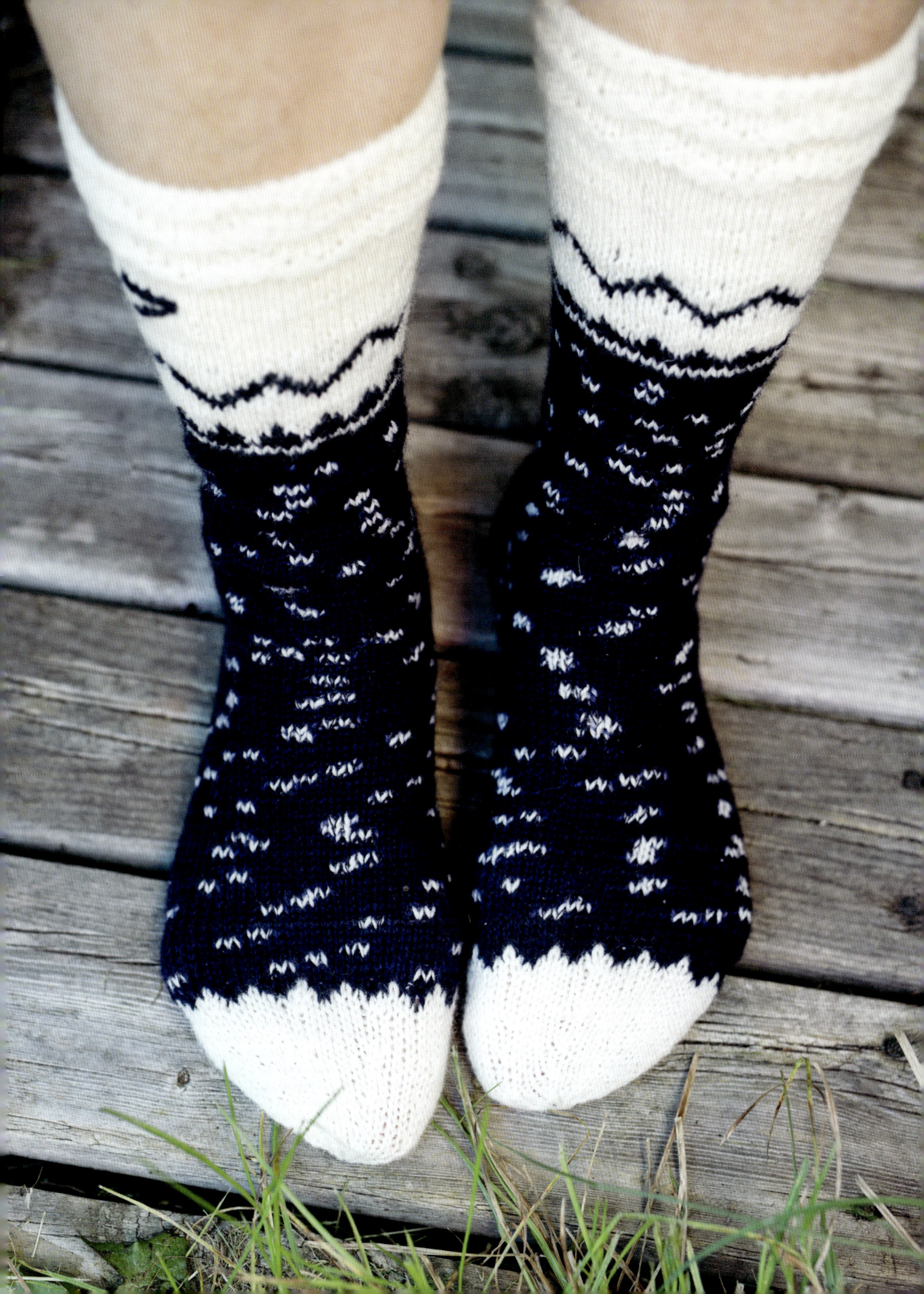

CHART 4

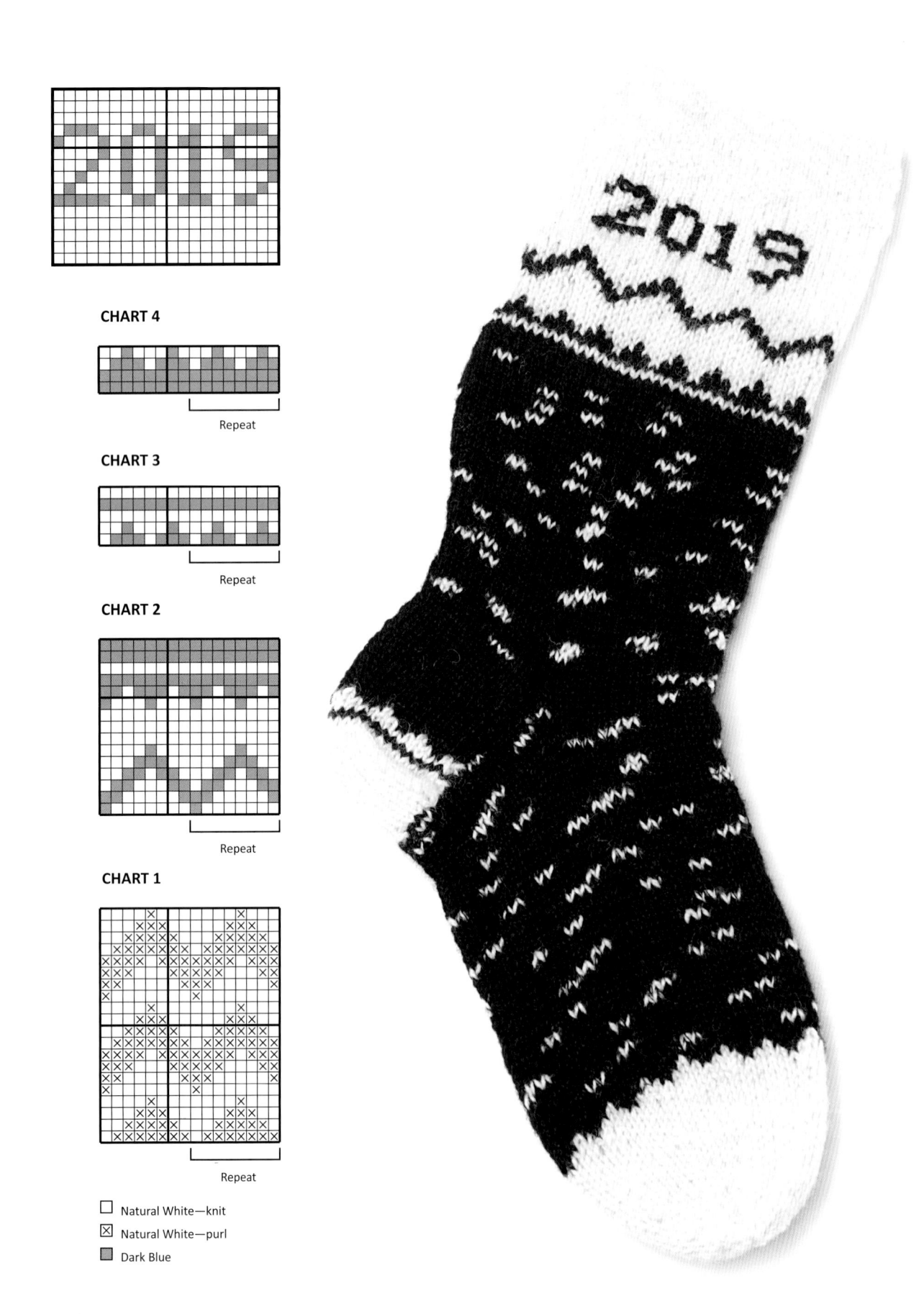

CHART 3

CHART 2

CHART 1

☐ Natural White—knit
☒ Natural White—purl
▨ Dark Blue

110

INSTRUCTIONS

Skill Level: Experienced

Sizes: Women's (Men's)

MATERIALS

Yarn:

CYCA #1 (fingering/2 ply), 2-ply Gammelserie from Rauma (100% wool, 175 yd/160 m / 50 g), Natural White 401: 50 (50) g

CYCA #1 (fingering/2 ply), Finullgarn from Rauma (100% wool, 191 yd/175 m / 50 g), Dark Blue 459: 50 (50) g

Flame yarn as for the Nordland's Bunad or similar: 100 (100) g

Reinforcing Thread: Mettler extra strong sewing thread, black and natural white or similar

Needles: U. S. size 1.5 (2.5) / 2.5 (3) mm: set of 5 dpn

Gauge: 25 (23) sts in pattern = 4 in / 10 cm. Adjust needle size to obtain correct gauge if necessary.

LEG

With Natural White, CO 64 sts. Divide sts evenly onto 4 dpn. Join, being careful not to twist cast-on row; pm for beginning of rnd. Work around in the knit/purl pattern shown on Chart 1 and then work 15 rnds in st st with Natural White.
Next, work following Chart 2 with Natural White and Dark Blue. Change to flame yarn. When the piece measures 6¼ in / 16 cm), decrease 2 sts at the center back.
Knit 3 rnds and then decrease 2 sts at center back on the 4th rnd; rep * to * until 8 sts have been decreased and 56 sts rem. Work 1½ in / 4 cm without decreasing.

BAND HEEL

After completing leg, place 28 sts on scrap yarn for the instep (to "rest" while you work the heel flap).

Heel Flap

Place rem 28 sts on one dpn and, with Dark Blue and darker reinforcing thread held together, work heel flap back and forth.
Begin with WS facing you.
Row 1 (WS): Sl 1 purlwise wyf, purl to end of row.
Row 2: Sl 1 purlwise wyb, knit to end of row.
Rep these 2 rows until there are 10 chain sts at each side of flap. Now work following Chart 3.

Heel Gusset:

With Natural White yarn and matching reinforcing thread held together, shape the gusset:
Row 1 (WS): Sl 1, purl until 10 sts rem, p2tog; turn.
Row 2: Sl 1, knit until 10 sts rem, ssk; turn.
Row 3: Sl 1, purl until 1 st before gap, p2tog; turn.
Row 4: Sl 1, knit until 1 st before gap, ssk; turn.
Rep Rows 3-4 until all the side sts have been eliminated.
Cut reinforcing threads.

FOOT

Divide the instep sts onto 2 dpn and divide the rem heel sts onto 2 dpn so you have half of each section on a needle. Now, continuing with flame yarn, work in the round with RS facing you. Begin rnd at center of sole. Pick up and knit 1 st in each chain st along side of heel flap. You can pick up the sts tbl or knit them tbl on next rnd. Knit across instep. Pick up and knit 1 st in each chain st of opposite side of flap and then complete rnd as est.

Gusset

Knit until 2 sts rem on Ndl 1, k2tog. Knit across instep (Ndls 2-3). Ndl 4: Ssk, knit to end of rnd. Knit the next rnd without decreasing. Repeat these 2 rnds until 56 sts rem. Work rest of foot without decreasing. When foot measures 7 (8) in / 17.5 (20) cm or desired length before 4 rnds of Chart 4 + toe, work following Chart 4 and then work star toe.

STAR TOE

Begin at the center of the sole and work only with Natural White.
Rnd 1: (K5, k2tog) around.
Rnds 2-6: Knit.
Rnd 7: (K4, k2tog) around.
Rnds 8-11: Knit.
Rnd 12: (K3, k2tog) around.
Rnds 13-15: Knit
Rnd 16: (K2, k2tog) around.
Rnds 17-18: Knit.
Rnd 19: (K1, k2tog) around.
Rnd 20: Knit.
Rnd 21: (K2tog) around.

FINISHING

Cut yarn and draw end through rem sts; tighten. Weave in all ends neatly on WS.
Embroider the year and initials on the white section at the outer side of the leg. Place the numbers or letters 5 rounds above the zigzag panel and with 3 rounds between the panel with purl stitches and the embroidery.

Make the second sock the same way.

Rose Socks with Lace Patterns

The Norwegian Museum of Cultural History has a knitting sampler with a large number of different lace patterns. It's knitted with very fine cotton yarn. The sampler is from Oslo and the museum acquired it in 1929.

Fine, tight cotton yarn began to be available at the end of the 18th century. This yarn was particularly well-suited to lace knitting. Complex pattern knitting was very common among women in the finer circles. No one sat idle with her hands clasped.

Elna Arbo Wildfeld (1884-1957) wrote about her family in Drammen in her book *Memories from Gulskoven*. Her grandmother and the two young girls, Jenny and Louise, secured their places at the window in the living room. They embroidered and they knitted. "Innumerable fine handwork pieces were completed over the many years while they sat at their three places by the window. (…) Their knitted work was light as spiderwebs, and one wonders how their eyes could tolerate the strain, particularly when one remembers that they sat around a single tallow candle in the evening."

About her aunt Jenny, born in 1830, she writes: "She crocheted impressively, despite the fact that she was suffering from weight gain and by then was rather heavy—at that time one didn't exercise, and it was considered most suitable to sit still and knit after the age of 40. We lost count of all the stockings Aunt Jenny had knitted for us children in the family—durable black wool stockings."

A number of private servants' schools taught fine knitting, and this knitting sampler might very well have been made in such a class.

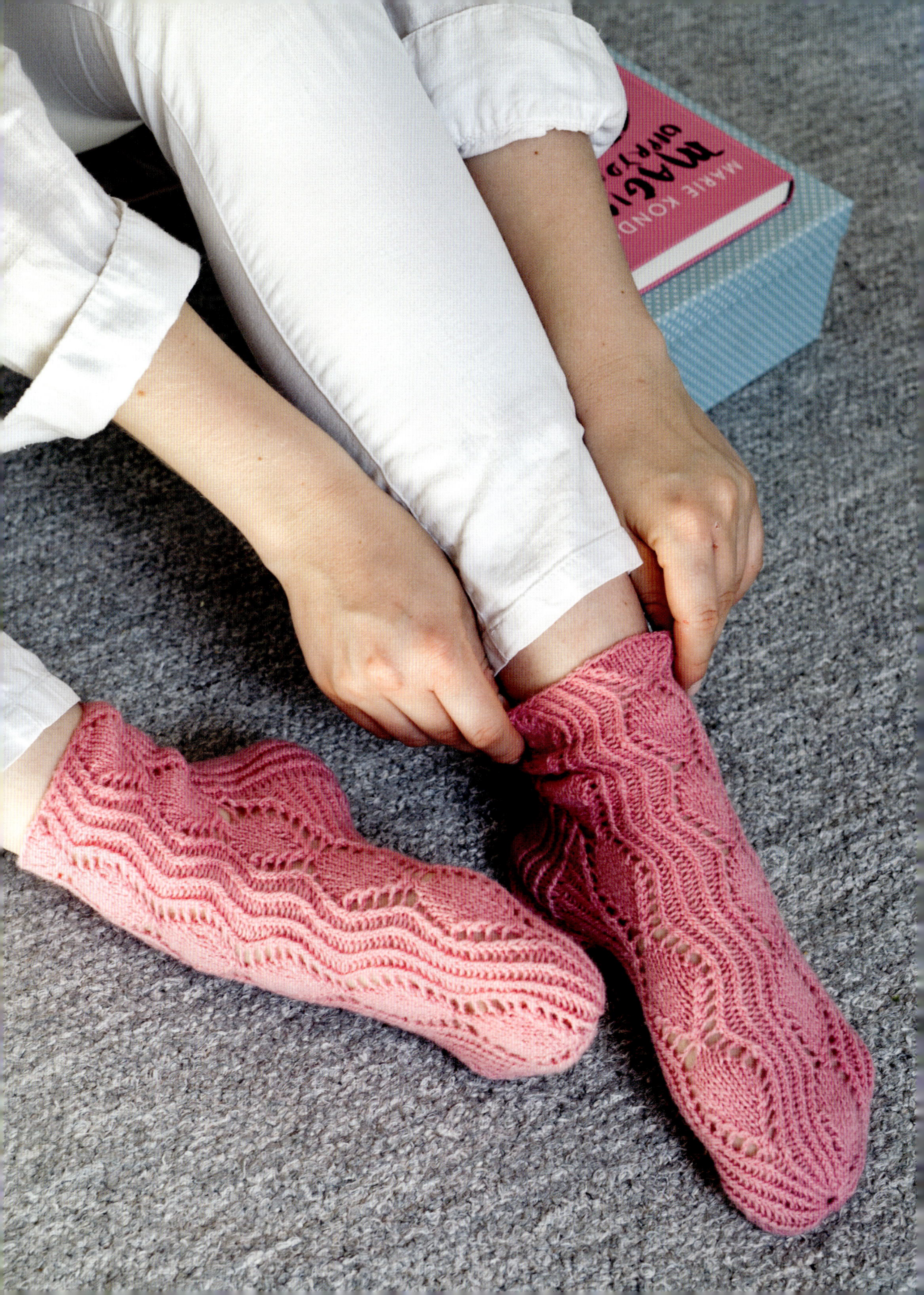
MARIE

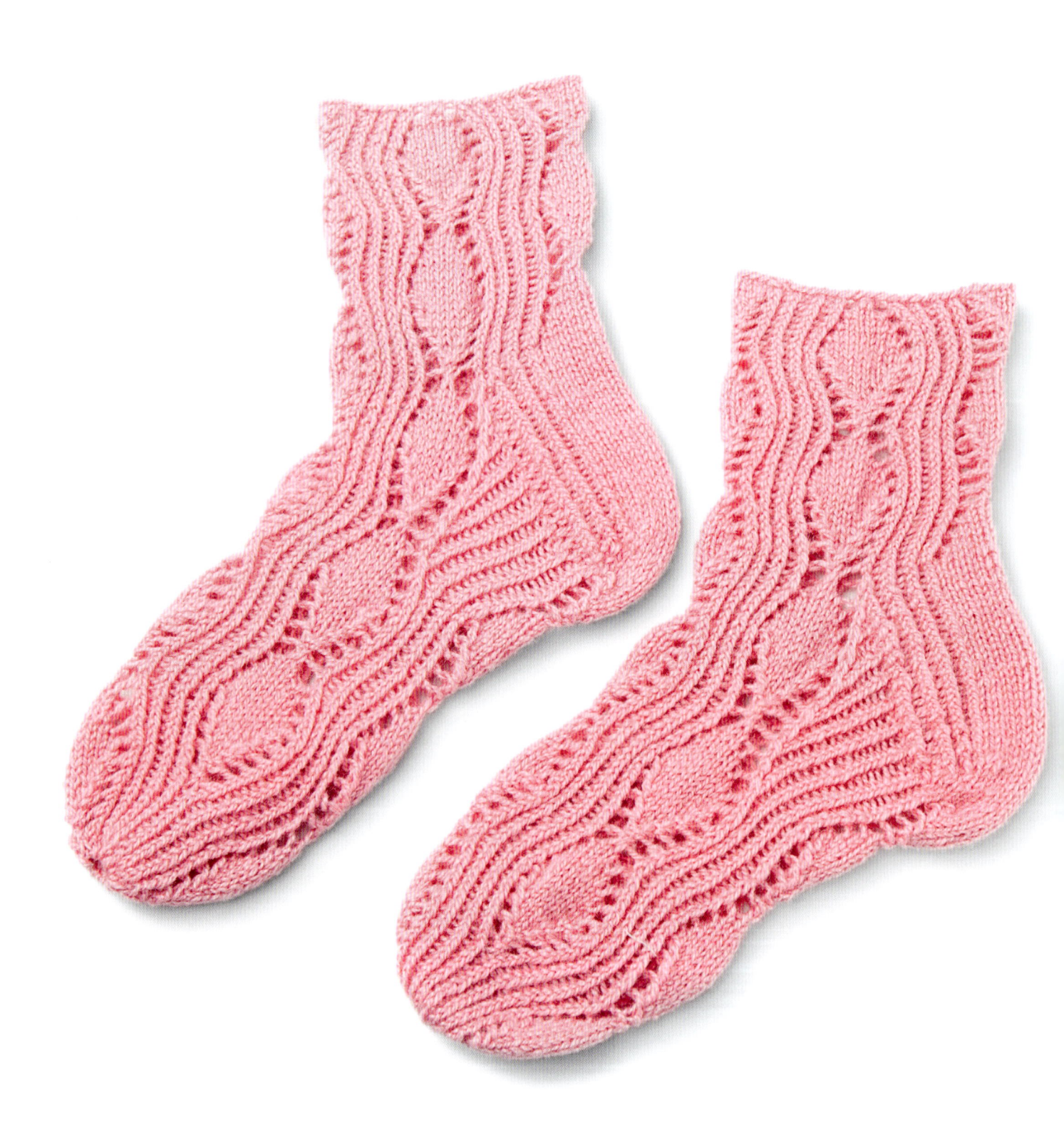

INSTRUCTIONS

Skill Level: Intermediate

Size: Women's

MATERIALS
Yarn:
CYCA #1 (fingering/2 ply), Finullgarn from Rauma (100% wool, 191 yd/175 m / 50 g), Rose Pink 479: 100 g

Needles: U. S. size 1.5 / 2.5 mm: set of 5 dpn

Gauge: 35 sts in pattern or 30 sts in st st = 4 in / 10 cm.
Adjust needle size to obtain correct gauge if necessary.

LEG
CO 56 sts. Divide sts evenly onto 4 dpn. Join, being careful not to twist cast-on row; pm for beginning of rnd. Work around in pattern as shown in chart.

GUSSET HEEL
After completing the leg, divide the stitches, placing the 31 instep stitches onto scrap yarn. These instep stitches will "rest" until the heel is complete.

Place the remaining 25 stitches onto one needle and work back and forth. Begin with the WS facing you.
Row 1 (WS): Sl 1 purlwise wyf, work in pattern following heel flap chart = (P1tbl, k1) 3 times, p1tbl, p11, (p1tbl, k1) 3 times, p1tbl.
Row 2: Sl 1 purlwise wyb, work following chart = (k1tbl, p1) 3 times, k1tbl, k11, (k1tbl, p1) 3 times, k1tbl.
Repeat these 2 rows until there are 15 chain sts at each side of the flap.

Shaping the Heel
Row 1: Sl 1, purl until 8 sts rem on the needle, p2tog, p1; turn.
Row 2: Sl 1, knit until 8 sts rem on needle, ssk, k1; turn.
Row 3: Sl 1, purl until 1 st before gap, p2tog, p1; turn.
Row 4: Sl 1, knit until 1 st rem before gap, ssk, k1; turn.
Repeat Rows 3-4 until all the side sts have been eliminated.

Gusset Shaping
Divide the instep sts from the holder onto 2 dpn; divide the sole sts onto 2 dpn with half of the sts on each. With RS facing, begin working in the round. Begin rnd at center of sole. With Ndl 1, knit to flap; pick up and knit 1 st in each chain up side of flap. You can pick up the chain sts through back loops, or knit them through back loops on the next rnd. With Ndls 2-3, work in pattern following gusset chart. Next, with Ndl 4, pick up and knit sts down opposite side of flap as for the first side. Knit to center of sole.

On the next rnd, begin decreasing to shape gusset while also following charted pattern: Knit until 2 sts rem on Ndl 1, k2tog. Work across instep sts on Ndls 2-3. With Ndl 4, ssk and then knit to end of rnd.
Work the next rnd without decreasing.
Repeat these 2 rnds until 56 sts rem. Continue without further shaping, with instep in pattern and sole in st st until you've completed 5 repeats at the sides. Shape toe as shown on the chart.

FINISHING
Cut yarn and draw end through rem sts; tighten. Weave in all ends neatly on WS. Make the second sock the same way.

FOOT

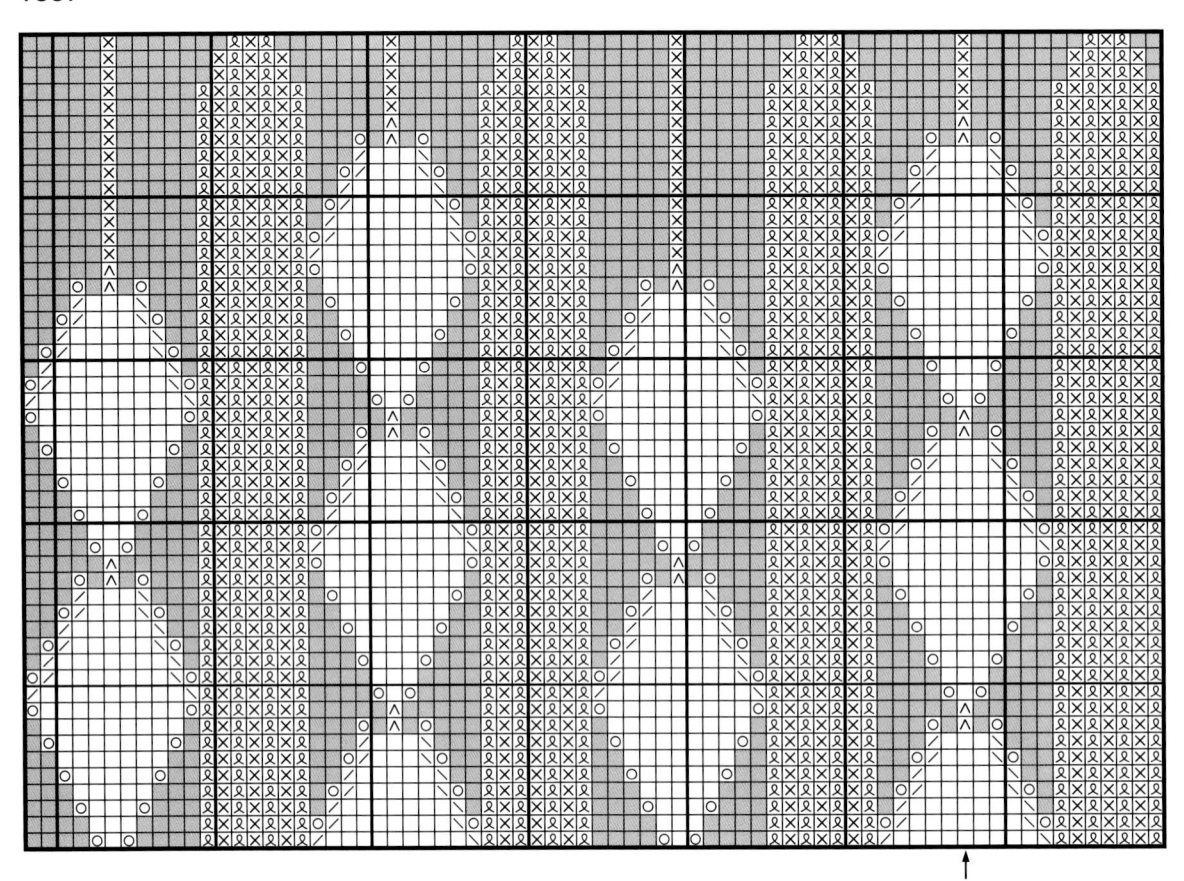

↑ Center back

- ☐ Knit on RS, purl on WS
- ℞ K1tbl on RS, p1tbl on WS
- ☒ Purl on RS, knit on WS
- ◯ Yo
- ╲ K2tog tbl
- ╱ K2tog
- ⋀ K2tog tbl, slip st back to left needle and slip the last (left) st over the first so you have 1 st again
- ▨ No stitch

GUSSET SHAPING

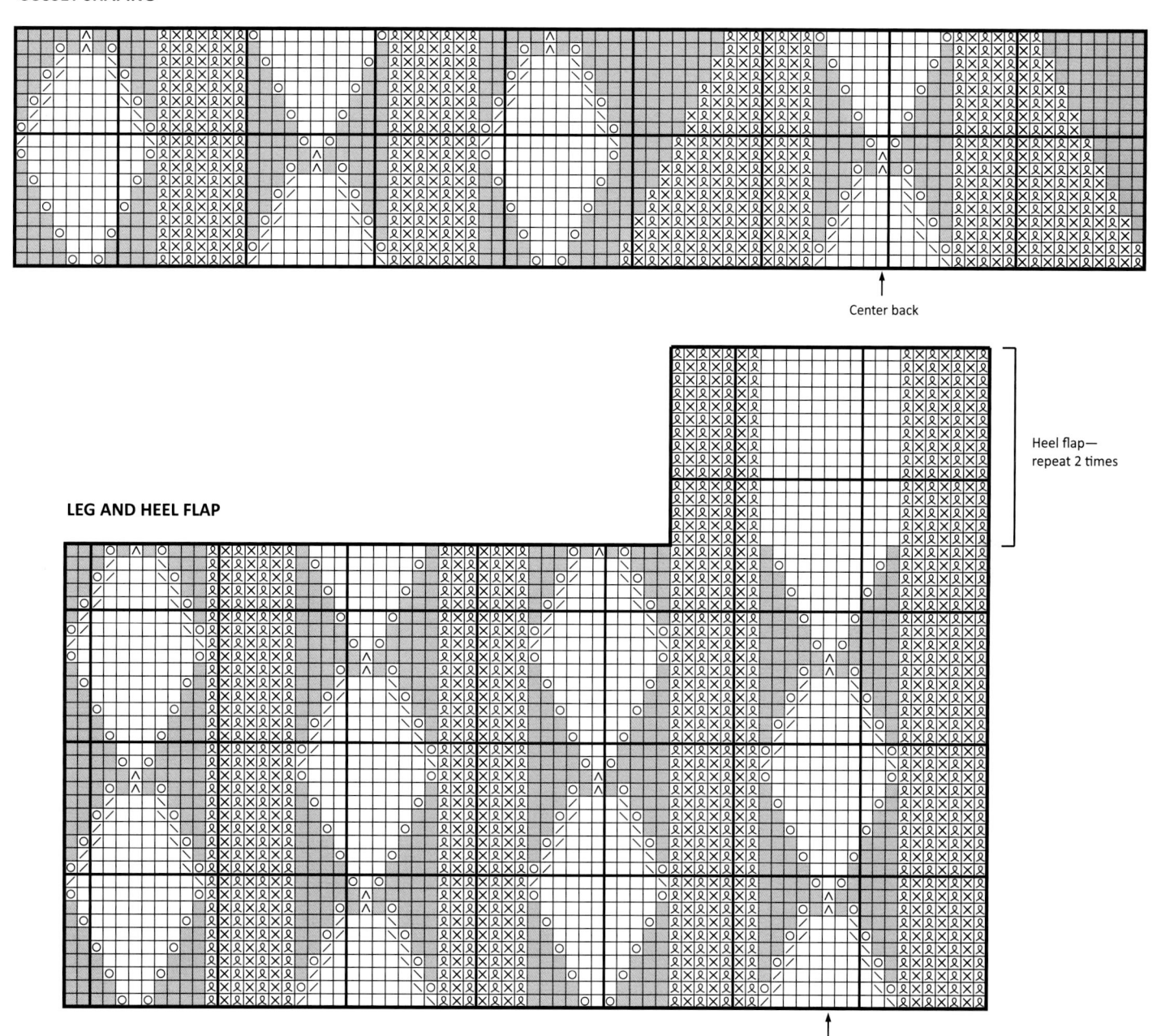

LEG AND HEEL FLAP

Center back

Heel flap—
repeat 2 times

Center back

Stockings from Voss

A pair of confirmation stockings from Voss was among the items registered in connection with Norway's Handcraft Association's exhibit, "Knitting Then and Now," in 1983-84. They were knitted by Maria Olsdatter Årmot (1884-1980) from Myrkjedalen for her daughter Kristi (born in 1909) when she was confirmed. The stockings must have been from the early 1920s.

According to the census of 1910, Maria, her husband Lars Bystølen, and their daughter Kristi lived on the Årmot farm with her parents. The couple had eight children. Kristi's later married name was Aksnes.

The yarn for these stockings was a handspun two-ply. The stockings, which are long and go well over the knees, were dyed after they were knitted. Eventually the feet were re-knitted.

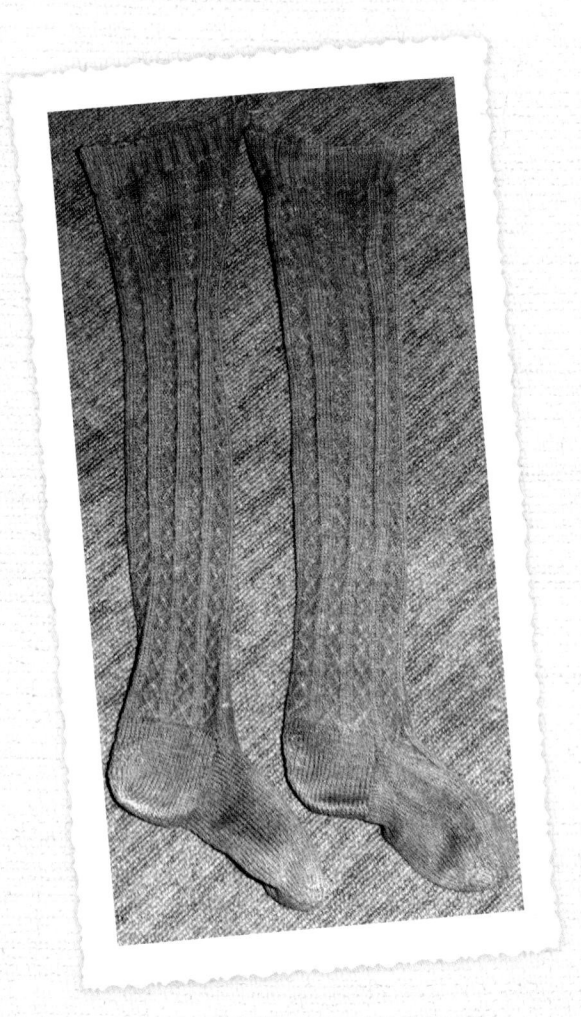

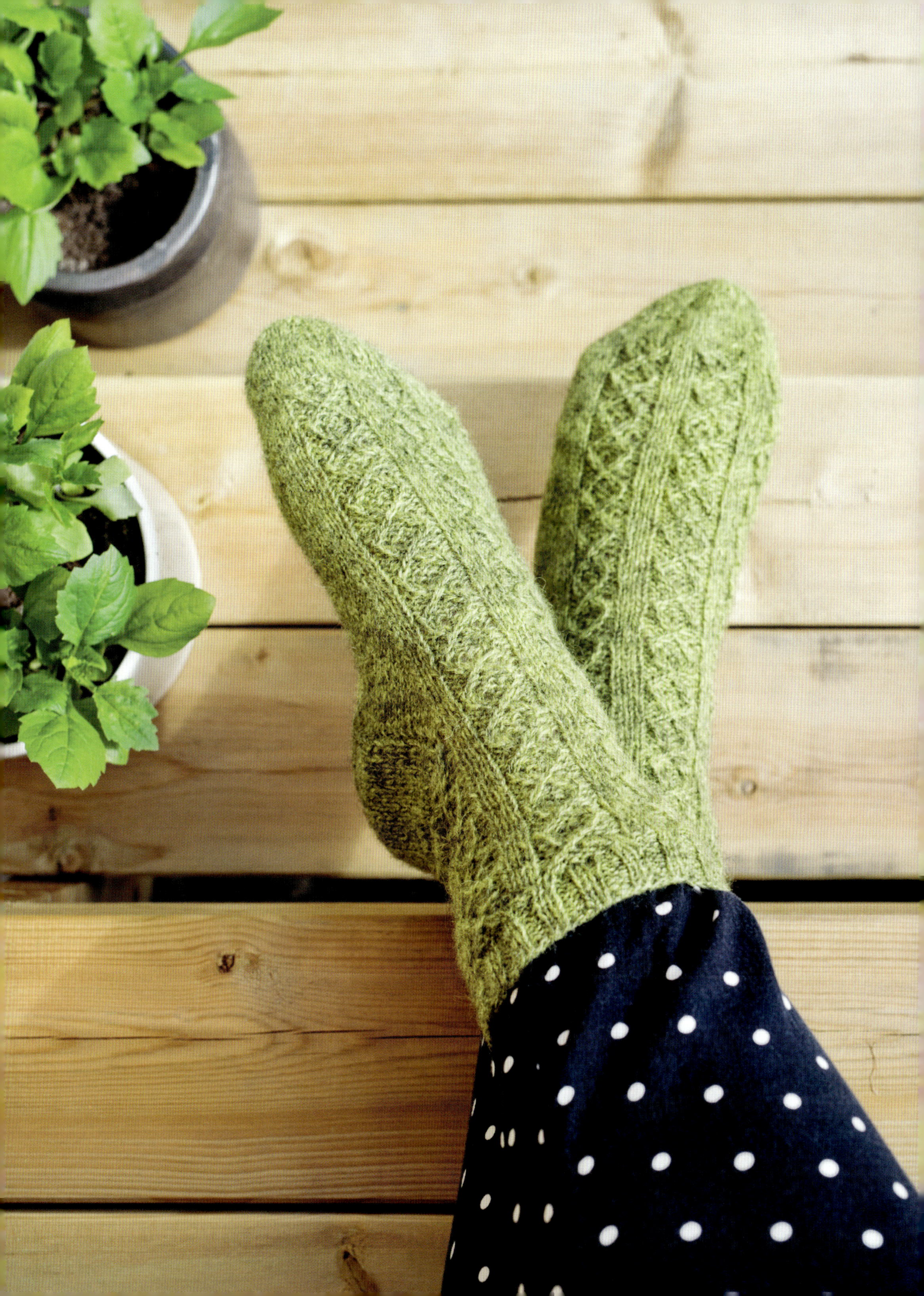

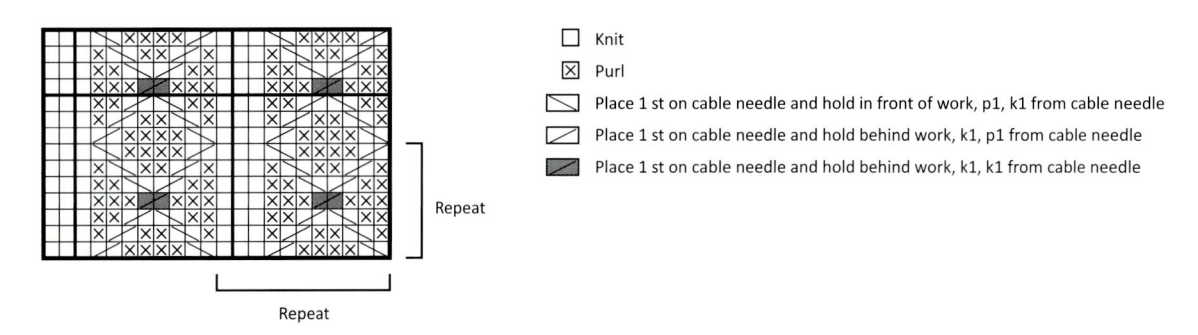

- Knit
- ☒ Purl
- Place 1 st on cable needle and hold in front of work, p1, k1 from cable needle
- Place 1 st on cable needle and hold behind work, k1, p1 from cable needle
- Place 1 st on cable needle and hold behind work, k1, k1 from cable needle

INSTRUCTIONS

Skill Level: Intermediate

Sizes: Women's (Men's)

MATERIALS
Yarn:
CYCA #1 (fingering/2 ply), Sølje from Hillesvåg Ullvarefabrikk (100% Norwegian Pels wool, 383 yd/350 m / 100 g), Lime Green 642107: 100 (150) g

Reinforcing Thread: Mettler extra strong sewing thread in black or similar thread

Needles: U. S. size 1.5 / 2.5 mm: set of 5 dpn; cable needle

Gauge: 26 sts in pattern = 4 in / 10 cm. Adjust needle size to obtain correct gauge if necessary.

CO 68 (80) sts. Divide sts evenly onto 4 dpn. Join, being careful not to twist cast-on row; pm for beginning of rnd. Work around in k2, p2 ribbing for 10 rnds and, on the last rnd, decrease evenly spaced around to 66 (77) sts. Work the 11-stitch pattern repeat 6 (7) times around. Work the repeat in length 5 times.

GUSSET HEEL
After completing the leg, divide the stitches, placing the 34 (45) instep stitches onto scrap yarn. These instep stitches will "rest" until the heel is complete.

Place the remaining 32 (32) stitches onto one needle and work back and forth with Sølje yarn and reinforcing thread held together. Begin with the WS facing you.
Row 1 (WS): Sl 1 purlwise wyf, p31 (31).
Row 2: Sl 1 purlwise wyb, k31 (31).
Repeat these 2 rows until there are 16 chain sts at each side of the flap.

Shaping the Heel
Row 1: Sl 1, purl until 11 sts rem on needle, p2tog, p1; turn.
Row 2: Sl 1, knit until 11 sts rem on needle, ssk, k1; turn.
Row 3: Sl 1, purl until 1 st before gap, p2tog, p1; turn.
Row 4: Sl 1, knit until 1 st rem before gap, ssk, k1; turn.
Repeat Rows 3-4 until all the side sts have been eliminated. Cut reinforcing thread.

Gusset Shaping
Divide the instep sts from the holder onto 2 dpn; divide the sole sts onto 2 dpn with half of the sts on each. With RS facing, begin working in the round. Begin rnd at center of sole with Lime Green yarn only. With Ndl 1, knit to flap; pick up and knit 1 st in each chain up side of flap. You can pick up the chain sts through back loops, or knit them through back loops on the next rnd. With Ndls 2-3, work across the instep in pattern as est. Next, with Ndl 4, pick up and knit sts down opposite side of flap as for the first side. Knit to center of sole.

On the next rnd, begin decreasing to shape gusset: Knit until 2 sts rem on Ndl 1, k2tog. Work across instep sts in pattern on Ndls 2-3. With Ndl 4, ssk and then knit to end of rnd. Work the next rnd without decreasing. Repeat these 2 rnds until 62 (73) sts rem. Continue without further shaping, with instep in pattern and sole in st st, until foot measures approx. 8 (9½) in / 20 (24) cm or desired length to toe shaping. End foot at the end of a complete pattern repeat.

STAR TOE
Begin at the center of the sole.
Rnd 1: (K5, k2tog) around. The 6 (3) sts rem on Ndl 4 will be decreased in subsequent rnds.
Rnds 2-6: Knit.
Rnd 7: (K4, k2tog) around.
Rnds 8-11: Knit.
Rnd 12: (K3, k2tog) around.
Rnds 13-15: Knit
Rnd 16: (K2, k2tog) around.
Rnds 17-18: Knit.
Rnd 19: (K1, k2tog) around.
Rnd 20: Knit.
Rnd 21: (K2tog) around.

FINISHING
Cut yarn and draw end through rem sts; tighten. Weave in all ends neatly on WS. Make the second sock the same way.

HORDALAND

Short *Skakareiker* Socks from Austevoll

Austevoll is a little island community out in the mouth of a fjord near Bergen. It consists of more than 650 islands, islets, and skerries. Fishing has been and remains the most important industry.

Kari Kristina Økland Vatsvik (1899-1988) learned to knit this type of sock from an old woman. She knitted long stockings for her own confirmation during the summer while at the mountain pastures. That must have been around 1913 or 1914. The pattern, literally "shaking furrows or stripes," is called *skakareiker* locally.

This information comes from Norway's Handcraft Association's registry of knitted textiles in private ownership around 1983.

The picture that was attached was quite poor quality and difficult to decipher. I've determined that the pattern is made with knit and purl stitches repeated over 11 stitches in width and 10 rounds in length.

The technique produces a very elastic result and can be used advantageously for long stockings or other textiles. Our version is a pair of short socks in alpaca silk yarn—the result is a delicate quality that works well for bed socks.

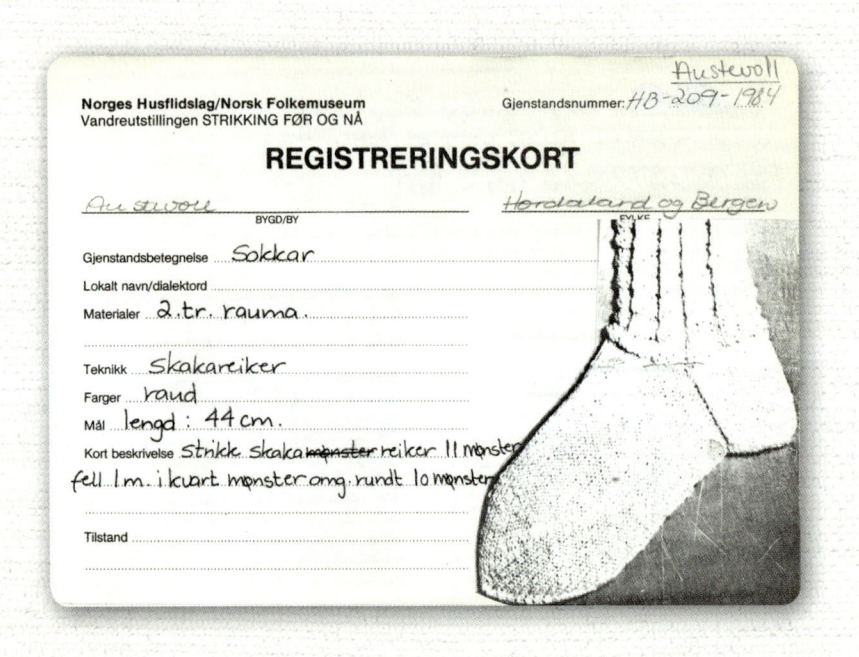

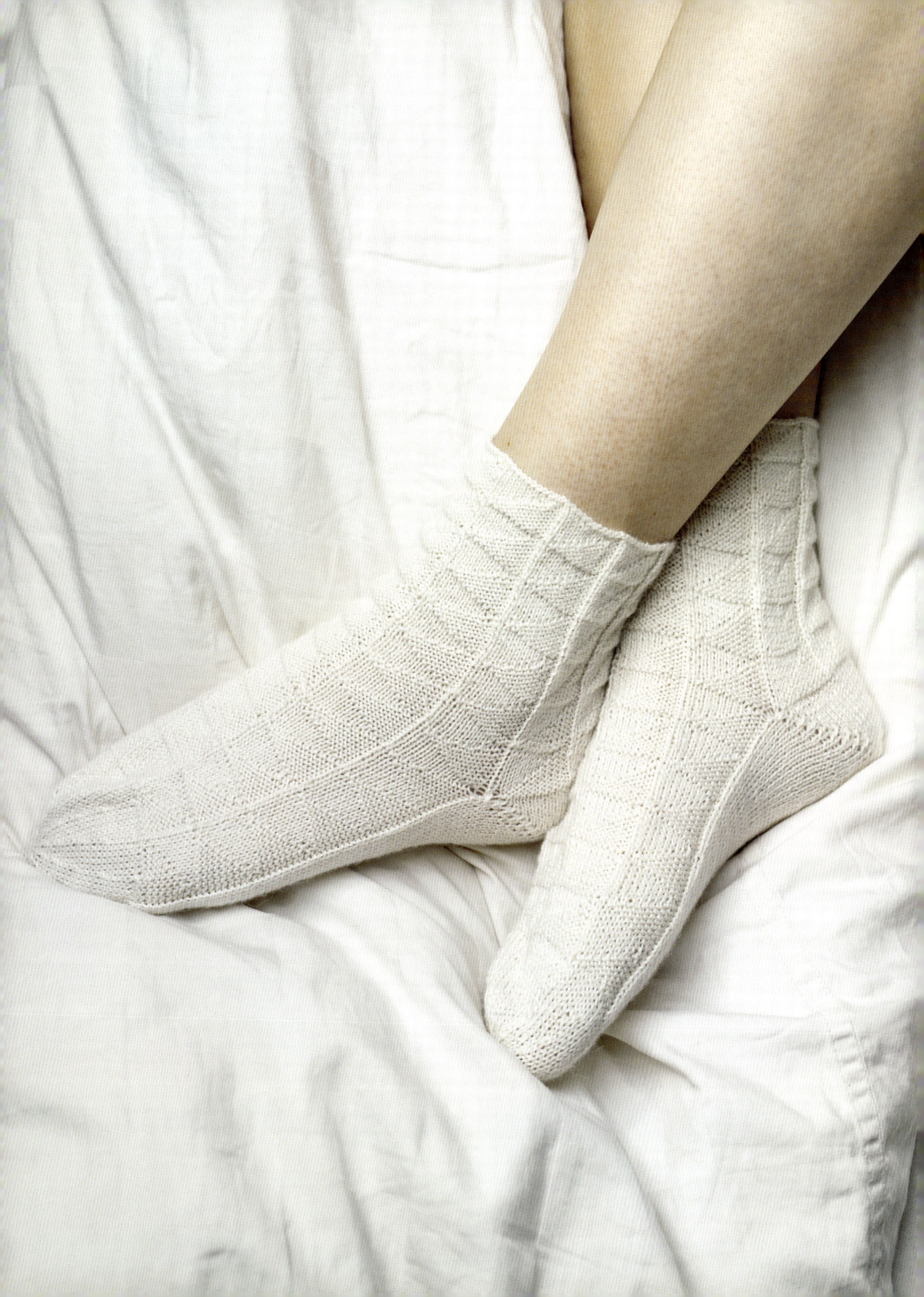

☐ Knit
☒ Purl

Repeat

Repeat

124

INSTRUCTIONS

Skill Level: Experienced

Size: Women's

MATERIALS
Yarn:
CYCA #1 (fingering/2 ply), Alpakka Silke from Sandnes Garn (70% alpaca, 30% silk, 218 yd/199 m / 50 g), White 1002: 100 g

Needles: U. S. size 0 / 2 mm: set of 5 dpn

Gauge: 34 sts in pattern = 4 in / 10 cm. Adjust needle size to obtain correct gauge if necessary.

LEG
CO 88 sts. Divide sts evenly onto 4 dpn. Join, being careful not to twist cast-on row; pm for beginning of rnd. Work around in charted pattern for 6 repeats in length.

After completing the leg, divide the stitches in half, placing the 44 instep stitches onto scrap yarn. These instep stitches will "rest" until the heel is complete.

HOURGLASS HEEL
Arrange rem 44 sts on one dpn and work back and forth.
Row 1 (RS): Knit across; turn.
Row 2: Sl 1 purlwise wyf, purl until 1 st rem; turn.
Row 3: Sl 1 purlwise wyb, knit until 1 st rem; turn.
Row 4: Sl 1, purl until 2 sts rem; turn.
Row 5: Sl 1, knit until 2 sts rem; turn.
Continue the same way with 1 less st before each turn until 16 sts rem at the center of the heel. Knit the last row.
Sl 1, purl as many sts as were last knitted (16). Pick up the strand between the last and next st, twist it and purl it tog with the next st; turn.
Sl 1, knit as many sts as last worked (16). Pick up the strand between the last st and the next, twist it and knit it together with the next st; turn.
Continue, repeating these 2 rows. You should have 1 more st each time before you turn.
NOTE: Tighten the yarn a bit each time you turn to avoid holes.
Continue with 1 st more on each row until you work all 44 sts on the last row.

FOOT
Now work around on all sts, working in pattern on the 44 instep sts and in st st on the 44 sole sts, until foot measures approx. 7½ in / 19 cm or desired length.

STAR TOE
Begin at the center of the sole.
Rnd 1: (K5, k2tog) around. The 4 sts rem on Ndl 4 will be decreased in subsequent rnds.
Rnds 2-6: Knit.
Rnd 7: (K4, k2tog) around.
Rnds 8-11: Knit.
Rnd 12: (K3, k2tog) around.
Rnds 13-15: Knit
Rnd 16: (K2, k2tog) around.
Rnds 17-18: Knit.
Rnd 19: (K1, k2tog) around.
Rnd 20: Knit.
Rnd 21: (K2tog) around.

FINISHING
Cut yarn and draw end through rem sts; tighten. Weave in all ends neatly on WS. Make the second sock the same way.

Kroneleistar from Øygarden

The Coast Museum in Øygarden has two pairs of children's socks knitted by Ingrid Mjøs. One pair is slightly larger than the other. Both pairs have "seafoam" patterns, locally referred to as *krone* patterns—the socks themselves are called *kroneleistar*. These socks were often made as christening socks because the *krone* pattern symbolized Jesus's crown, which protected the child.

The technique is also well known in other countries. When the Norwegian Handcraft Association registered knitted textiles in connection with the exhibit "Knitting Then and Now" in 1983-84, they took in a pair of "best" or "Sunday" socks in a men's size from Herand in Hardanger. The stockings were knitted with white cotton yarn in 1922 or 1923 by Inger Trå (born in 1891). The stockings later appeared in Haugesund.

At the same time, they registered a pair of elegant child's stockings in Stavanger. Some were knitted with 3-ply "mackerel" yarn and some with bleached cotton yarn. These stockings were knitted by Olga Vidvei from Tunheim in Time in 1919. Olga wore stockings with the same type of seafoam pattern for her wedding in 1917, as recounted by her daughter.

Another example of the seafoam pattern is a pair of white cotton stockings with a monogram knitted into the top, which has been registered by The Norwegian Institute for Bunad and Folk Costume. They are from Grong in North Trøndelag.

It's difficult to say how old the seafoam pattern is, but we find wave patterns in the earliest knitting books published in the Nordic countries: Sine Andresen's *Knitting Book for School and Household Use* came out in Denmark in 1845. The pattern also appears in Caroline Halvorsen's *Norwegian Knitting Book for Elementary Schools and Home* in 1901. She calls the pattern "waves". Several variations of the pattern are described in Johanna Schreiner's *Knitting Patterns from Great-Grandmother's Time*, which was published ten years later. Today, you'll find the pattern used for several traditional bunad folk costume stockings.

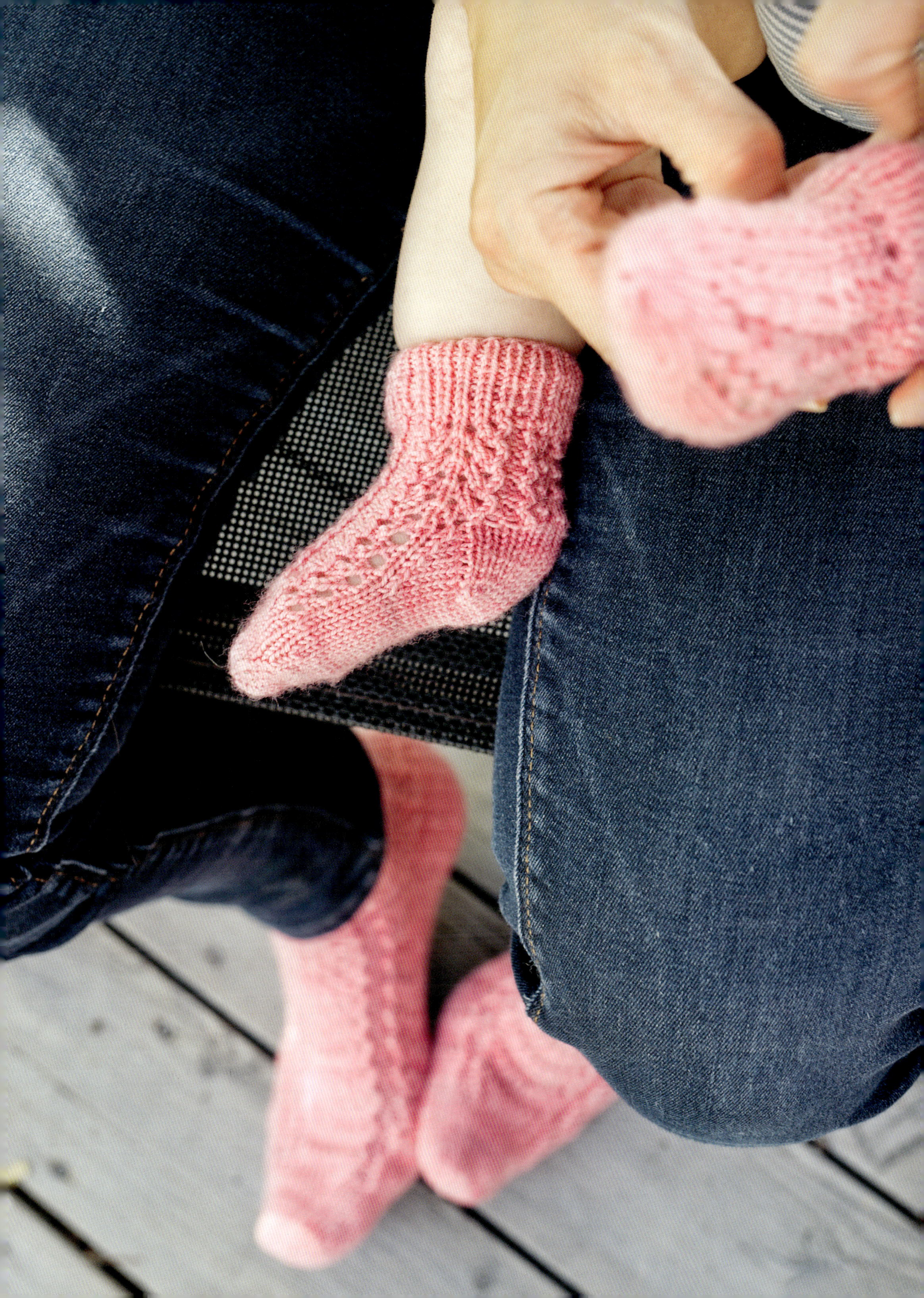

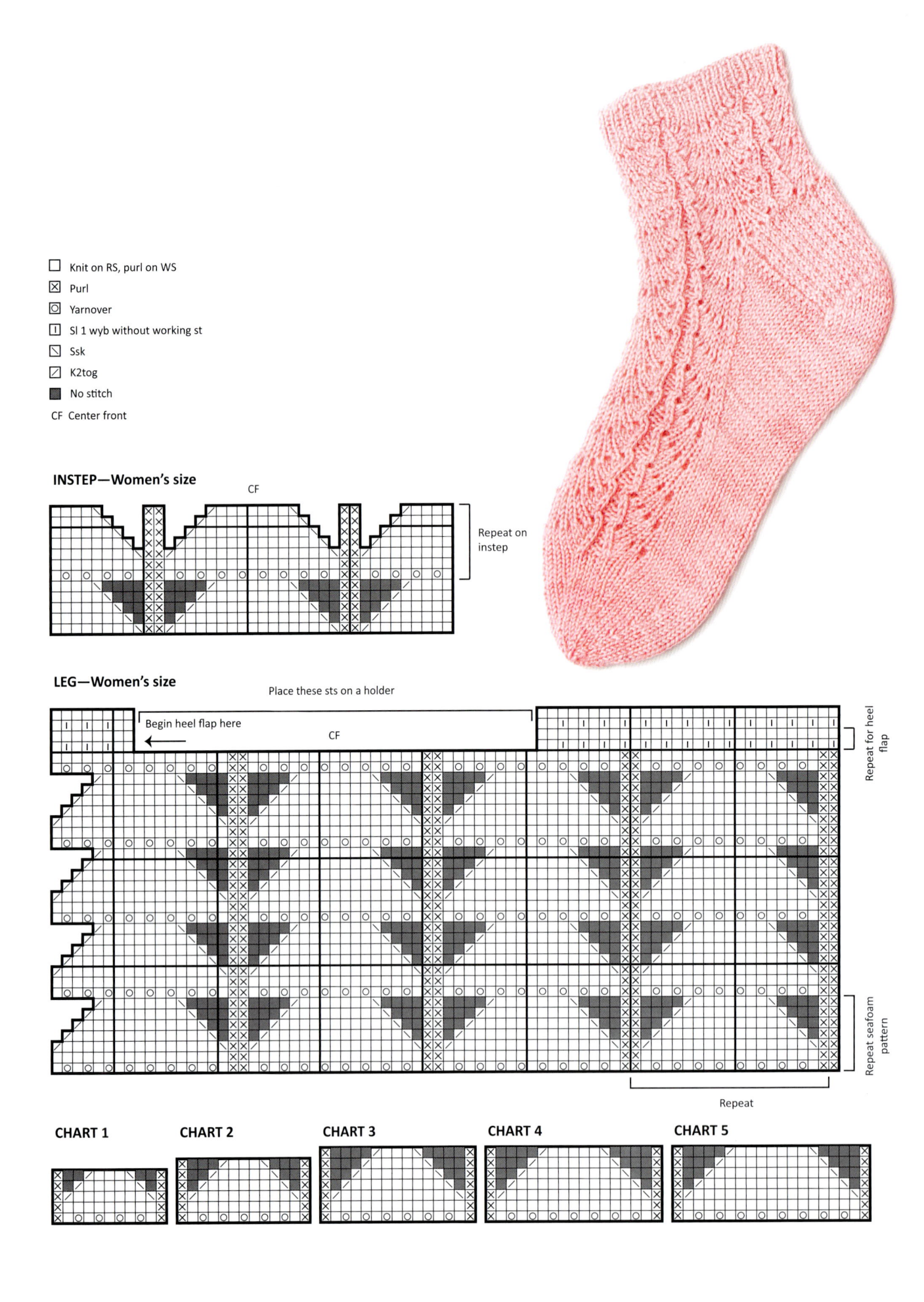

☐ Knit on RS, purl on WS
☒ Purl
⊙ Yarnover
│ Sl 1 wyb without working st
◺ Ssk
◿ K2tog
■ No stitch
CF Center front

INSTEP—Women's size

Repeat on instep

LEG—Women's size

Place these sts on a holder
Begin heel flap here
CF
Repeat for heel flap
Repeat seafoam pattern
Repeat

CHART 1 **CHART 2** **CHART 3** **CHART 4** **CHART 5**

128

INSTRUCTIONS

Skill Level: Intermediate

Sizes: 1-3 months (1-2, 3-6, 7-10 years; women's)

MATERIALS
Yarn:
CYCA #1 (fingering/2 ply), Sheila's Gold from Wool2dye4 (80% Merino Wool, 20% nylon, 400 yd/366 m / 100 g), February Rose hand-dyed by Kate Fredriksen: 50 (50, 50, 50, 100) g

Needles: U. S. size 0 / 2 mm: set of 5 dpn

Gauge: 30 sts in pattern = 4 in / 10 cm. Adjust needle size to obtain correct gauge if necessary.

LEG
CO 44 (52, 60, 68, 72) sts. Divide sts evenly onto 4 dpn. Join, being careful not to twist cast-on row; pm for beginning of rnd. Work around in k1, p1 ribbing for 8 rnds. Knit the next rnd, decreasing evenly spaced around to 28 (32, 36, 40, 44) sts. Now work seafoam pattern, following Chart 1 (2, 3, 4, 5). **NOTE:** Only the women's size is completely charted in pattern. If you want a longer leg for the socks, work the repeat one or several times extra. When the leg is finished, there are 44 (52, 60, 68, 76) sts.

GUSSET HEEL
After completing the leg, divide the stitches, placing the 23 (27, 31, 35, 39) instep stitches onto scrap yarn. These instep stitches will "rest" until the heel is complete.
Place the remaining 21 (25, 29, 33, 37) sts onto one needle and work back and forth. The leg chart shows which sts are worked for the heel flap on the women's size. **NOTE:** The center front of the sock is also the center of a repeat.
Begin with the RS facing you.
Row 1 (RS): Sl 1 purlwise wyb, *k1, sl 1*; rep * to * across, ending with k2.
Row 2: Sl 1 purlwise wyf, purl to end of row.
Repeat these 2 rows until there are 7 (9, 11, 13, 15) chain sts at each side of the flap.
End with Row 1.

Shaping the Heel
Row 1 (WS): Sl 1, purl until 7 (8, 10, 11, 12) sts rem on the needle, p2tog, p1; turn.
Row 2: Sl 1, knit until 7 (8, 10, 11, 12) sts rem on needle, ssk, k1; turn.

Row 3: Sl 1, purl until 1 st before gap, p2tog, p1; turn.
Row 4: Sl 1, knit until 1 st rem before gap, ssk, k1; turn.
Repeat Rows 3-4 until all the side sts have been eliminated.

Gusset Shaping
Divide the instep sts from the holder onto 2 dpn; divide the sole sts onto 2 dpn with half of the sts on each. With RS facing, begin working in the round. Begin rnd at center of sole. With Ndl 1, knit to flap; pick up and knit 1 st in each chain up side of flap. You can pick up the chain sts through back loops, or knit them through back loops on the next rnd. With Ndls 2-3, work across the instep in pattern as shown on chart. Next, with Ndl 4, pick up and knit sts down opposite side of flap as for the first side. Knit to center of sole.

On the next rnd, begin decreasing to shape gusset: Knit until 2 sts rem on Ndl 1, k2tog. Work across instep sts on Ndls 2-3 as shown on chart. With Ndl 4, ssk and then knit to end of rnd. Work the next rnd without decreasing.
Repeat these 2 rnds until 12 (14, 16, 20, 24) sts total rem on Ndls 1 and 4 = 35 (41, 47, 55, 63) sts total. Continue without further shaping, with instep in pattern and sole in st st until foot measures 2½ (3¼, 4, 4¾, 6) in / 6 (8, 10, 12, 15) cm or desired length to toe shaping. Try to end the foot with a complete pattern repeat.

STAR TOE
Begin at the center of the sole.
Rnd 1: (K5, k2tog) around. Sts rem on Ndl 4 will be decreased in subsequent rnds.
Rnds 2-6: Knit.
Rnd 7: (K4, k2tog) around.
Rnds 8-11: Knit.
Rnd 12: (K3, k2tog) around.
Rnds 13-15: Knit
Rnd 16: (K2, k2tog) around.
Rnds 17-18: Knit.
Rnd 19: (K1, k2tog) around.
Rnd 20: Knit.
Rnd 21: (K2tog) around.

FINISHING
Cut yarn and draw end through rem sts; tighten. Weave in all ends neatly on WS.
Make the second sock the same way.

HORDALAND

Hardanger Socks

Today we connect complex cable patterns first and foremost with Ireland and the Aran Islands. Most historians agree that Aran garments first appeared in the islands west of Ireland at the end of the 19th century, around 1890. At that time, a number of British people came to the islands to contribute to the development of the fishing industry. New methods of knitting sweaters arrived with them.

The first commercially available Aran patterns that we know of were published at the beginning of the 1940s. After *Vogue* described these garments in the 1950s, their desirability increased exponentially.

Here in Norway, we have several examples of cable patterns that were knitted long before then. A great number of carefully knitted stockings from Telemark in the early 19th century have been preserved. Cable techniques were well developed in Setesdal even earlier. These patterns are complex and locally referred to as *vriuband*.

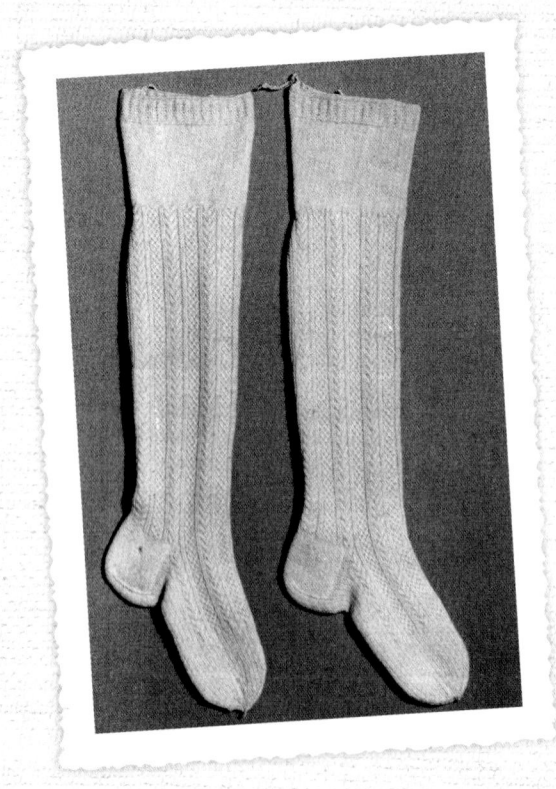

Copying these stockings isn't easy, because they were knitted with extremely fine wool yarn. It's likely they were knitted with needles size 00000 / 1 mm or finer.

One pair of Hardanger stockings from the Norwegian Museum of Cultural History can be distinguished from the characteristic Setesdal or Telemark stockings. While the other stockings have distinct sections of different pattern elements, this pair is more unassuming in its composition. The same pattern, which consists of two different cable panels, is repeated all around the stocking.

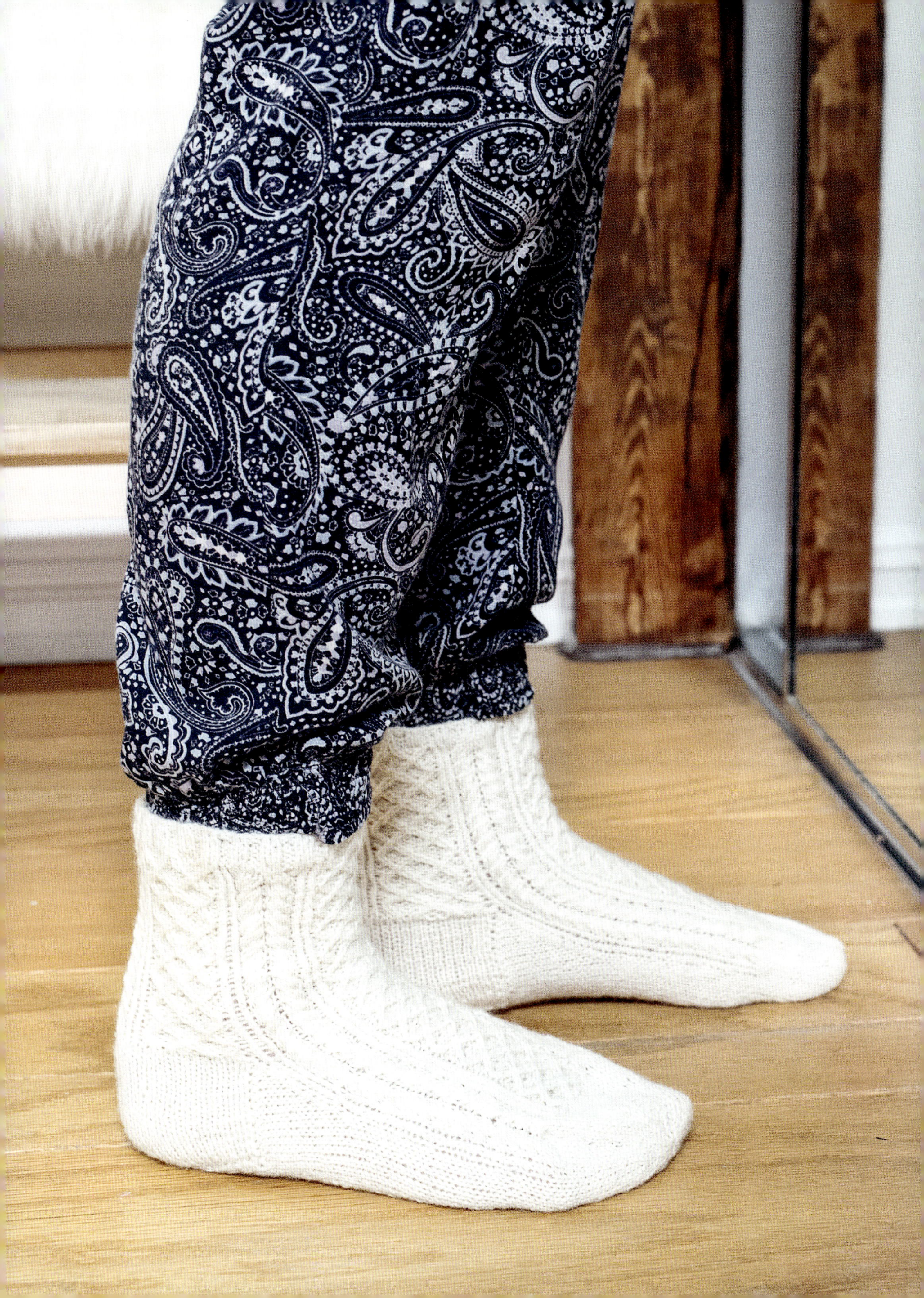

FOOT

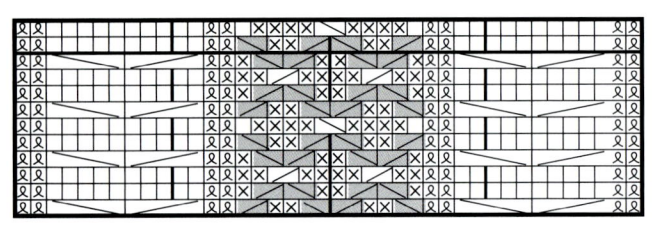

LEG

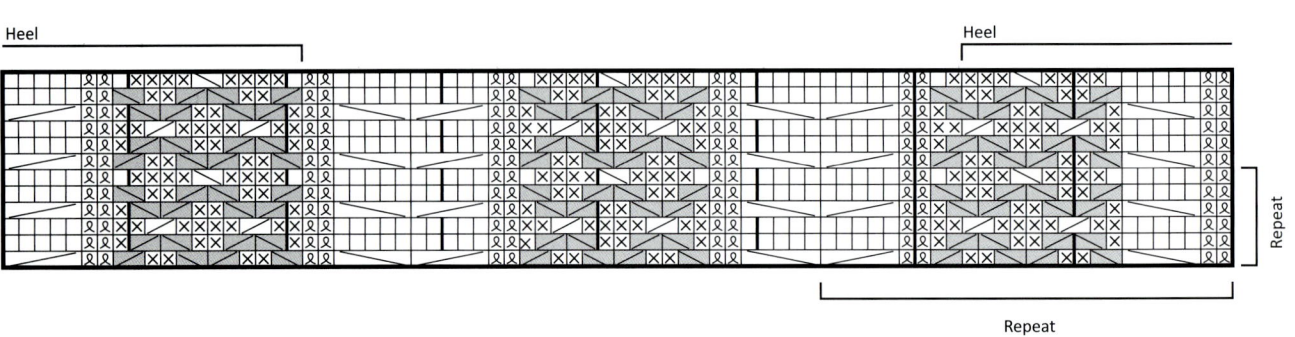

Heel

Repeat

Repeat

- ☐ Knit
- ⍉ Twisted Knit (k1tbl)
- ☒ Purl
- Place 1 st on cable needle and hold in front of work, k1, k1 from cable needle
- Place 1 st on cable needle and hold in back of work, k1, k1 from cable needle
- Place 1 st on cable needle and hold in front of work, pk1, k1 from cable needle
- Place 1 st on cable needle and hold in back of work, p1, k1 from cable needle
- Place 3 sts on cable needle and hold in front of work, k2, k3 from cable needle
- Place 2 sts on cable needle and hold in back of work, k3, k2 from cable needle

INSTRUCTIONS

Skill Level: Intermediate

Sizes: Women's (Men's)

MATERIALS
Yarn:
CYCA #1 (fingering/2 ply), 2-ply Gammelserie from Rauma (100% wool, 175 yd/160 m / 50 g), Natural White 401: 100 (150) g

Reinforcing Thread: Mettler extra strong sewing thread, Natural White: 33 (66) yd / 30 (60) m

Needles: U. S. 0 (1.5) / 2 (2.5) mm: set of 5 dpn; cable needle

Gauge: 26 (24) sts in pattern = 4 in / 10 cm. Adjust needle size to obtain correct gauge if necessary.

LEG
CO 76 sts. Divide sts evenly onto 4 dpn. Join, being careful not to twist cast-on row; pm for beginning of rnd. Work around in k2, p2 ribbing for 6 rnds, increasing 2 sts at center back on the last rnd. Continue in charted pattern, working 6 repeats of the pattern + Rnds 1-2.

GUSSET HEEL
After completing the leg, divide the stitches, placing the 40 instep stitches onto scrap yarn. These instep stitches will "rest" until the heel is complete.

Place the remaining 38 sts onto one needle and work back and forth. Hold reinforcing thread with working yarn.
Begin with the WS facing you.
Row 1 (WS): Sl 1 purlwise wyf, purl to end of row.
Row 2: Sl 1 purlwise wyb, knit to end of row.
Repeat these 2 rows until there are 13 chain sts at each side of the flap.

Shaping the Heel
Row 1 (WS): Sl 1, purl until 13 sts rem on the needle, p2tog, p1; turn.
Row 2: Sl 1, knit until 13 sts rem on needle, ssk, k1; turn.
Row 3: Sl 1, purl until 1 st before gap, p2tog, p1; turn.
Row 4: Sl 1, knit until 1 st rem before gap, ssk, k1; turn.

Repeat Rows 3-4 until all the side sts have been eliminated.
Cut reinforcing thread.

Gusset Shaping
Divide the instep sts from the holder onto 2 dpn; divide the sole sts onto 2 dpn with half of the sts on each. With RS facing, begin working in the round. Begin rnd at center of sole. With Ndl 1, knit to flap; pick up and knit 1 st in each chain up side of flap. You can pick up the chain sts through back loops, or knit them through back loops on the next rnd. With Ndls 2-3, work across the instep in pattern as shown on chart. Next, with Ndl 4, pick up and knit sts down opposite side of flap as for the first side. Knit to center of sole.

On the next rnd, begin decreasing to shape gusset: Knit until 2 sts rem on Ndl 1, k2tog. Work across instep sts on Ndls 2-3 as shown on chart. With Ndl 4, ssk and then knit to end of rnd.
Work the next rnd without decreasing.
Repeat these 2 rnds until 78 sts rem. On the next rnd, at only one side of instep, dec 1 st = 77 sts rem. Continue without further shaping, with instep in pattern and sole in st st until foot measures 7½ (8¾) in / 19 (22) cm or desired length to toe shaping. Try to end the foot with a complete pattern repeat.

STAR TOE
Begin at the center of the sole.
Rnd 1: (K5, k2tog) around.
Rnds 2-6: Knit.
Rnd 7: (K4, k2tog) around.
Rnds 8-11: Knit.
Rnd 12: (K3, k2tog) around.
Rnds 13-15: Knit
Rnd 16: (K2, k2tog) around.
Rnds 17-18: Knit.
Rnd 19: (K1, k2tog) around.
Rnd 20: Knit.
Rnd 21: (K2tog) around.

FINISHING
Cut yarn and draw end through rem sts; tighten. Weave in all ends neatly on WS. Make the second sock the same way.

SOGN AND FJORDANE

Sunnfjord Socks

The first Norwegian knitting patterns came out in 1888. The first and second editions of Marie Blom's cookbook, *Household Book for Town and Country*, has a short addendum, "Various Patterns for Knitting." That part follows a long section about dealing with corns on the feet, cold and complaining feet, warts, toothache, and dandruff. Patterns were written for large men's stocking sizes with heavy 4-ply yarn, women's stockings of fine Scottish yarn, Scottish wool stockings for a large 6-year-old boy, and smaller baby socks or oversocks. There were even knee sock patterns for arthritic patients.

Socks and stockings were some of the most important items one could knit, so it wasn't unusual to find instructions for them alongside patterns for wool sweaters, skirts, gloves, and hats, as in this book. Charts, however, were not included. Knitters then were expected to work these things out on their own.

Patterns wander. If someone sees a pattern she likes, she'll copy pattern elements. A knitter might add a little panel, a date, or some letters. We know that in Selbu they had small rose books for sketching in motif variations. The samplers most girls had to sew during handcraft sessions at school were used as sources of inspiration and pattern collections.

From Surnadal in Nordmøre and Gaular in Sogn and Fjordane, we recognize a pattern that's constructed like stones in a wall. The elements of the pattern are arranged in bands; on every other row, the "stones" are shifted so there are no stacked vertical *fuger*, or joints, as they say in masonry jargon. This pattern appears on mittens in both Surnadal and Gaular. The University Museum in Bergen also has a pair of stockings with exactly the same pattern. It's a pair from Sunnfjord, knitted in red and black homespun wool yarn.

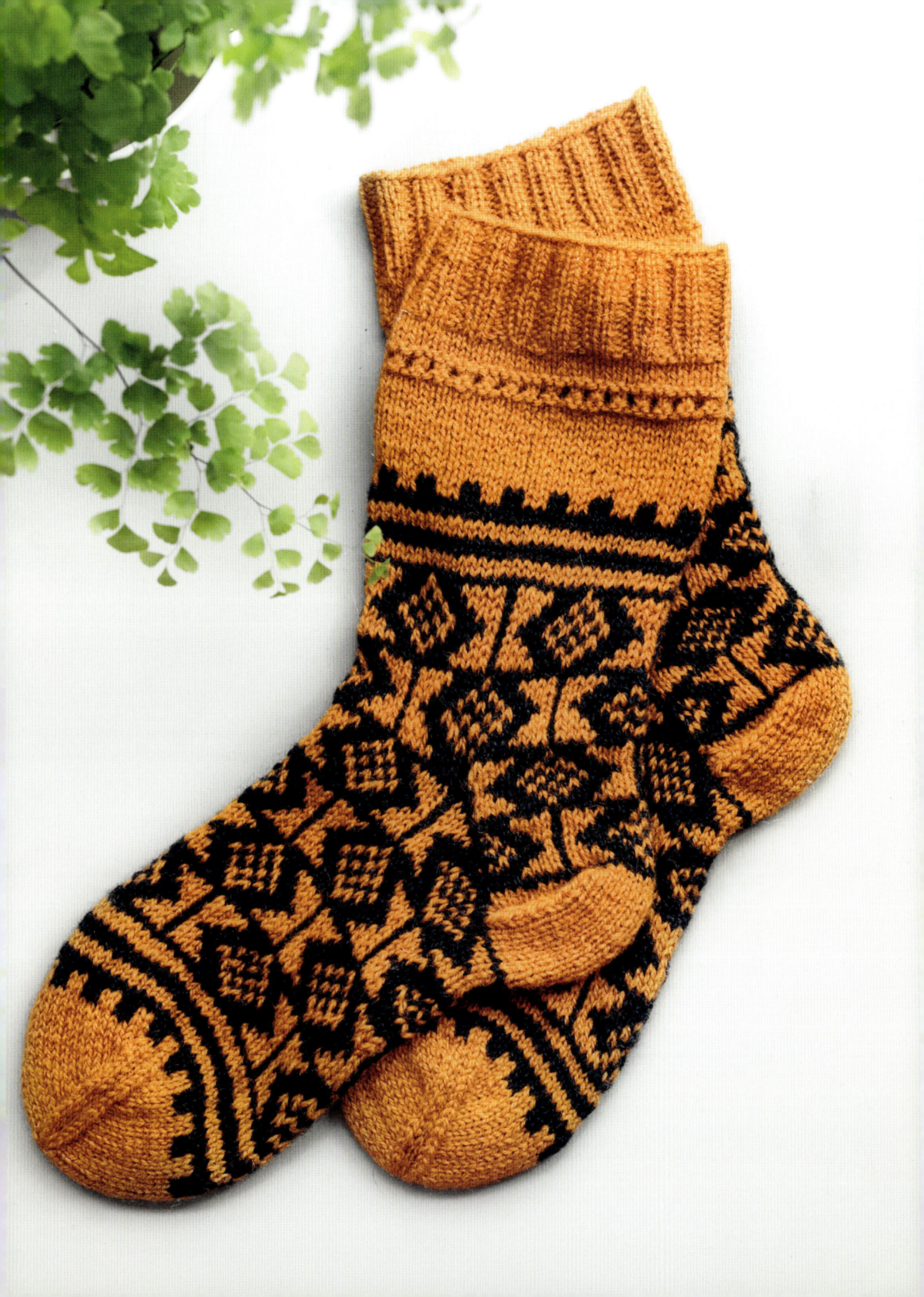

FOOT

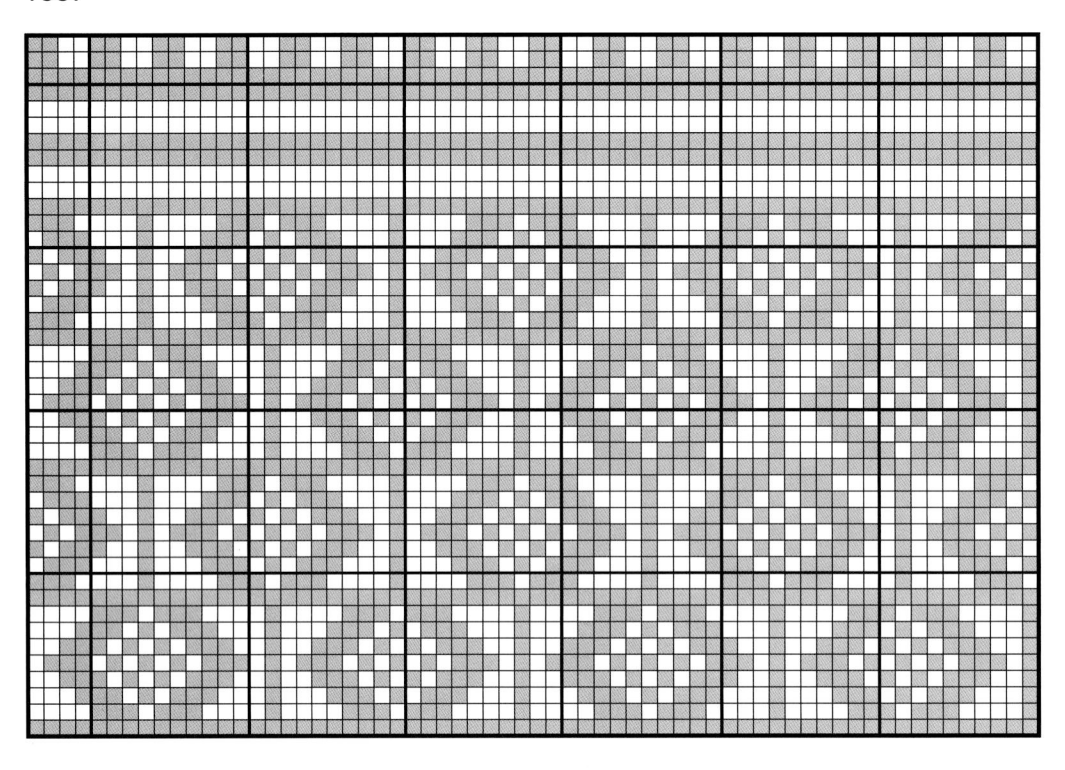

HEEL FLAP

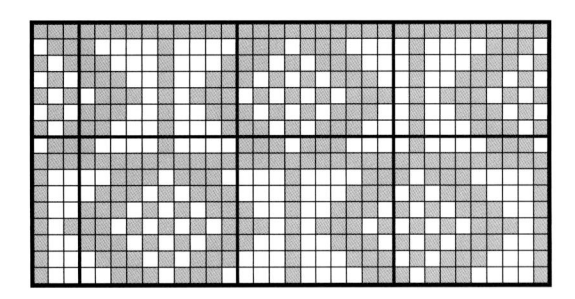

☐ Orange—knit on RS and purl on WS
▨ Black—knit on RS and purl on WS

LEG

Place these instep stitches on a holder "to rest" while you knit the heel flap

INSTRUCTIONS

Skill Level: Experienced

Sizes: Women's (Men's)

MATERIALS
Yarn:
CYCA #1 (fingering/2 ply), Finullgarn from Rauma (100% wool, 191 yd/175 m / 50 g)

Yarn Colors and Amounts:
Orange 461: 100 (100) g
Black 4387: 50 (50) g

Reinforcing Thread: black silk or similar thread

Needles: U. S. size 1.5 (2.5) / 2.5 (3) mm: set of 5 dpn

Gauge: 30 (28) sts in colorwork pattern = 4 in / 10 cm.
Adjust needle size to obtain correct gauge if necessary.

LEG
With Orange, CO 64 sts. Divide sts evenly onto 4 dpn. Join, being careful not to twist cast-on row; pm for beginning of rnd. Work around in k2, p2 ribbing for 1½ in / 4 cm. Knit 4 rnds in st st and then work an eyelet panel as follows: Purl 1 rnd, knit 1 rnd, work eyelet rnd: (k2tog, yo) around, purl 1 rnd.
Continue in st st until piece measures 3¼ in / 8 cm long. Now work in leg pattern, as shown on chart.

BAND HEEL
After completing leg, place 31 sts on scrap yarn for the instep (see chart). These sts will "rest" until the heel is finished (see top of leg chart, which indicates instep sts).

Heel Flap
Place the rem 33 sts on one dpn and work the heel flap back and forth. Begin on RS. Work heel flap in pattern as shown on the chart, carrying the reinforcing thread with the black yarn. Work the last st of each row with doubled yarn (1 strand each Orange and Black). Begin on RS as follows:
Row 1 (RS): Sl 1 purlwise wyb, knit to last st, end k1 with both colors.
Row 2: Sl 1 purlwise wyf, purl to last st, end p1 with both colors.

Rep these 2 rows until there are 10 chain sts at each side of flap. Cut black yarn and reinforcing thread; continue with Orange only.

Now decrease to shape the band:
Row 1: Sl 1, knit until 11 sts rem, ssk; turn.
Row 2: Sl 1, purl until 11 sts rem, p2tog; turn.
Row 3: Sl 1, knit until 1 st before gap, ssk; turn.
Row 4: Sl 1, purl until 1 st before gap, p2tog; turn.
Rep Rows 3-4 until all the side sts have been eliminated; cut yarn.

FOOT
Divide the instep sts onto 2 dpn and divide the rem heel sts onto 2 dpn so you have half of each section on a needle. Now work the charted pattern in the round with RS facing you. Begin rnd at center of heel. Pick up and knit 1 st in each chain st along side of heel flap. You can pick up the sts tbl or knit them tbl on next rnd. Work across instep, following chart. Pick up and knit 1 st in each chain st of opposite side of flap and then complete rnd as est = 64 sts total. Continue in foot pattern to end of foot chart. If necessary, you can add a whole or half repeat before the final stripe. Cut Black.

WEDGE TOE
Divide the sts, with 16 sts on each needle
*Ndl 1: Knit until 3 sts rem on needle, k2tog, k1.
Ndl 2: K1, ssk, knit to end of needle.
Ndl 3: Work as for Ndl 1.
Ndl 4: Work as for Ndl 2.
Knit 2 rnds without decreasing*.
Rep * to * 3 times and then decrease on every other rnd until 3 sts rem on each needle. Cut yarn and draw end through rem sts; tighten.

FINISHING
Weave in all ends neatly on WS.
Make the second sock the same way.

SOGN AND FJORDANE

Spiral Socks from Nordfjord

In 1993, the Nordfjord Museum acquired a pair of long hand-knitted white spiral socks from Hole in Byrkjelo. They're women's stockings that were never completely finished and were never worn, 39 in / 99 cm long and knitted with fine white wool yarn.

The stockings don't have a heel, and the pattern spirals around from the ribbed cuff all the way down to the toe. "At the top, a horizontal row of large holes. Directly below that, wide diagonal stripes down to the toes and tapering at the toe tips" is all the information we have about these stockings.

I'd always imagined spiral socks were a new discovery, perhaps having been designed in the 1970s or 80s. However, similar socks have been popular at various times. Here we have an example of this type of stocking, knitted earlier. It's difficult to say when these stockings were made, but by comparing them to other knitted items, we can estimate that they were likely made before WWII.

Heelless stockings are very practical for small children. No matter how you pull them onto their feet, they'll conform to the foot shape. They're particularly useful for very small children, because the socks don't slide off easily.

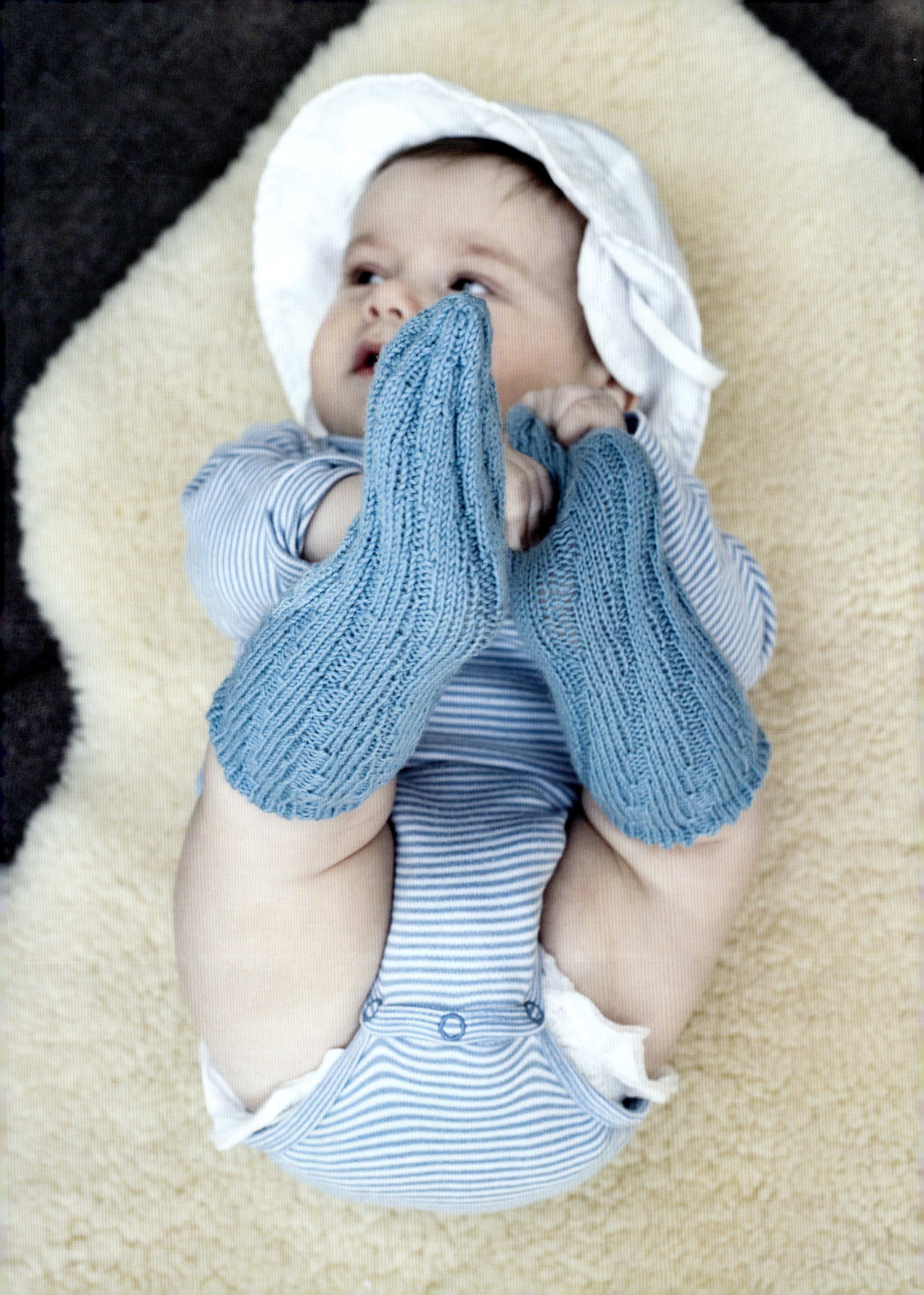

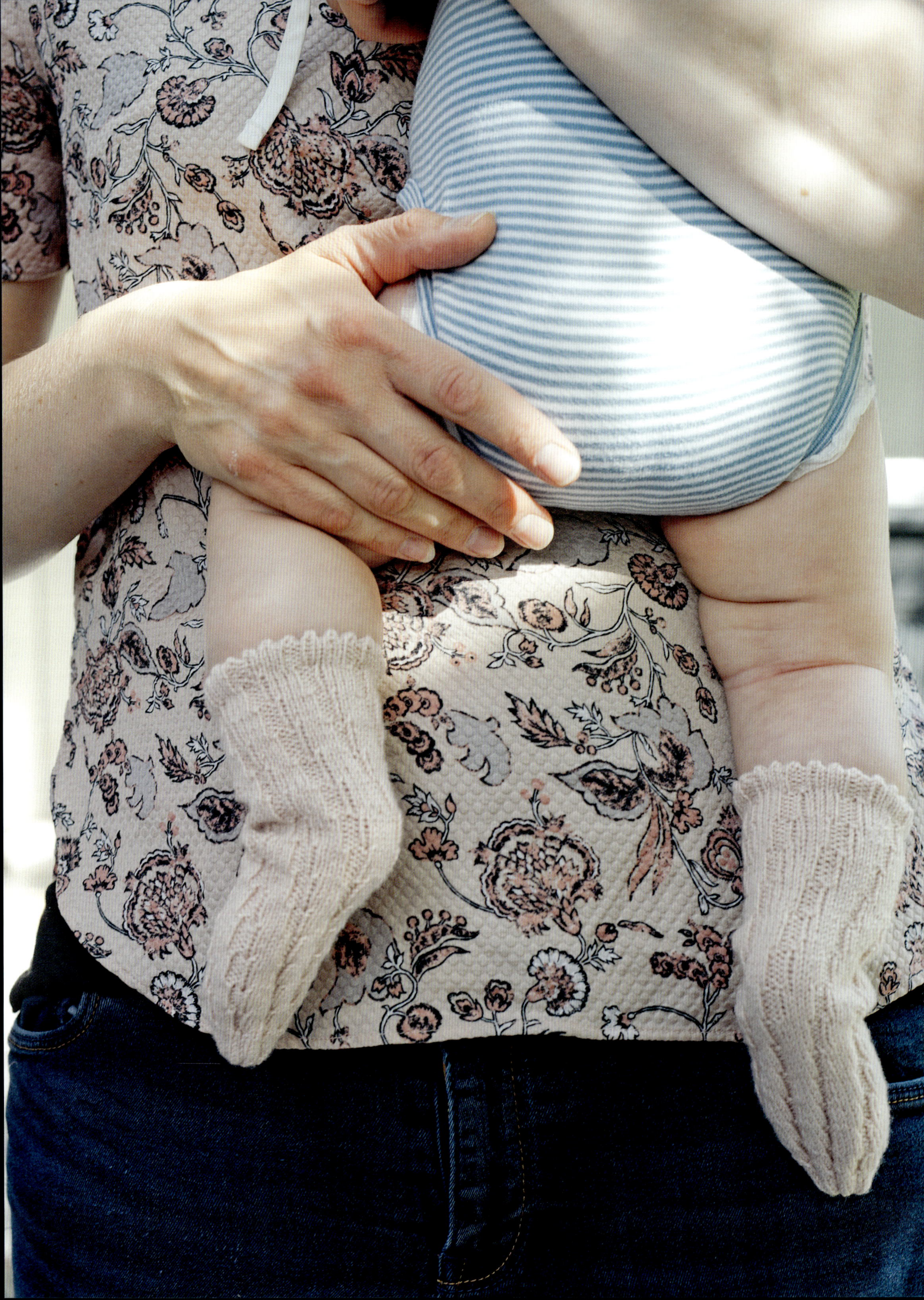

Shaping for left sock

Shaping for right sock

Left sock

Right sock

Repeat

Repeat

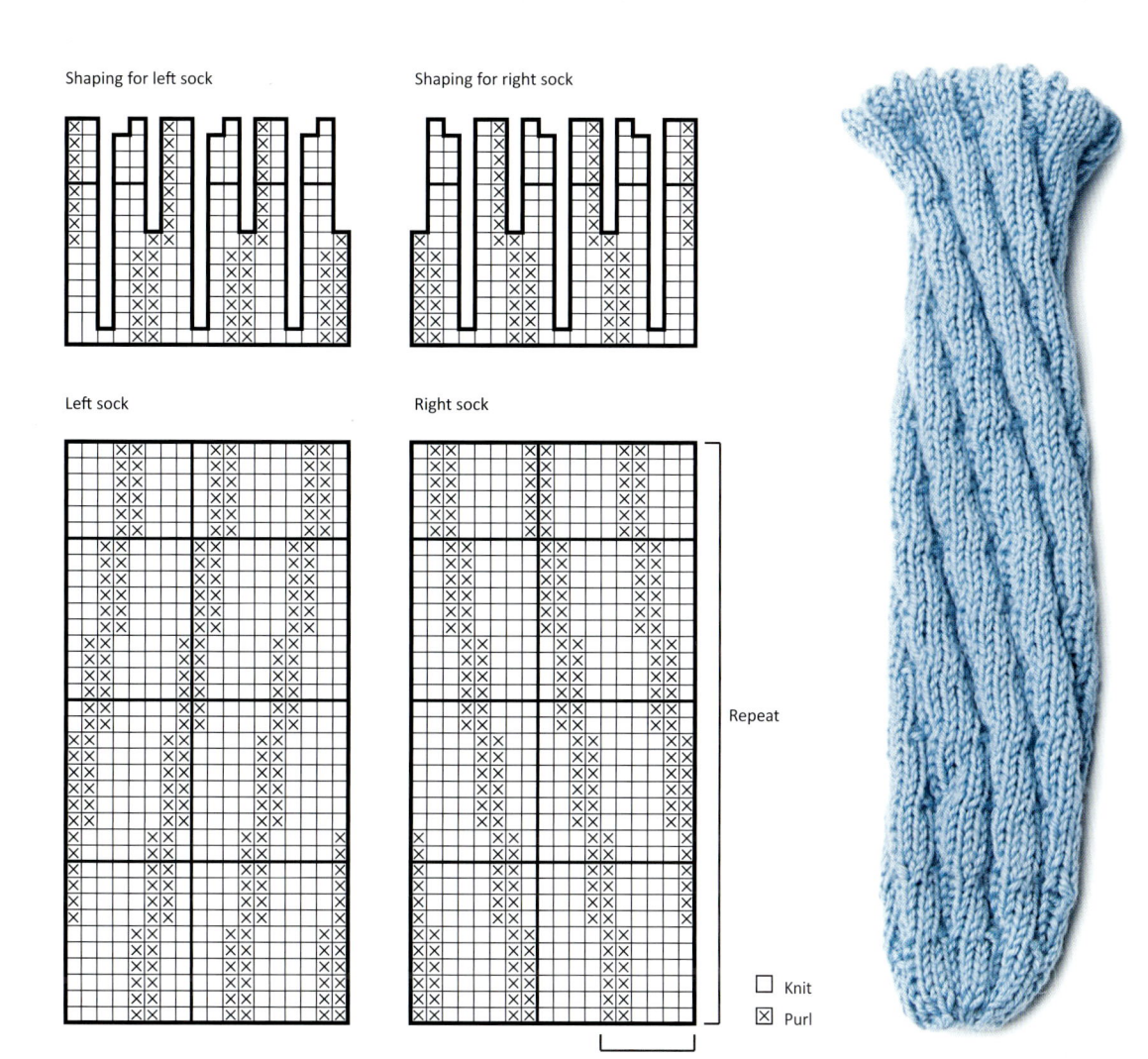

☐ Knit
☒ Purl

INSTRUCTIONS

Skill Level: Intermediate

Sizes: 0-3 (3-6, 6-12, 12-18) months

MATERIALS
Yarn:
CYCA #1 (fingering/2 ply), Hot Socks Pearl with Cashmere from Four Seasons Gründl (75% Merino wool, 20% polyamide, 5% cashmere, 218 yd/ 199 m / 50 g)

Yarn Color and Amount:
Pink 15: 50 g for all sizes
Or Light Blue 12: 50 g for all sizes

Needles: U. S. size 0 (1.5, 1.5, 1.5) / 2 (2.5, 2.5, 2.5) mm: set of 5 dpn

Gauge: 30 sts in pattern = 4 in / 10 cm.
Adjust needle size to obtain correct gauge if necessary.

CO 48 (48, 54, 60) sts. Divide sts as evenly as possible onto 4 dpn. Join, being careful not to twist cast-on row; pm for beginning of rnd.
Knit 4 rnds and then make an eyelet rnd: (K2tog, yo) around.
Now work in k4, p2 ribbing for 6 rnds and then continue as shown on the chart.
Work in pattern until there are 13 (13, 16, 20) shifts of the ribbing or to desired length.

TOE SHAPING FOR RIGHT SOCK
See chart.
Decrease Rnd 1: Work (K1, k2tog, k1, p2) around.
Next 5 rnds: (K3, p2).
Decrease Rnd 2: P1, (k3, p2tog) around. End by working the last st tog with the 1st purl.
Next 5 rnds: P1, (k3, p1) around, ending with k3.
Decrease Rnd 3: P1, (k2tog, k1, p1) around.
Cut yarn and draw end through rem sts; tighten.

Finish left sock following chart. The right and left socks spiral in opposite directions.

FINISHING
Weave in all ends neatly on WS. Fold cuff at eyelet rnd and sew down neatly on WS.

MØRE AND ROMSDAL

Children's Socks from Nordmøre

In 2014, Lisbet Harang auctioned a selection of items from Nestu Harang in Surnadal, the farm she had inherited from her father Geir. Among the items which are now owned by the Nordmøre Museum Foundation are a pair of hand-knitted children's wool socks. They were knitted with a blue pattern on a white background. The socks have three typical eight-petal roses with rounded forms over each sock front and two on the back of the leg.

Early in the 1500s, the first pattern books came out in Germany, just a few decades after Johann Gutenberg developed an effective method for printing with loose fonts. The books immediately became a success in the western world, both among professional handworkers and women who were responsible for their family's clothing and textiles. Among the upper classes, embroidery was extremely popular, but the designs were also used for weaving and in knitted garments.

We've found the different variations of traditional eight-petal roses and the rose used on these stockings in the earliest pattern books. The eight-petal rose pattern is easy to copy, easy to remember, and can be arranged in endless ways. For that reason, we find this pattern all over Europe.

19

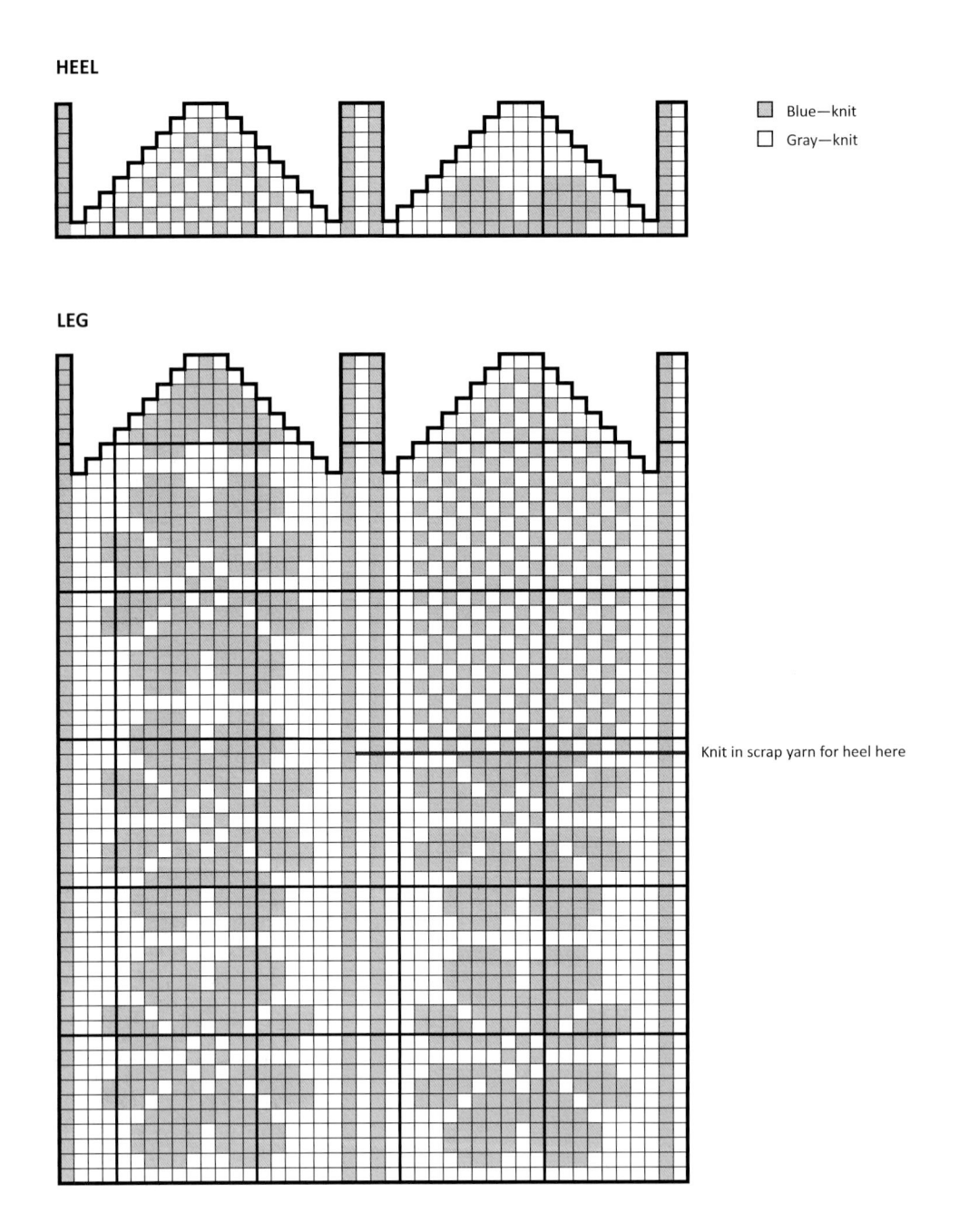

HEEL

LEG

☐ Blue—knit
☐ Gray—knit

Knit in scrap yarn for heel here

INSTRUCTIONS

Skill Level: Experienced

Sizes: 2-4 (5-6) years

MATERIALS
Yarn:
CYCA #3 (DK, light worsted), Sterk from Du Store Alpakka (40% Merino wool, 40% alpaca, 20% nylon, 150 yd/137 m / 50 g)

Yarn Colors and Amounts:
Blue 833: 50 g
Light Gray 841: 50 g

Needles: 2.5 (4) / 3 (3.5) mm: set of 5 dpn

Gauge: 26 (24) sts in pattern = 4 in / 10 cm. Adjust needle size to obtain correct gauge if necessary.

LEG
With Gray, CO 44 sts. Divide sts evenly onto 4 dpn. Join, being careful not to twist cast-on row; pm for beginning of rnd. Work around in k1, p1 ribbing for 1¼ in / 3 cm. Continue in charted pattern. At the red line on the chart, knit across indicated 23 sts with smooth scrap yarn (see details on page 20). Slide those sts back onto left needle and work in pattern. Continue with the flower pattern on the instep sts and k1 Blue, k1 Gray on the sole as shown on the chart. Shape toe as shown on the chart and as follows: Decrease at the beginning of a needle with ssk and at end of needle with k2tog.

AFTERTHOUGHT HEEL
With one dpn, pick up 23 sts on instep side of scrap yarn and, with a second dpn, pick up and knit 21 sts tbl on sole side of scrap yarn. Divide the sts evenly onto 4 dpn and work around in pattern as shown on heel chart (see details on page 20). After completing shaping, cut yarn and draw end through rem sts; tighten.

FINISHING
Weave in all ends neatly on WS. Make the second sock the same way.

SOUTH TRØNDELAG

Socks from Budalen

In 1987, the Norwegian Museum of Cultural History held a large fieldwork expedition in Budalen in Central Gauldal. All kinds of textiles, tools, furniture and personal property were registered. The list of items included a pair of children's socks and stockings knitted as one. They're from Innistu on Storrø and were knitted in 1928 or 1929. Short socks were popular then, but at that time it was also common to wear long stockings. Instead of knitting a pair of long stockings and a pair of short socks—which would certainly have been difficult to fit together into shoes—the stockings were made as for two pairs.

Similar socks with a large eight-petal rose as the motif on the front of the foot are also familiar from Selbu. In this example, however, no small pattern details were added, in order to make it easier to knit the design. The dark eight-petal rose is almost a graphic element on the light background.

The original socks were knitted with very fine yarn and are for a child. By varying the thickness of the yarn and needles, these socks can also be sized for adults.

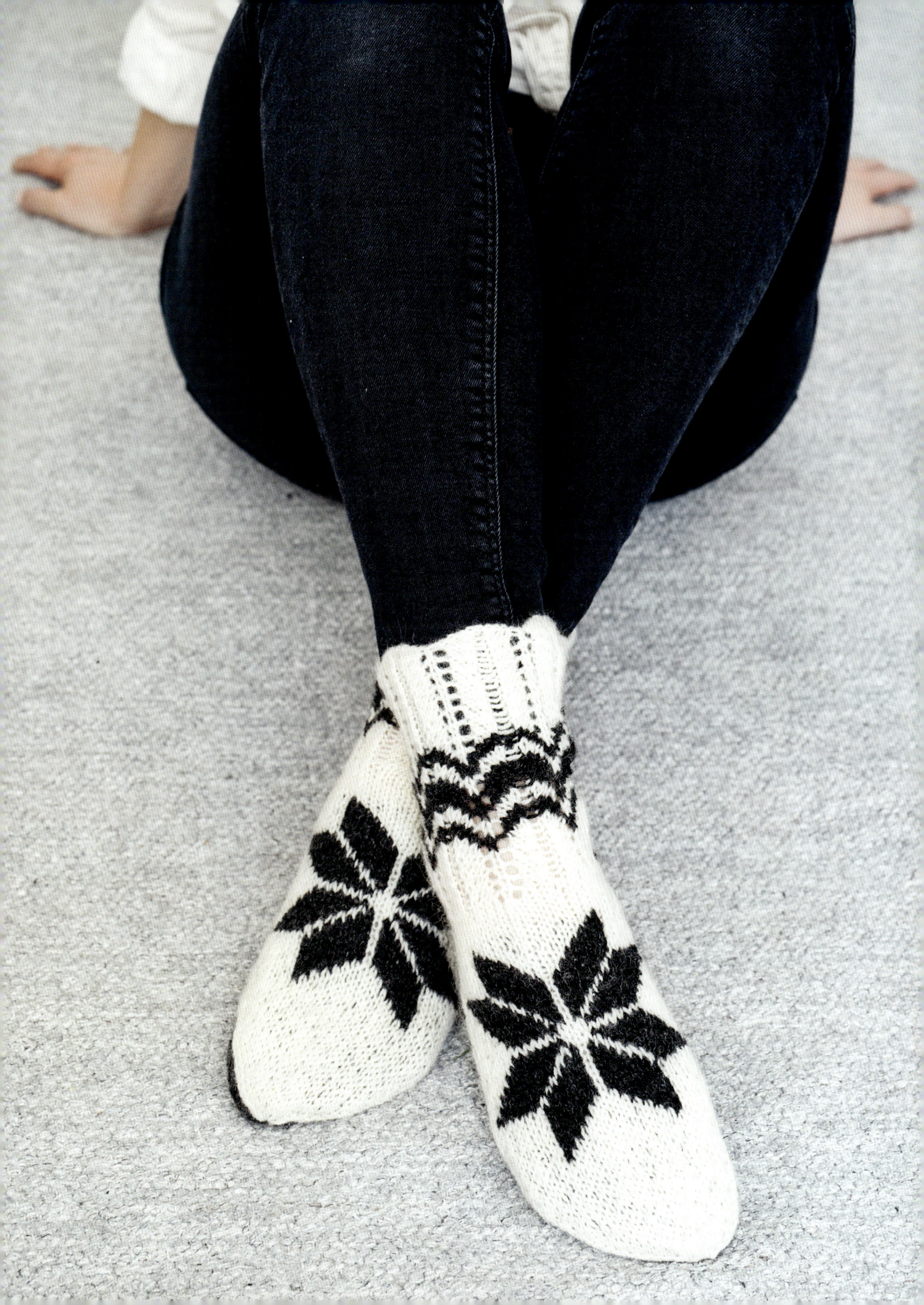

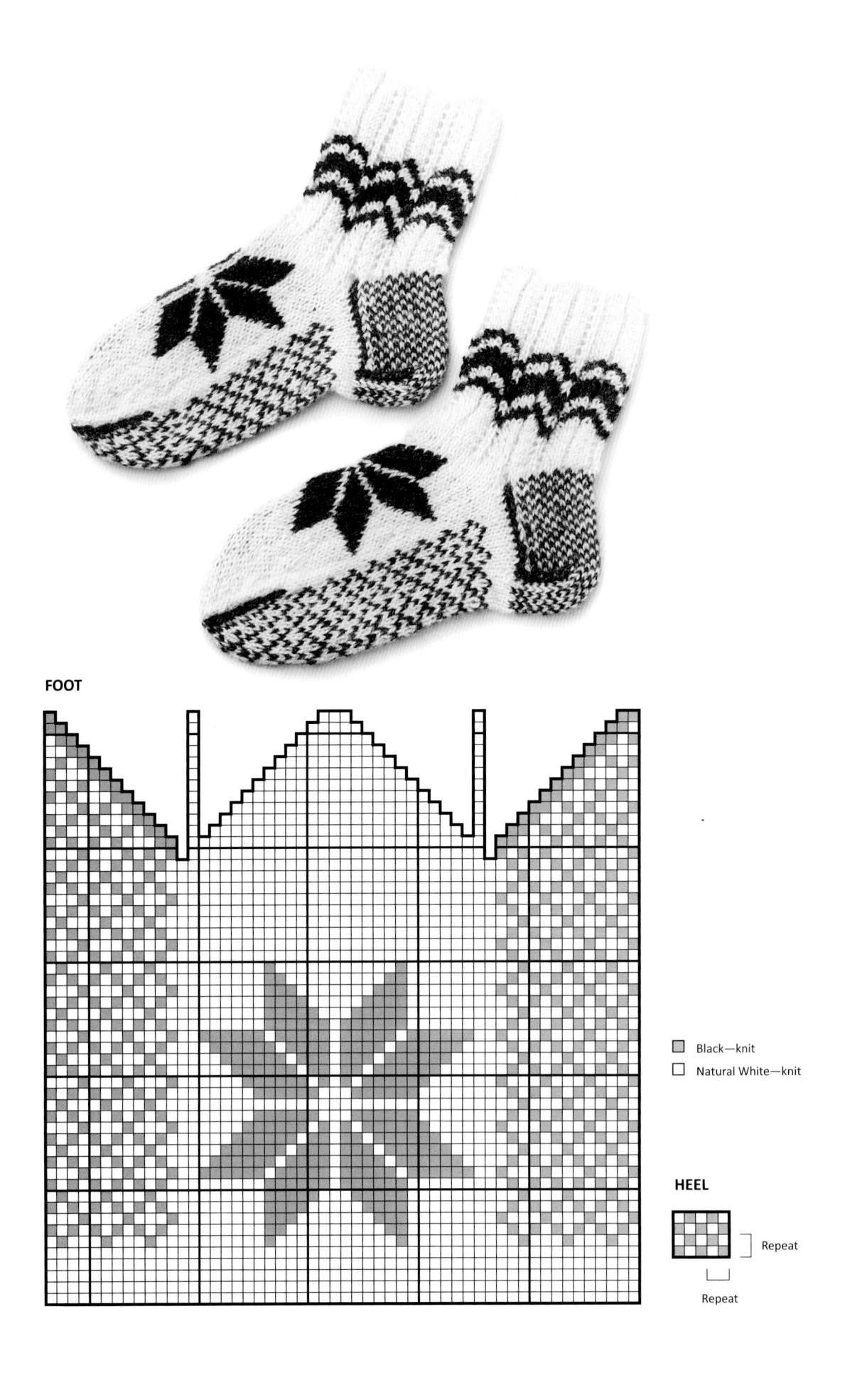

FOOT

Black—knit
Natural White—knit

HEEL

Repeat

Repeat

148

INSTRUCTIONS

Skill Level: Experienced

Size: Women's

MATERIALS
Yarn:
CYCA #2 (sport/4 ply), Ask Hifa 2 from Hillesvåg Ullvarefabrikk (100% Norwegian wool, 344 yd/315 m / 100 g)

Yarn Colors and Amounts:
Natural White 316057: 100 g
Charcoal Gray 316056: 100 g

Needles:
U. S. size 2.5 / 3 mm: set of 5 dpn

Gauge: 22 sts in pattern = 4 in / 10 cm. Adjust needle size to obtain correct gauge if necessary.

LEG
With Natural White, CO 60 sts. Divide sts evenly onto 4 dpn. Join, being careful not to twist cast-on row; pm for beginning of rnd. Work around in the lace cuff as follows:
Rnd 1: *K2tog, k2, yo, k1, yo, k2, ssk, p1*; rep * to * around.
Rnd 2: *K9, p1*; rep * to * around.
These two rnds form 1 repeat. Work the repeat 8 times.
Now work repeat in color sequence:
Change to Charcoal and work 1 repeat.
Change to White and work 1 repeat.
Change to Charcoal and work 2 repeats.
Change to White and work 1 repeat.
Change to Charcoal and work 1 repeat.
Change to White and work 4 repeats.

BAND HEEL
After completing leg, place 31 sts on scrap yarn for the instep. These sts will "rest" until the heel is finished.

Heel Flap
Place the rem 29 sts on one dpn and work the heel flap back and forth. Work heel flap in pattern as shown on the chart. Work the last st of each row with doubled yarn (1 strand each White and Charcoal). Begin on WS as follows:

Row 1 (WS): Sl 1 purlwise wyf, purl to last st, end p1 with both colors.
Row 2: Sl 1 purlwise wyb, knit to last st, end k1 with both colors.
Rep these 2 rows until there are 10 chain sts at each side of flap.

Now decrease to shape the band:
Row 1: Sl 1, purl until 11 sts rem, p2tog; turn.
Row 2: Sl 1, knit until 11 sts rem, ssk; turn.
Row 3: Sl 1, purl until 1 st before gap, p2tog; turn.
Row 4: Sl 1, knit until 1 st before gap, ssk; turn.
Rep Rows 3-4 until all the side sts have been eliminated.

FOOT
Divide the instep sts onto 2 dpn and divide the rem heel sts onto 2 dpn so you have half of each section on a needle. Now work in the round with RS facing you. Begin rnd at center of heel. With White (= 1st row of foot chart), pick up and knit 1 st in each chain st along side of heel flap. You can pick up the sts tbl or knit them tbl on next rnd. Knit across instep sts. Pick up and knit 1 st in each chain st of opposite side of flap and then complete rnd.

Gusset Shaping
Knit until 2 sts rem on Ndl 1, k2tog. Knit across Ndls 2 and 3. Begin Ndl 4 with ssk and knit to end of rnd. Knit the next rnd without decreasing.

Repeat these 2 rnds, working in charted pattern, until 54 sts rem.

WEDGE TOE
Shape the toe as shown on the chart.
At the right side, decrease with ssk and, on the left side, k2tog. Cut yarn and draw end through rem sts; tighten.

FINISHING
Weave in all ends neatly on WS. Make the second sock the same way.

SOUTH TRØNDELAG

Ragg Socks from Hitra

These days, when we want sturdy sock and stocking yarns that will be strong and long-lasting, we choose yarn with polyamide (nylon) or polyester, synthetic fibers derived from petroleum. These synthetic fibers came onto the market in the 1930s. Before that time, we used natural fibers. Cow hair, tangled cattle hair, hair from horses' tails, and tangled hair from goats—all longer, stronger fibers than wool from sheep—were often blended in with wool when spinning yarn. Women also used their own hair to make extra strong mittens or socks. Usually the hair was collected as it accumulated on a brush or comb.

The Norwegian word *ragg* signifies goat hair blended with wool. Today the word is associated with thick, warm wool socks.

The Coast Museum in South Trøndelag has a pair of relatively coarse gray wool socks in their collection. The feet are knitted in stockinette (stocking stitch) and the rest in ribbing. The letter O is embroidered with red thread at the top of each leg. The socks are from Glørstad on the north side of the island of Hitra—other than that, there is no information.

We can find socks of this type all around the country. They were warm, everyday socks without any unnecessary ornamentation. The embroidery was only to indicate whose socks they were, not for embellishment. The ribbing meant the socks fit the feet especially well. Certainly along the coast it was important to have sturdy socks. When out cod fishing for several months, it was typical to have several pairs stowed away in the equipment chest.

Professional fishermen from the entire Norwegian coast participated in winter fishing, which included upwards of 30,000 men. A woman took as many work days to produce all the clothing needed by a man as the men took to fish over the winter. It's been calculated that each woman needed to put in about 400 hours of work for each man who went out. Several pairs of mittens, stockings, wool underwear, and shirts had to be prepared, and most of these items were produced starting with the raw materials.

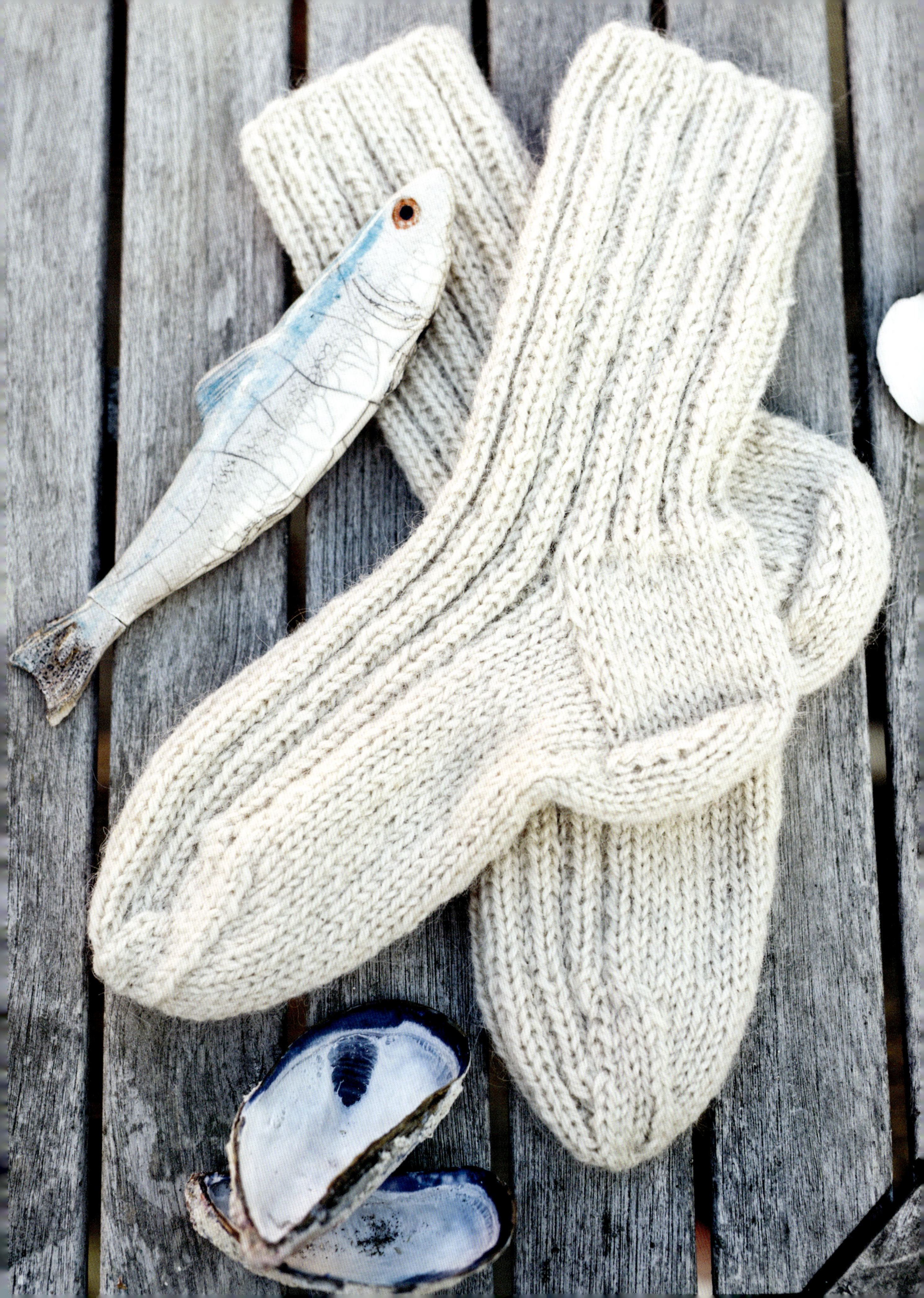

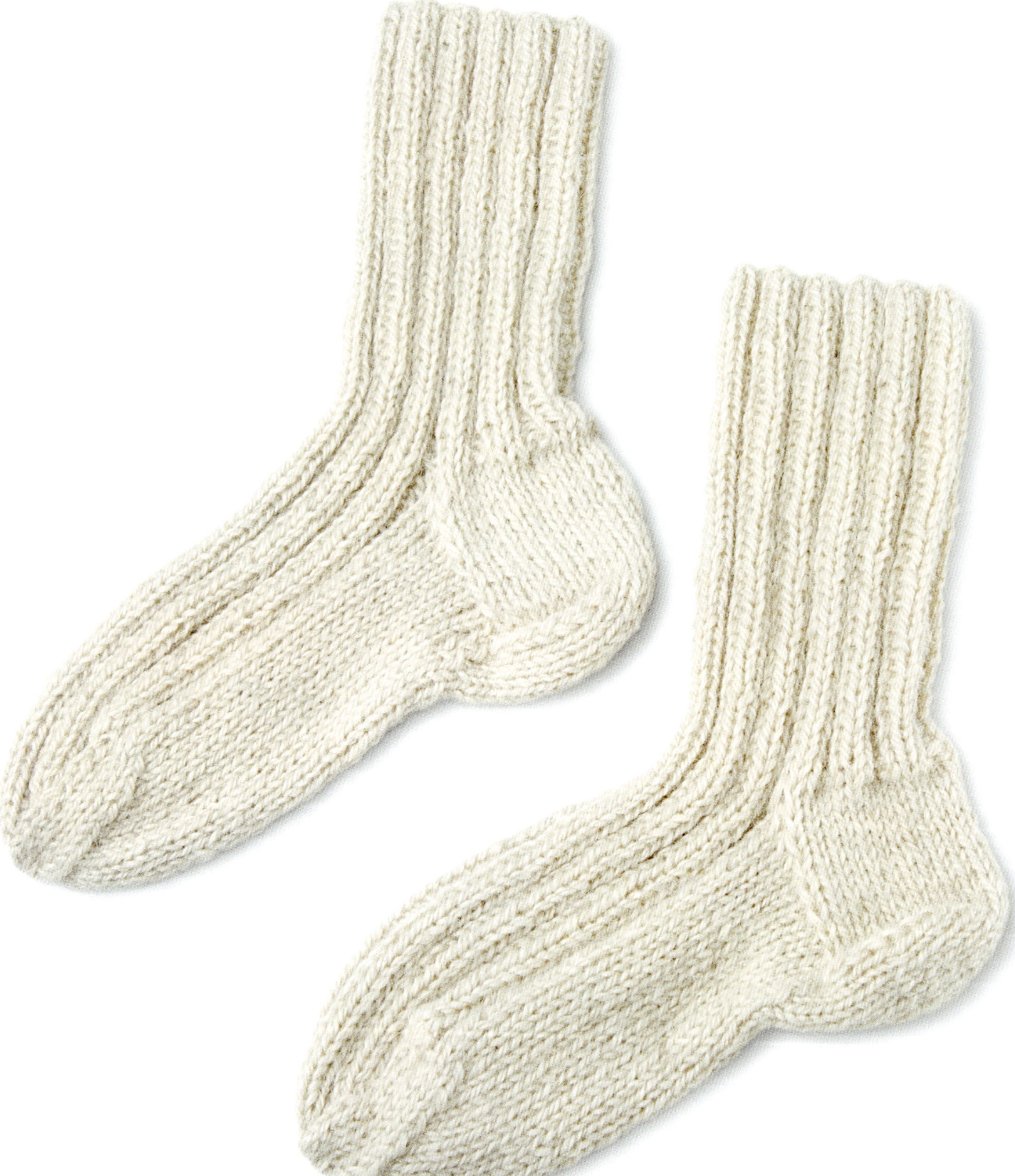

INSTRUCTIONS

Skill Level: Intermediate

Sizes: Women's (Men's)

MATERIALS
Yarn:
CYCA #2 (sport/4 ply), 3-ply Sand Spelsau yarn from Lofoten Wool (100% Spelsau wool, 142 yd/ 130 m / 100 g), Sand: 150 (150) g

Needles:
U. S. size 4 / 3.5 mm: set of 5 dpn

Gauge: 17 sts in pattern = 4 in / 10 cm. Adjust needle size to obtain correct gauge if necessary.

LEG
CO 48 (52) sts. Divide sts evenly onto 4 dpn. Join, being careful not to twist cast-on row; pm for beginning of rnd. Work around in k2, p2 ribbing for 5½ in / 14 cm.

BAND HEEL WITH SHORT HEEL FLAP
After completing leg, place 26 (30) sts on scrap yarn for the instep (to "rest" while you work the heel flap).

Heel Flap
Place rem 22 sts on one dpn and work heel flap back and forth.
Begin with WS facing you.
Row 1 (WS): Sl 1 purlwise wyf, purl to end of row.
Row 2: Sl 1 purlwise wyb, knit to end of row.
Rep these 2 rows until there are 8 chain sts at each side of flap.

Heel Gusset:
Row 1: Sl 1, purl until 8 sts rem, p2tog; turn.
Row 2: Sl 1, knit until 8 sts rem, ssk; turn.
Row 3: Sl 1, purl until 1 st before gap, p2tog; turn.
Row 4: Sl 1, knit until 1 st before gap, ssk; turn.
Rep Rows 3-4 until all the side sts have been eliminated.

FOOT
Divide the instep sts onto 2 dpn and divide the rem heel sts onto 2 dpn so you have half of each section on a needle. Work in the round with RS facing you. Begin rnd at center of sole. Knit to heel flap. Pick up and knit 1 st in each chain st along side of heel flap. You can pick up the sts tbl or knit them tbl on next rnd. Work in ribbing as est across instep. Pick up and knit sts in chain sts of opposite side of flap and then knit to end of rnd = 50 (54) sts.

Begin at the center of the sole. K2, k2tog, k8, work 26 (30) sts in ribbing, k8, ssk, k2 = 48 (52) sts rem.
Now work foot with ribbing across instep and st st on sole until sock measures 9 (9) in / 20 (23) cm or desired length to toe shaping.

WEDGE TOE
Divide the sts evenly onto 4 dpn.
*** Ndl 1:** Knit until 3 sts rem on needle, k2tog, k1.
Ndl 2: K1, ssk, work ribbing to end of needle.
Ndl 3: Work ribbing to last 3 sts and end with k2tog, k1.
Ndl 4: K1, ssk, knit to end of needle.
Knit 1 rnd without decreasing*.
Rep * to * 3 times and then decrease on every rnd until 4 sts rem on each needle. Cut yarn and draw end through rem sts; tighten.

FINISHING
Weave in all ends neatly on WS. Make the second sock the same way.

SOUTH TRØNDELAG

Striped Socks from Orkladalen

Stripes are one of the easiest ways to add patterning to knitted items. Horizontal stripes became quite the trend in the second half of the nineteenth century and a large number of striped socks have survived from that period. All sorts of striping sequences were used from simple stripes all the same width to a variety of stripe repeats.

It is easy to be inspired by good stripe patterning. The starting point for these stockings is a pair from Meldal/Rennebu that was registered at The Norwegian Institute for Bunad and Folk Costume on Fagneres. The stockings are owned by the Meldal Town Museum. They were knitted with red and white wool yarn. At the top is a wide section of diagonally striped lace followed by an elegant two-color panel, making the stockings distinctive.

The stockings were quite durable. Everyday stockings were usually single-color, sheep's white. But often people had a pair that had been made more carefully. It could be a pair knitted for confirmation or a wedding, and then used as Sunday or festival day stockings.

Girls had to learn how to knit stockings early on. By the age of 5 or 6, they were expected to contribute to the production process. Knitting was often done while girls minded cattle.

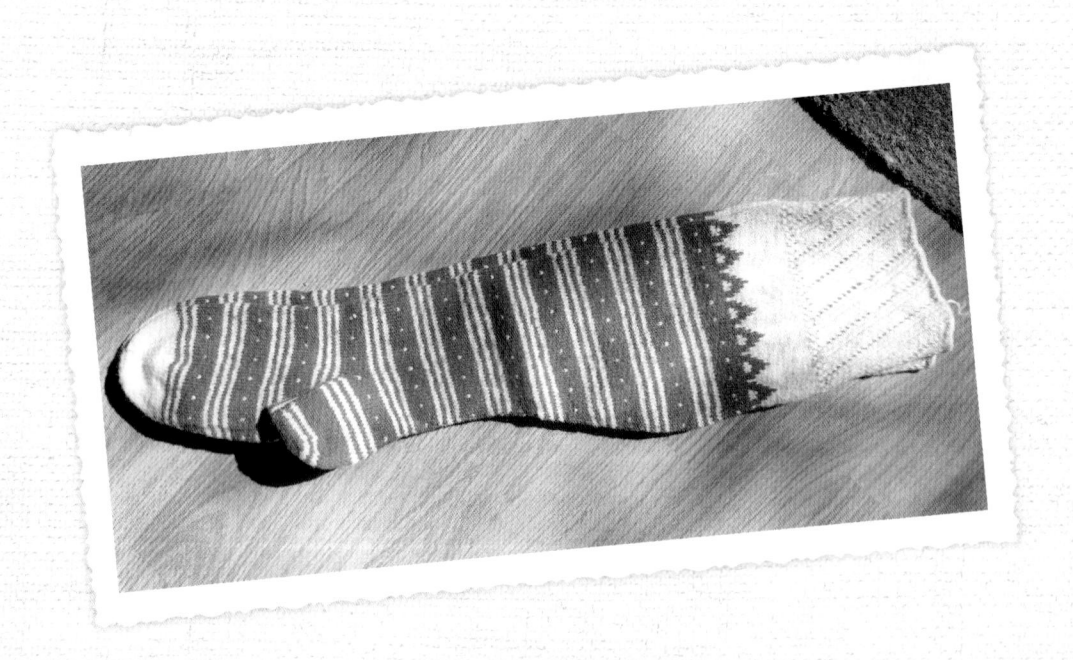

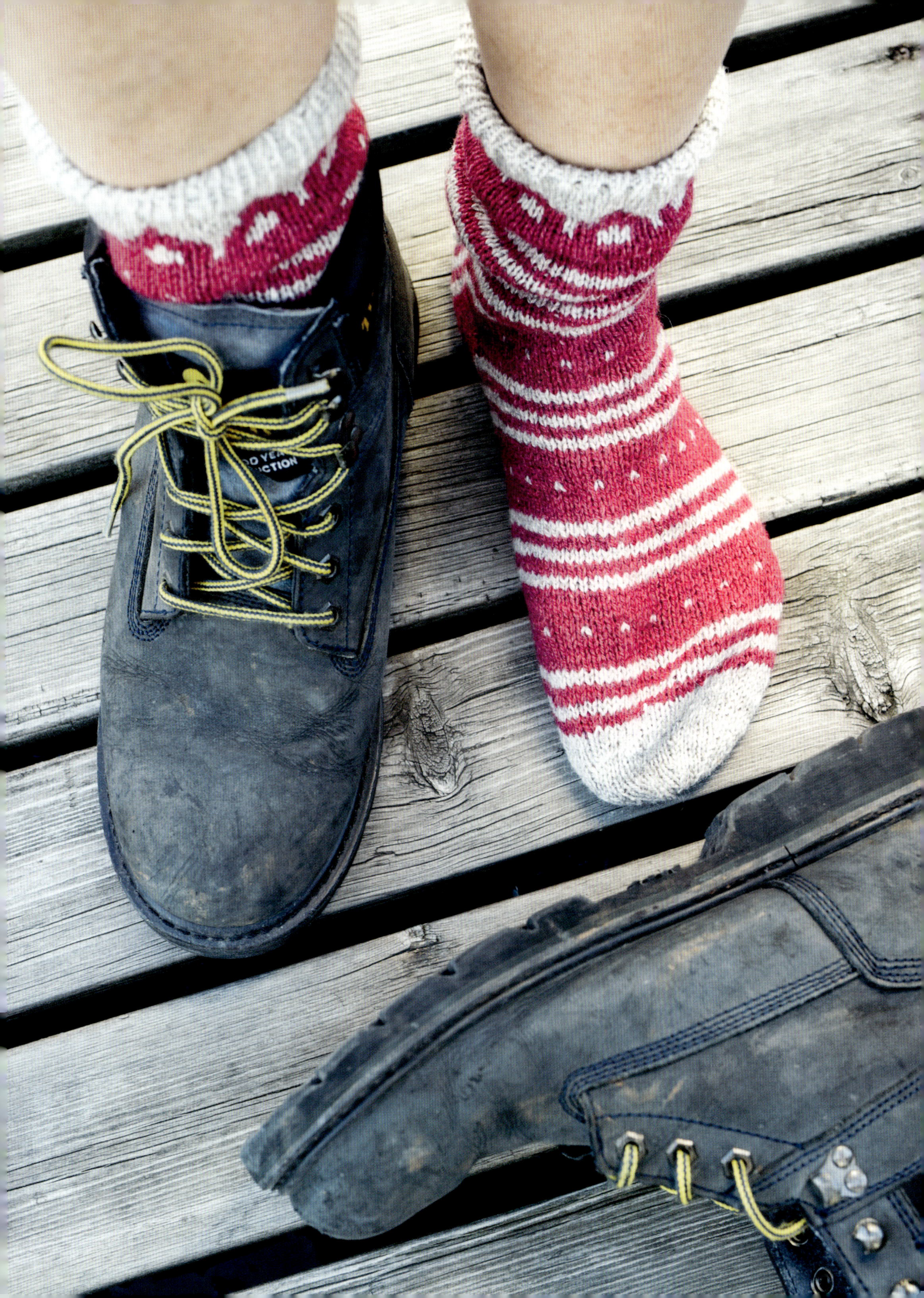

Repeat

☐ Natural White—knit
■ Burgundy—knit

Decrease 8 sts evenly spaced around on men's size

Repeat

INSTRUCTIONS

Skill Level: Experienced

Sizes: Women's (men's)

MATERIALS
Yarn:
CYCA #1 (light fingering/2 ply), Samite Silk Blend from Blacker Yarns (40% Shetland wool, 30% Blue-faced Leicester wool, 20% Eri silk, 10% Gotland wool, 503 yd/460 m / 100 g)

Yarn Colors and Amounts:
Aspen's Shiver, Natural White: 100 (100) g
Fiery Dew, Burgundy: 100 (100) g

Needles: U. S. size 1.5 / 2.5 mm: set of 5 dpn

Gauge: 24 sts in pattern = 4 in / 10 cm. Adjust needle size to obtain correct gauge if necessary.

LEG
With Natural White, CO 64 (72) sts. Divide sts evenly onto 4 dpn. Join, being careful not to twist cast-on row; pm for beginning of rnd. Work around in k1, p1 ribbing for 10 rnds. Now work an eyelet rnd: K1, (yo, k2tog) around. End by slipping the 1st st (the single knit st) to Ndl 4, yo, k2tog. Next, work in pattern following the chart. On the men's size, decrease 8 sts evenly spaced around on the last rnd [= (k7, k2tog) around = 64 sts rem] before beginning with the Burgundy yarn.

GUSSET HEEL
After completing the leg, divide the stitches in half, placing the 32 (32) instep stitches onto scrap yarn. These instep stitches will "rest" until the heel is complete.
Place the remaining 32 (32) sts onto one needle and work back and forth. Work heel flap with Natural White only.
Begin with the WS facing you; work the reinforced heel pattern.
Row 1 (WS): Sl 1 purlwise wyf, purl to end of row.
Row 2: Sl 1 purlwise wyb, (k1, sl 1) to last st; end k1.
Repeat these 2 rows until there are 15 (16) chain sts at each side of the flap.

Shaping the Heel
Row 1 (WS): Sl 1, purl until 11 sts rem on the needle, p2tog, p1; turn.
Row 2: Sl 1, knit until 11 sts rem on needle, ssk, k1; turn.
Row 3: Sl 1, purl until 1 st before gap, p2tog, p1; turn.
Row 4: Sl 1, knit until 1 st rem before gap, ssk, k1; turn.

Repeat Rows 3-4 until all the side sts have been eliminated.

Gusset Shaping
Divide the instep sts from the holder onto 2 dpn; divide the sole sts onto 2 dpn with half of the sts on each. With RS facing and Natural White, begin working in the round. Begin rnd at center of sole. With Ndl 1, knit to flap; pick up and knit 1 st in each chain up side of flap. You can pick up the chain sts through back loops, or knit them through back loops on the next rnd. With Ndls 2-3, knit across the instep. Next, with Ndl 4, pick up and knit sts down opposite side of flap as for the first side. Knit to center of sole.

On the next rnd, begin decreasing to shape gusset: Knit until 2 sts rem on Ndl 1, k2tog. Knit across instep sts on Ndls 2-3. With Ndl 4, ssk and then knit to end of rnd.
Attach Burgundy and work the next rnd in charted pattern without decreasing.
Repeat these 2 rnds, working in charted pattern, until 58 (64) sts rem. Continue in pattern without further shaping until foot measures approx. 7 (9½) in / 18 (24) cm or desired length to toe shaping. Decrease 2 (1) sts before you begin the last stripe = 56 (63) sts rem.

STAR TOE
Begin at the center of the sole with Natural White.
Rnd 1: (K5, k2tog) around.
Rnds 2-6: Knit.
Rnd 7: (K4, k2tog) around.
Rnds 8-11: Knit.
Rnd 12: (K3, k2tog) around.
Rnds 13-15: Knit
Rnd 16: (K2, k2tog) around.
Rnds 17-18: Knit.
Rnd 19: (K1, k2tog) around.
Rnd 20: Knit.
Rnd 21: (K2tog) around.

FINISHING
Cut yarn and draw end through rem sts; tighten. Weave in all ends neatly on WS. Make the second sock the same way.

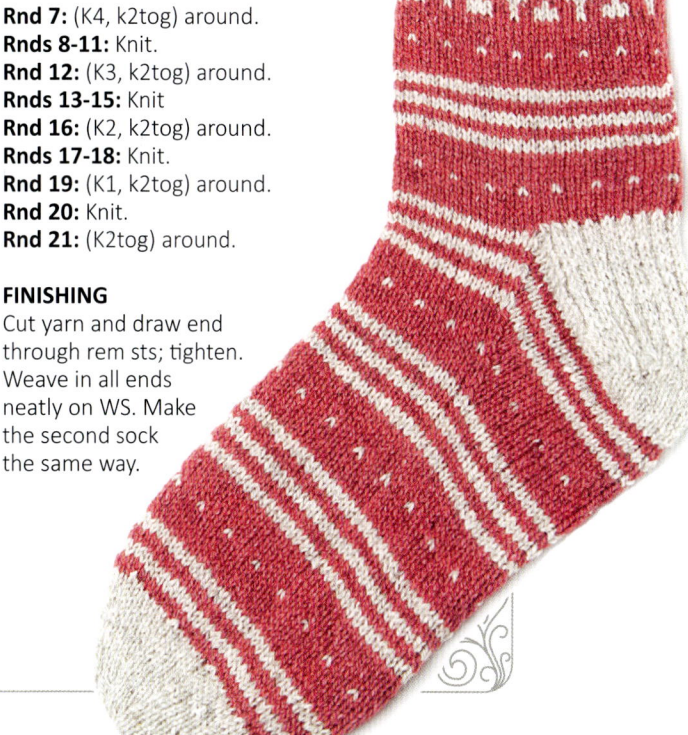

NORTH TRØNDELAG

Maria's Stockings from Lierne

"Hen knitting" was a style popularized in the 1970s. The Danish author Kirsten Hofstatter was angry because it wasn't possible to buy knitting patterns without also buying the yarn at the same time. She wrote her own knitting book in 1973 and tried to have it published by Red Rooster, but the book was rejected—so Hofstatter decided to start her own publishing company. She named her company the Red Hen in protest but eventually changed it to Hen Publishing Company. The book was titled *Hen Knitting* (see also *Knit Yourself In*, Trafalgar Square, 2015 / *Creative Colour Knitting*, Search Press, 2015).

Hofstatter's goal was to help knitters free themselves from traditional pattern instructions by imaginatively composing their own designs. She felt patterns didn't have to be symmetrical, and encouraged knitters to use leftover yarn and colors not traditionally considered as "going together." Hen knitting came to symbolize the 1968 generation's revolt against previous norms, and was particularly popular among feminists in the 1970s.

Long before that time, Maria Magdalena Mortensdatter had knitted a pair of stockings that could easily be considered "hen" knitting. The initials MMMDT and the year 1899 were knitted in at the top of the stockings. After that, she knitted a series of panels, some with relatively tricky pattern sequences. The motifs were clearly derived from pattern books of the time, samplers, or similar design sources. We recognize the panels with acorns at the center of the legs and the leaf panels on the feet, both of which were taken from a German pattern booklet from the beginning of the 1500s. The wave panels at the top of each stocking are also familiar.

The following written information was included with the stockings: "Mr. Holand. Here is a pair of stockings that I am donating to the museum in Nordli. The handwork was done by Maria Magdalena Mortensdater. Tunsjøn 1899 (…) Respectfully, Olga Nygård. Overhalla, August 1955."

In the census for 1910, Maria Mortensdatter is listed as an unmarried servant girl at the Tunnsjø farm in Skogen, at the home of the farmer and proprietor Jens Olsen and the farmer's wife Ane Maria Rustad. She was born on 6 February 1886 in Sweden. So she was only 13 years old when she knitted these stockings. Perhaps they were for her confirmation.

Maria's wool stockings have red patterns against a white background and are only 18¼ in / 46 cm long.

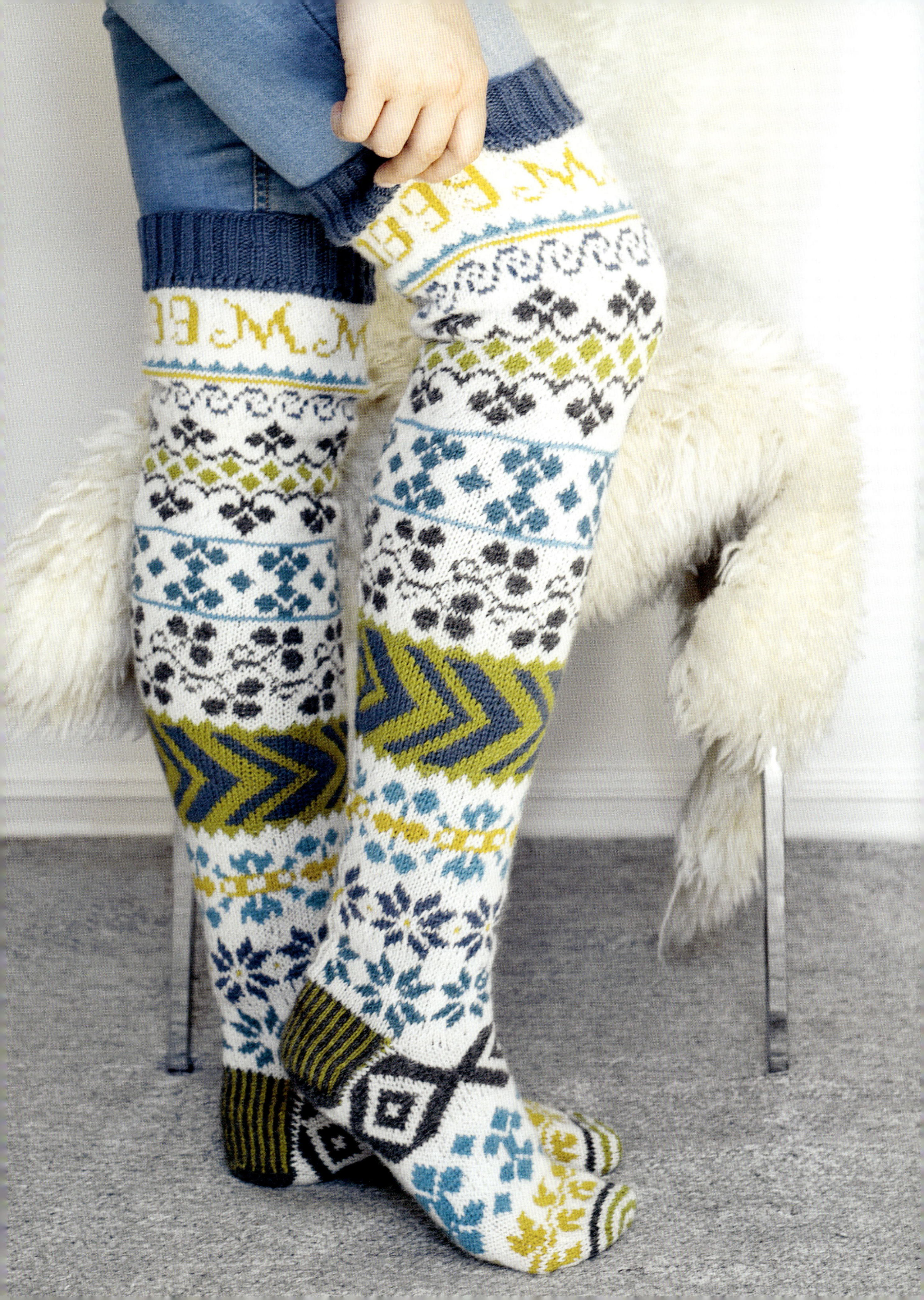

INSTRUCTIONS

Skill Level: Experienced

Sizes: Women's small (women's large)

Finished Measurements:
Width at top of stocking: 13¾ (15) in / 35 (38) cm

MATERIALS
Yarn:
CYCA #1 (fingering/2 ply), Eco Baby Wool from Dale Garn (100% wool, 175 yd/160 m / 50 g), Blue 1315: 50 (50) g

CYCA #1 (fingering/2 ply), Mini Sterk from Du Store Alpakka (40% alpaca, 40% Merino wool, 20% polyamide, 182 yd/166 m / 50 g)

Yarn Colors and Amounts:
Natural 806: 150 (150) g
Golden Yellow 835: 50 (50) g
Charcoal 807: 50 (50) g
Dark Sea Green 857: 50 (50) g
Turquoise 834: 50 (50) g
Yellow-Green 843: 50 (50) g

Needles: U. S. size 0 (1.5) / 2 (2.5) mm: set of 5 dpn

Gauge: 32 (30) sts in pattern = 4 in / 10 cm. Adjust needle size to obtain correct gauge if necessary.

LEG

With Blue, CO 112 sts. Divide sts evenly onto 4 dpn. Join, being careful not to twist cast-on row; pm for beginning of rnd. Work around in k2, p2 ribbing for 2 in / 5 cm. Knit 1 rnd and then work eyelet rnd: (k2tog, yo) around.
Change to st st, increasing 1 st at center back on the first rnd. Work in pattern following the chart for the leg (see pages 162-163), always purling the center back stitch. Decrease as indicated on the chart. Work decrease rounds as: K2tog, work in pattern until 3 sts rem; end rnd with ssk, p1.

GUSSET HEEL

After completing the leg, 73 sts rem. Decrease the purl st at center back. Place the 36 instep stitches onto scrap yarn. These instep stitches will "rest" until the heel is complete.
Place the remaining 36 sts onto one needle and work back and forth. Work heel flap with Charcoal and Yellow-Green, following chart (see pages 161-162).
Begin with the WS facing you.
Row 1 (WS): Sl 1 purlwise wyf, purl to end of row.
Row 2: Sl 1 purlwise wyb, knit to end of row.
Repeat these 2 rows until there are 18 (18) chain sts at each side of the flap. Continue with Charcoal only.

Shaping the Heel

Row 1 (WS): Sl 1, purl until 12 sts rem on the needle, p2tog, p1; turn.
Row 2: Sl 1, knit until 12 sts rem on needle, ssk, k1; turn.
Row 3: Sl 1, purl until 1 st before gap, p2tog, p1; turn.
Row 4: Sl 1, knit until 1 st rem before gap, ssk, k1; turn.
Repeat Rows 3-4 until all the side sts have been eliminated = 24 sts rem.

FOOT

Change to Natural. Divide the instep sts from the holder onto 2 dpn; divide the sole sts onto 2 dpn with half of the sts on each. With RS facing, begin working in the round. Begin rnd at center of sole. With Ndl 1, k12; pick up and knit 18 sts through back loops in chains up side of flap. With Ndls 2-3, work across the 36 instep sts. Next, with Ndl 4, pick up and knit 18 sts tbl down opposite side of flap as for the first side. K12 to center of sole. Continue in pattern as shown on the chart, decreasing as indicated.

STAR TOE

Just before completing the foot chart, decrease 10 sts as shown on the chart. After completing charted rows, continue shaping as described below *at the same time* as working the stripe sequence: 2 rnds Charcoal, 2 rnds Natural, 2 rnds Yellow-Green, 2 rnds Natural, 2 rnds Yellow-Green, 2 rnds Natural, and then work only with Yellow-Green.

Begin at the center of the sole.
Rnd 1: (K4, k2tog) around. The 5 sts rem at the end of Ndl 4 will be decreased in subsequent rounds.
Rnds 2-5: Knit.
Rnd 6: (K3, k2tog) around.
Rnds 7-9: Knit.
Rnd 10: (K2, k2tog) around.
Rnds 11-12: Knit
Rnd 13: (K1, k2tog) around.
Rnd 14: Knit.
Rnd 15: (K2tog) around.

FINISHING

Cut yarn and draw end through rem sts; tighten. Weave in all ends neatly on WS. Make the second sock the same way.

For a longer foot, work more stripes before beginning the toe shaping. For a shorter foot, begin decreasing a bit sooner, and, if necessary, omit the last pattern panel.

FOOT

Work only for large size

Small size: decrease every 10th st

- ☐ Natural
- ▦ Golden Yellow
- ⊙ Turquoise
- ◁ Blue
- N Charcoal
- ⊟ Yellow-Green
- ⋈ Dark Sea Green
- ⊠ Purl

Gusset shaping

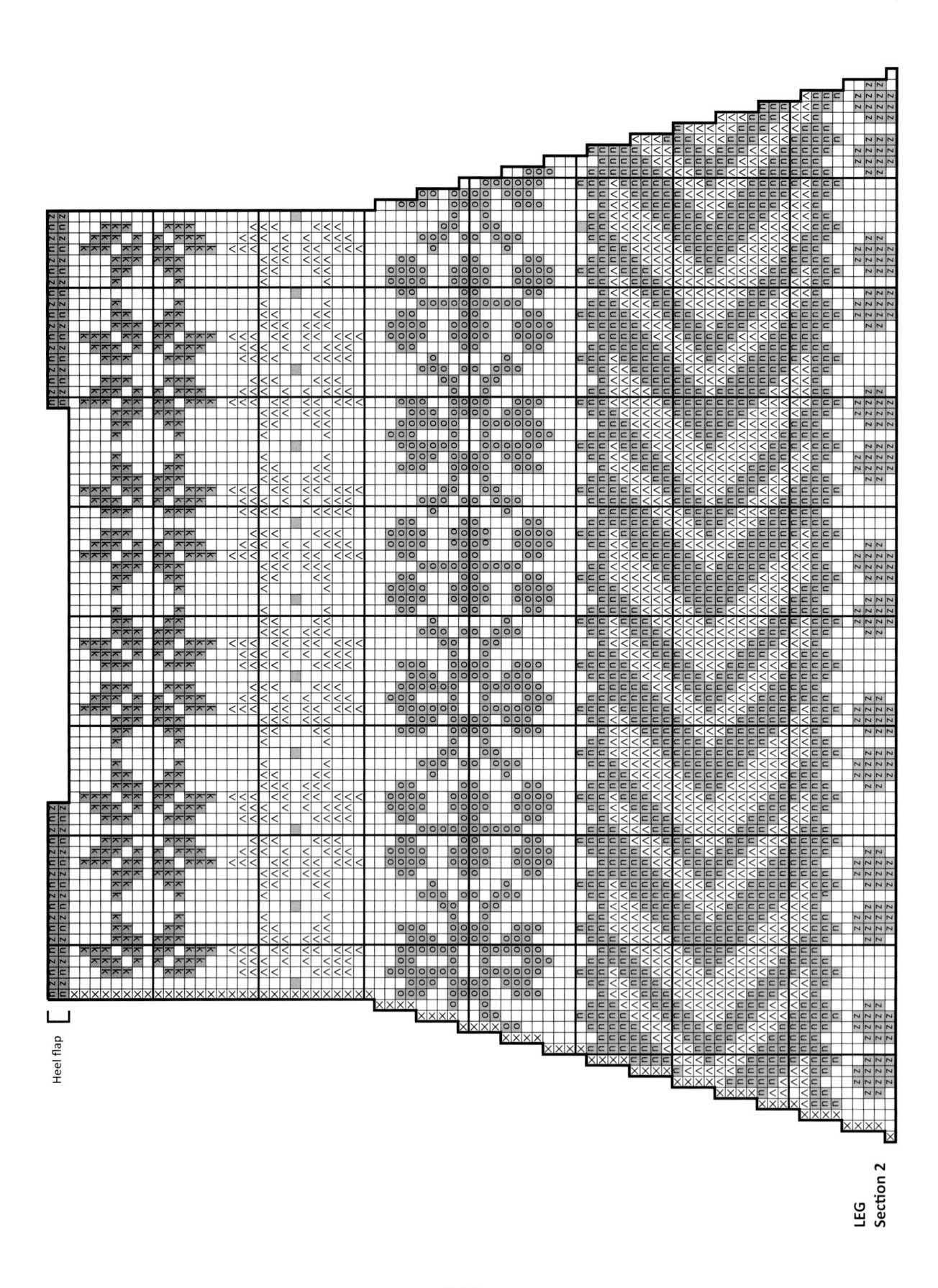

Heel flap

LEG
Section 2

← Begin here

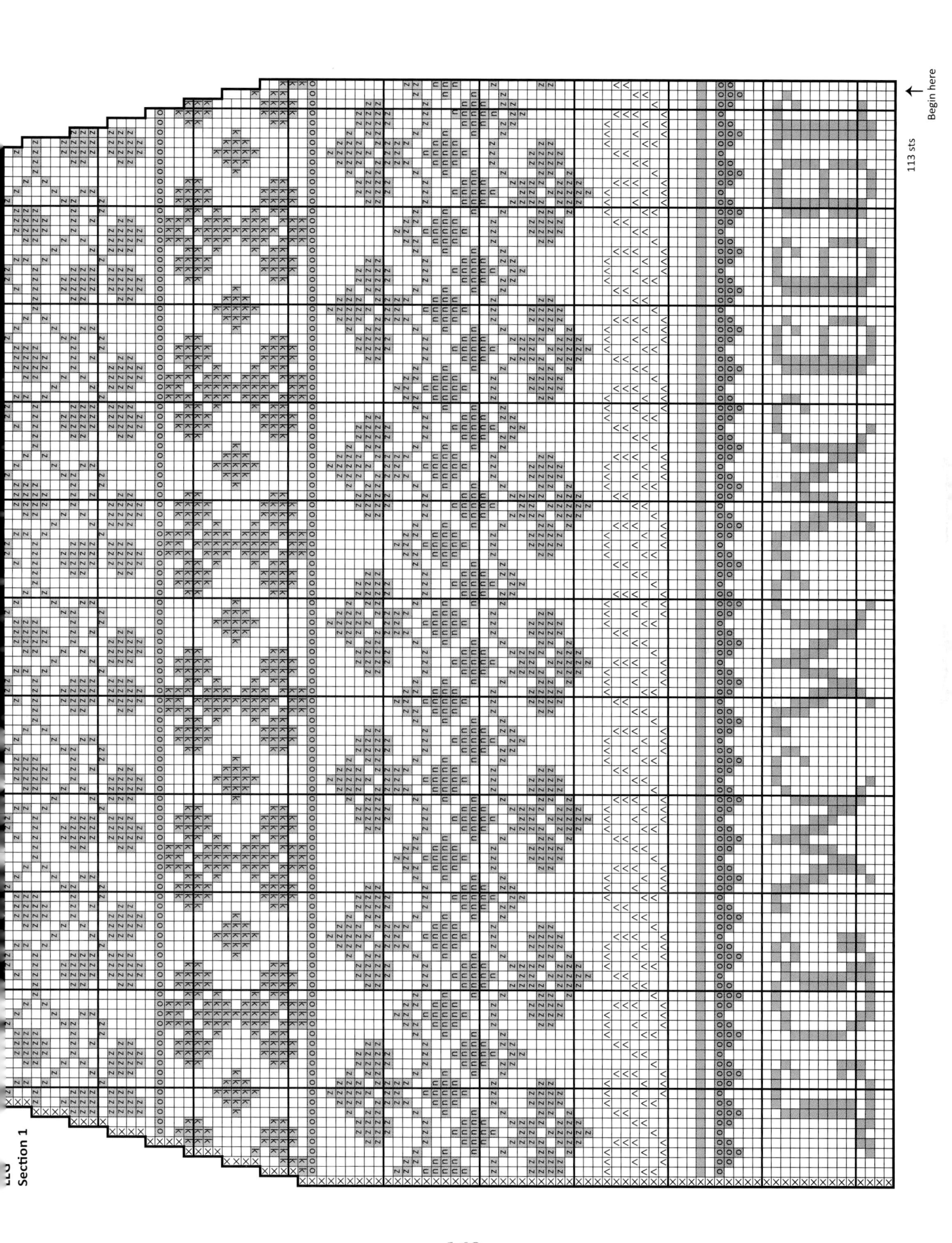

113 sts

Section 1

NORTH TRØNDELAG

Trønder Socks

The Sverresborg Trøndelag Folk Museum has two pairs of stockings in fine red and white cotton yarn. The basic pattern for these stockings is the same but they have slightly different finishing at the top. It's possible the same person knitted both pairs.

The wave pattern panels can be found in a number of knitted garments. Such panels were also very common on samplers, and it wasn't unusual to take inspiration from these when learning to knit. A variation of the little wave panel at the top of these stockings has also been featured in a small German pattern booklet for cross stitch embroidery, published in the second half of the 1800s.

The information that came with the stockings is sparse. About one pair it says: "From Karen Aune's estate." These stockings have an extra rose panel at the top. The other pair is listed as: "Inherited from Mrs. Paulsen, née Brenne, who had received them from an old woman in Hegra."

These Hegra stockings were the inspiration for our stockings.

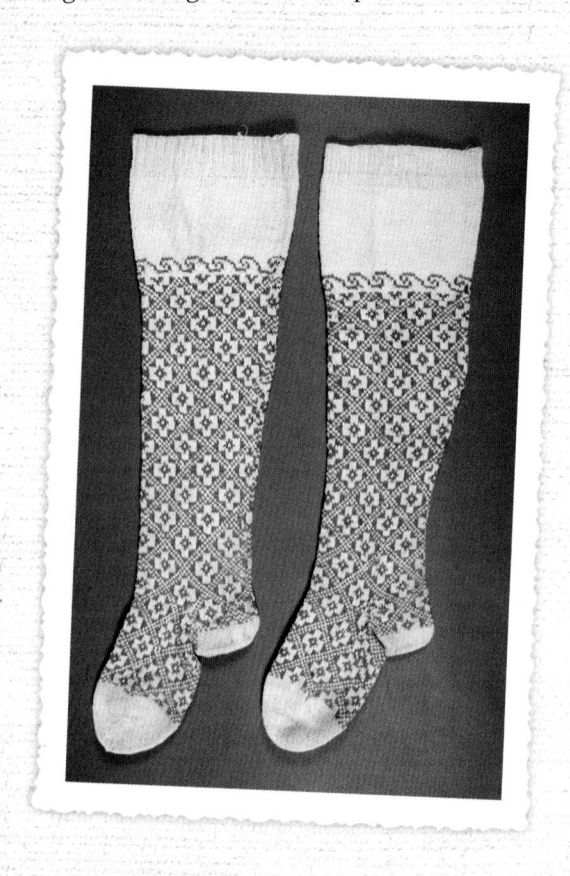

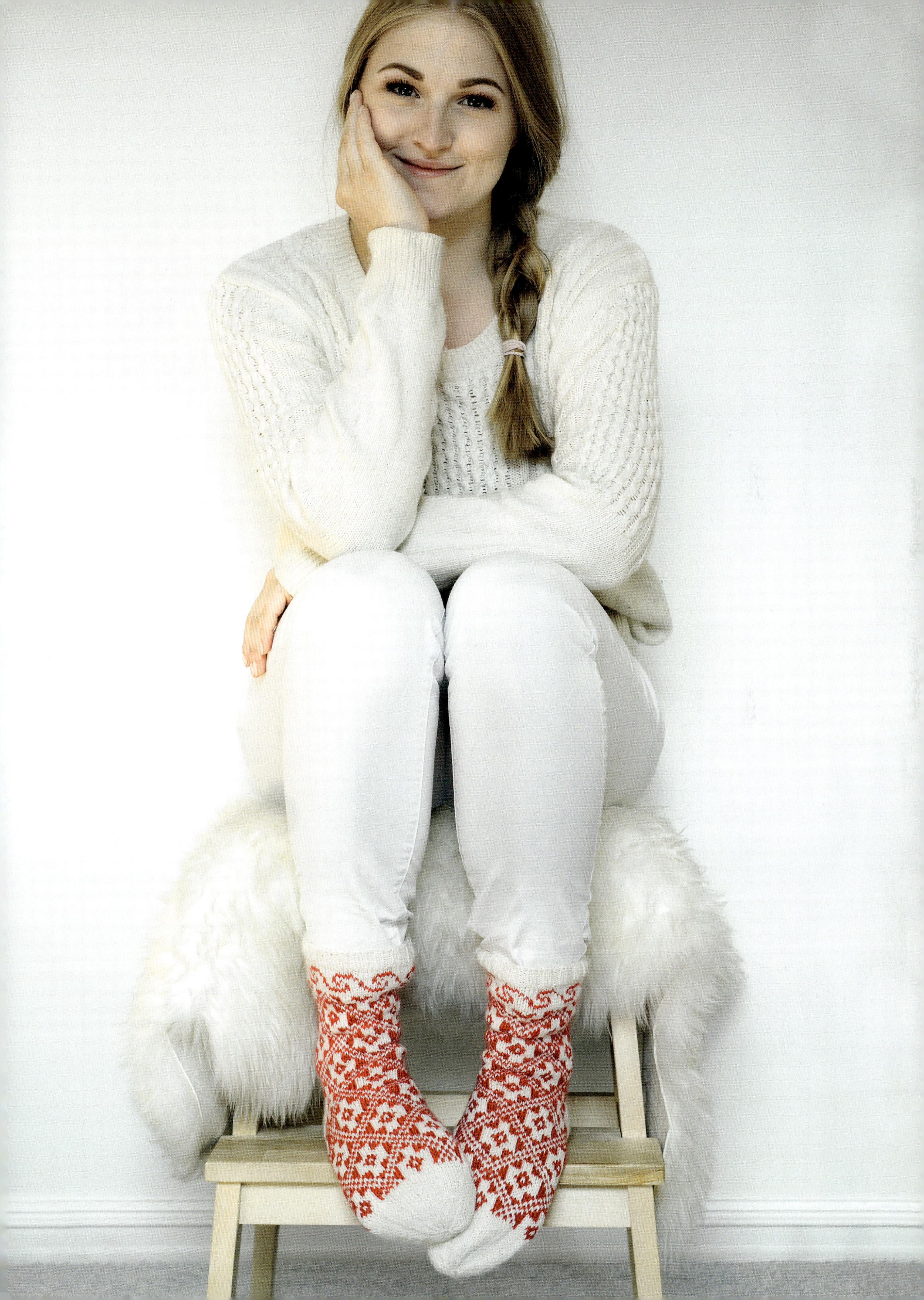

☐ Natural—knit
☒ Natural—purl
▨ Red—knit

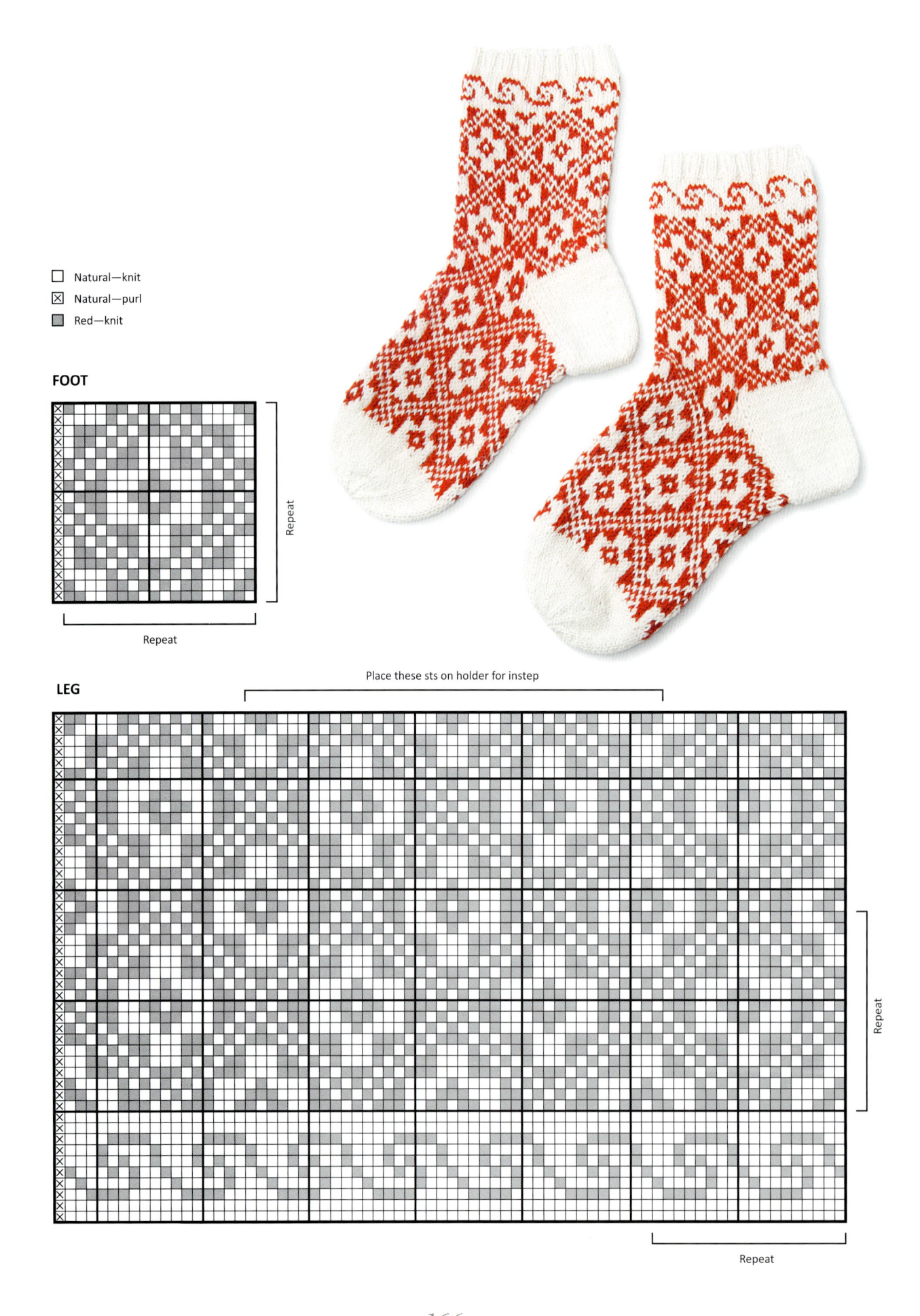

FOOT

Repeat

LEG

Place these sts on holder for instep

Repeat

Repeat

166

INSTRUCTIONS

Skill Level: Experienced

Sizes: Women's (men's)

MATERIALS
Yarn:
CYCA #1 (fingering/2 ply), Mini Sterk from Du Store Alpakka (40% alpaca, 40% Merino wool, 20% polyamide, 182 yd/166 m / 50 g)

Yarn Colors and Amounts:
Natural White 806: 50 (50) g
Red 828: 50 (50) g

Needles: U. S. size 1.5 (2.5) / 2.5 (3) mm: set of 5 dpn

Gauge: 34 (32) sts in pattern = 4 in / 10 cm. Adjust needle size to obtain correct gauge if necessary.

LEG
With Natural, CO 72 sts. Divide sts evenly onto 4 dpn. Join, being careful not to twist cast-on row; pm for beginning of rnd. Work around in k2, p2 ribbing for 8 rnds. Increasing 2 sts at center back on the first rnd, work following the leg chart. Always purl the center back stitch.

COMMON HEEL
After completing sock leg, divide the sts, placing 39 sts on scrap yarn (see chart) for instep. These sts will "rest" until the heel is finished.

Heel Flap
Decrease 1 st at center back. Divide the remaining 34 stitches onto two dpn (Ndls A and B with 17 sts on each) and work back and forth with Natural. Begin with the RS facing you.
Row 1 (RS): Sl 1 purlwise wyb, knit rem sts on Ndls A and B.
Row 2: Sl 1 purlwise wyf, purl all rem sts on Ndls A and B.
Repeat these 2 rows until there are 13 chain sts at each side of the flap.

Shaping the Heel
Now you will shape the center back by decreasing as follows:
Row 1: Sl 1, knit until 5 sts rem on Ndl A, k2tog, k3. On Ndl B, k3, ssk, knit to end of needle.
Row 2: Sl 1, purl to end of row.
Row 3: Sl 1, knit until 4 sts rem on Ndl A, k2tog, k2. On Ndl B, k2, ssk, knit to end of needle.
Row 4: Sl 1, purl to end of row.
Row 5: Sl 1, knit until 3 sts rem on Ndl A, k2tog, k1. On Ndl B, k1, ssk, knit to end of needle.
Row 6: Sl 1, purl to end of row.
Row 7: Sl 1, knit until 2 sts rem on Ndl A, k2tog. On Ndl B, ssk, knit to end of needle.
Row 8: Sl 1, purl to end of Ndl B. Yarn is now at center of heel flap.
Hold the two dpn with RS facing in (so WS faces out on each side). Join the sets of sts with 3-needle BO: K2tog with 1 st from each needle, *k2tog with next st from each needle, pass first st over the second*. Repeat from * to * until 1 st loop rem.

FOOT
Divide the instep sts onto 2 dpn. With RS facing, Natural (carrying Red), and Ndl 1, beginning at the center of the sole, pick up and knit 1 st in each chain st on the side of the flap. You can pick up the chain sts through back loops or knit them tbl on the next rnd. Work the instep sts on Ndls 2-3, in pattern following the chart. With Ndl 4, pick up and knit sts on opposite side of heel flap = 74 sts total.
Work foot in pattern following the foot chart until length is 7-8 in / 18-20 cm or desired length before toe.

STAR TOE
With Natural, begin at the center of the sole. Knit 1 rnd before you begin toe shaping.
Rnd 1: (K5, k2tog) around. The 4 sts rem on Ndl 4 will be decreased in subsequent rnds.
Rnds 2-6: Knit.
Rnd 7: (K4, k2tog) around.
Rnds 8-11: Knit.
Rnd 12: (K3, k2tog) around.
Rnds 13-15: Knit
Rnd 16: (K2, k2tog) around.
Rnds 17-18: Knit.
Rnd 19: (K1, k2tog) around.
Rnd 20: Knit.
Rnd 21: (K2tog) around.

FINISHING
Cut yarn and draw end through rem sts; tighten. Weave in all ends neatly on WS. Make the second sock the same way.

Children's Socks from Helgeland

Between 1920 and 1930, Martin Åbodsvik took a photo of a good-natured little lad on a bench in Ågskaret in Meløy. The boy is dressed in knitted clothing from head to toe. In another photo, he's sitting, embraced by a woman who was most likely his mother. She also wore knitted stockings under a dark, smooth dress with a lace collar.

Meløy is north of Rana towards Svartisen, and Norway's largest water power station is here. Construction on it began in 1920; perhaps the boy's family went there to work.

The boy is wearing a pair of long stockings on his legs and a pair of short socks on top of them. It almost looks like there's not quite enough room for both of them in his fine shiny shoes. Both stockings and socks are ribbed. Long stockings under a skirt or short trousers were not uncommon up to the 1950s. Stockings were held up by a bodice with ribbons and buttons—a type of undergarment that was usually knitted.

Only children and women wore such bodices. The garment was most often white, minimally shaped and sleeveless. As a rule, it would open and close with clasps, buttons, or a tie cord at the front. Often it came with some buttons to which the stocking bands could attach.

The boy's socks are knitted with two colors and have two narrow stripes on one leg and a wide stripe on the other. The background color is presumably sheep's natural white.

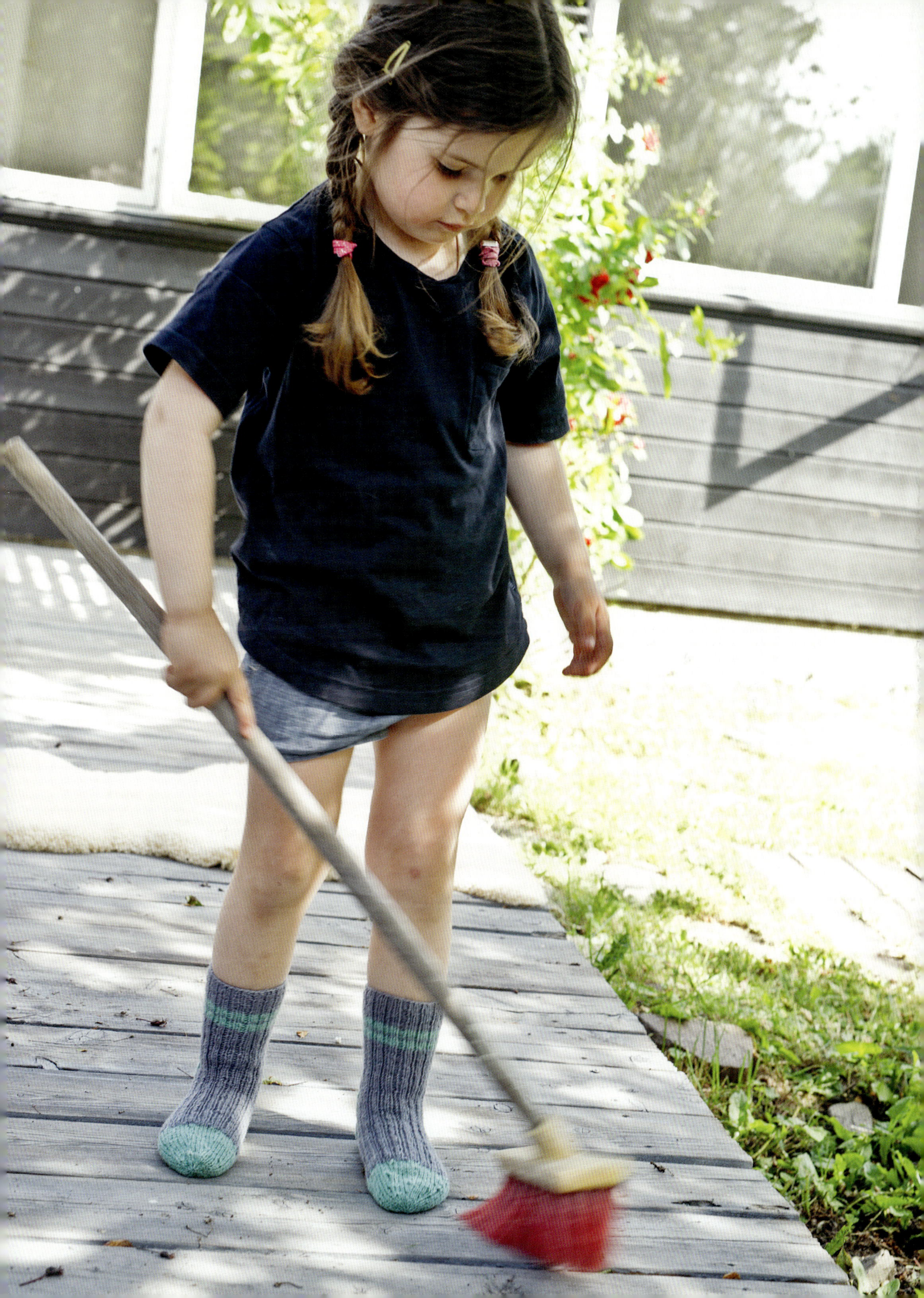

BREVKORT

INSTRUCTIONS

Skill Level: Intermediate

Sizes: 3-4 (5-6, 7-8, 9-10, 11-12) years

MATERIALS
Yarn:
CYCA #1 (fingering/2 ply), Finullgarn from Rauma (100% wool, 191 yd/175 m / 50 g):

Yarn Colors and Amounts:
Blue 4287: 50 (50, 50, 50, 50) g
Green 4887: 50 (50, 50, 50, 50) g

Reinforcing Thread: Mettler extra strong sewing thread, Blue 0350 or similar: 33 yd/30 m for all sizes

Needles: U. S. size 1.5 / 2.5 mm: set of 5 dpn

Gauge: 26 sts in pattern = 4 in / 10 cm.
Adjust needle size to obtain correct gauge if necessary.

LEG
With Blue, CO 45 (48, 51, 54, 60) sts. Divide sts as evenly as possible onto 4 dpn. Join, being careful not to twist cast-on row; pm for beginning of rnd. Work around in k2, p1 ribbing for 12 rnds. Now continue ribbing as est with stripes: 3 rnds Green, 1 rnd Blue, 3 rnds Green. Cut Green and continue in ribbing with Blue until leg measures 4 in / 10 cm.

GUSSET HEEL
After completing the leg, divide the sts, placing the 23 (25, 27, 27, 31) instep stitches onto scrap yarn. These instep stitches will "rest" until the heel is complete. Make sure the ribbing pattern is balanced on each side.
Place the remaining 22 (23, 24, 27, 29) sts onto one needle and work back and forth with Green held together with reinforcing thread.

Begin with the WS facing you.
Row 1 (WS): Sl 1 purlwise wyf, purl to end of row.
Row 2: Sl 1 purlwise wyb, knit to end of row.
Repeat these 2 rows until there are 12 (for all sizes) chain sts at each side of the flap.

Shaping the Heel
Row 1 (WS): Sl 1, purl until 8 sts rem on the needle, p2tog, p1; turn.
Row 2: Sl 1, knit until 8 sts rem on needle, ssk, k1; turn.
Row 3: Sl 1, purl until 1 st before gap, p2tog, p1; turn.
Row 4: Sl 1, knit until 1 st rem before gap, ssk, k1; turn.
Repeat Rows 3-4 until all the side sts have been eliminated. Cut reinforcing thread.

FOOT
Change to Blue. Divide the instep sts from the holder onto 2 dpn; divide the sole sts onto 2 dpn with half of the sts on each. With RS facing, begin working in the round. Begin rnd at center of sole. With Ndl 1, knit to heel flap; pick up and knit 1 st in each chain up side of flap. You can pick up the chain sts through back loops or knit them tbl on the next rnd. With Ndls 2-3, work across the instep sts in ribbing. Next, with Ndl 4, pick up and knit sts down opposite side of flap as for the first side. Knit to center of sole.

Gusset Shaping
On the next rnd, begin decreasing to shape gusset: Knit until 2 sts rem on Ndl 1, k2tog. Work across instep sts on Ndls 2-3 in ribbing. With Ndl 4, ssk and then knit to end of rnd. Work next rnd without decreasing. Repeat these 2 rnds until 45 (48, 51, 54, 60) sts rem. Continue as est with ribbing on instep and st st on sole, until sock foot measures 4 (4¾, 6, 7, 8¼) in / (12, 15, 18, 21) cm or desired length to toe shaping.

STAR TOE
Begin at the center of the sole. Change to Green.
Rnd 1: (K5, k2tog) around. The 3 (6, 2, 5, 4) sts rem on Ndl 4 will be decreased in subsequent rnds.
Rnds 2-6: Knit.
Rnd 7: (K4, k2tog) around.
Rnds 8-11: Knit.
Rnd 12: (K3, k2tog) around.
Rnds 13-15: Knit
Rnd 16: (K2, k2tog) around.
Rnds 17-18: Knit.
Rnd 19: (K1, k2tog) around.
Rnd 20: Knit.
Rnd 21: (K2tog) around.

FINISHING
Cut yarn and draw end through rem sts; tighten. Weave in all ends neatly on WS. Make the second sock the same way.

NORDLAND

Entrelac Stockings from Helgeland

Entrelac stockings can be found in many places in Norway. The earliest known source showing this technique with its distinctive block pattern is a travel sketch Johannes Flintoe made in Hjartdal in Telemark in 1828. We have almost no information about how the technique came to Norway, not even whether it was from the east or the west. Perhaps Finnish immigrants brought the tradition with them, or maybe it was Scots who'd shipwrecked on the west coast. Museums all around the country have entrelac knitted stockings in their collections, including the Rana Museum and the Vefsn Museum in Helgeland.

It has been said that only the most experienced knitters can work entrelac. The technique is slow, but the result makes lovely stockings that fit the feet well. It is, therefore, not surprising that stockings in this technique were well regarded and valued more highly than many others. As a rule, only two colors were used: black and white. To make the stockings extra fine, they could be dyed afterwards—with red, for example, so white blocks would become red and black blocks would deepen in color. There are also examples of entrelac stockings knitted with several colors.

The girl in the photo is wearing particularly lovely entrelac stockings. They're long and extend up beneath her dress, so we can't see the edging on them. This photo was taken on Hugløya in Nesna in 1913 or 1914, and the little girl is Gudrun Sylvestersen, née Ellingsen. The photographer was Barbara Bostrøm Baarsen, who was born in Bergen in 1876. Baarsen was known for her many portraits from Helgeland. She had studios in several places, but for this photo the model is sitting in a tent the photographer brought along on many of her travels.

Inspired by this picture, I knitted a pair of short entrelac stockings. In the photo, you can see that the foot is single-color, but I added a few extra pattern panels.

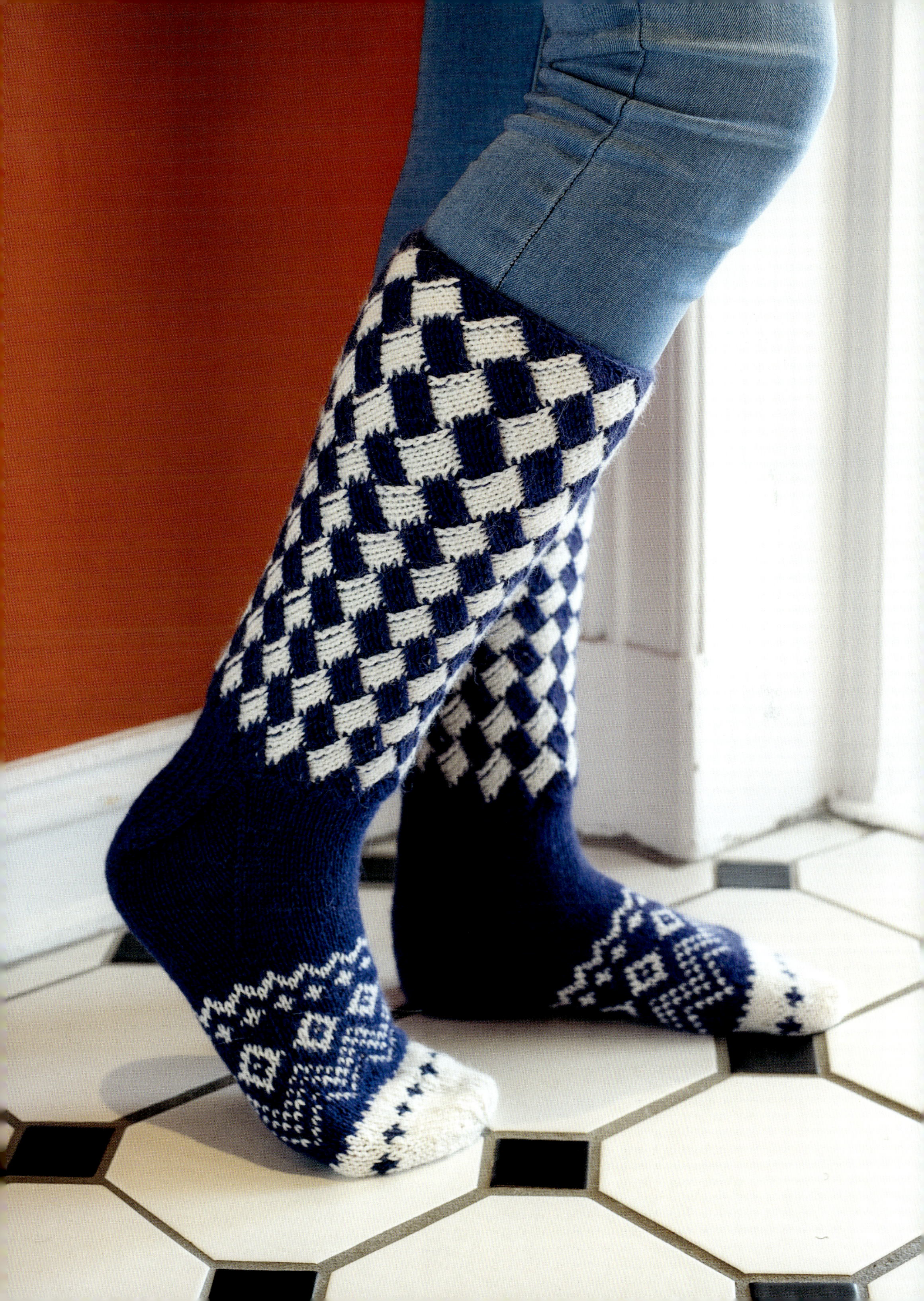

← Second decrease on star toe

← First decrease on star toe

Repeat

☐ Natural White
■ Blue

174

INSTRUCTIONS

Skill Level: Experienced

Sizes: Women's (men's)

MATERIALS
Yarn:
CYCA #3 (DK, light worsted), Sterk from Du Store Alpakka (40% Merino wool, 40% alpaca, 20% nylon, 150 yd/137 m / 50 g)

Yarn Colors and Amounts:
Dark Blue 815: 100 (150) g
Natural White 806: 100 (100) g

Needles: U. S. size 2.5 / 3 mm: set of 5 dpn

Gauge: 26 sts in pattern = 4 in / 10 cm. Adjust needle size to obtain correct gauge if necessary.

LEG
With Blue, CO 70 sts. Work back and forth in garter st (knit all rows) until there are 2 ridges on the RS. Now divide sts as evenly as possible onto 4 dpn. Join, being careful not to twist cast-on row; pm for beginning of rnd. Knit 1 rnd, decreasing evenly spaced around to 60 sts [= (k5, k2tog) around].
Change to entrelac (see instructions on page 10). Work the first triangles with Blue over 5 sts (producing 12 blocks) and then continue with tiers of White and Blue blocks until there are 2 (3) Blue and 3 (4) White tiers of blocks in addition to the triangles at the cast-on edge.
Next Tier: Pick up 4 Blue sts, instead of 5, and work the last 2 White sts tog with 1 Blue.
After completing the tier, 48 sts rem. Continue, working blocks of 4 sts until there are a total of 7 Blue and 6 White tiers over 4 sts = 18 tiers total, in addition to the triangles at the cast-on edge. Complete the entrelac by picking up 4 sts on each of the Blue blocks so that you have 48 + (4 x 12) = 96 sts.
On the next rnd, decrease 36 sts evenly spaced around (decrease every 2nd and 6th st) = 60 sts rem.

GUSSET HEEL
After completing the leg, divide the sts in half, placing the 30 instep stitches onto scrap yarn. These instep stitches will "rest" until the heel is complete.

Place the rem 30 sts onto one needle and work back and forth with Blue.
Begin with the WS facing you.
Row 1 (WS): Sl 1 purlwise wyf, purl to end of row.
Row 2: Sl 1 purlwise wyb, *k1, sl 1*; rep * to * to last st and end k1.
Repeat these 2 rows until there are 15 chain sts at each side of the flap.

Shaping the Heel
You can work the heel shaping in the heel pattern above or in stockinette.
Row 1 (WS): Sl 1, purl until 10 sts rem on the needle, p2tog, p1; turn.
Row 2: Sl 1, knit until 10 sts rem on needle, ssk, k1; turn.
Row 3: Sl 1, purl until 1 st before gap, p2tog, p1; turn.
Row 4: Sl 1, knit until 1 st rem before gap, ssk, k1; turn.
Repeat Rows 3-4 until all the side sts have been eliminated.

FOOT
Divide the instep sts from the holder onto 2 dpn; divide the sole sts onto 2 dpn with half of the sts on each. With RS facing, begin working in the round. Begin rnd at center of sole. With Ndl 1, knit to heel flap; pick up and knit 1 st in each chain up side of flap. You can pick up the chain sts through back loops or knit them tbl on the next rnd. With Ndls 2-3, knit across the instep sts. Next, with Ndl 4, pick up and knit sts down opposite side of flap as for the first side. Knit to center of sole.

Gusset Shaping
On the next rnd, begin decreasing to shape gusset: Knit until 2 sts rem on Ndl 1, k2tog. Knit across instep sts on Ndls 2-3. With Ndl 4, ssk and then knit to end of rnd. Work next rnd without decreasing.
Repeat these 2 rnds until 60 (68) sts rem. Continue around in st st until sock foot measures approx. 3½ (4¾) in / 9 (12) cm and then work charted pattern to first toe decrease (see arrow on chart).

STAR TOE
Begin at the center of the sole.
Rnd 1: (K5, k2tog) around. The 4 sts rem on Ndl 4 will be decreased in subsequent rnds.
Rnds 2-6: Knit.
Rnd 7: (K4, k2tog) around.
Rnds 8-11: Knit.
Rnd 12: (K3, k2tog) around.
Rnds 13-15: Knit
Rnd 16: (K2, k2tog) around.
Rnds 17-18: Knit.
Rnd 19: (K1, k2tog) around.
Rnd 20: Knit.
Rnd 21: (K2tog) around.

FINISHING
Cut yarn and draw end through rem sts; tighten. Weave in all ends neatly on WS. Make the second sock the same way.

Spider Socks from Troms

A rather common pattern element we find in several places around Norway is called *skarttrell* or *kongoro* in Selbu. *Kongro* is an old Norse name for a spider or daddy longlegs.

One pair of women's stockings from Troms, registered by The Norwegian Institute for Bunad and Folk Costume, features *kongro* patterns in a tight block net—a type of spiderweb, if you will. The stockings were knitted with heathery light and dark gray wool yarns.

Daddy longlegs or *kongro* spiders were considered lucky insects in many religions. When Mohammed fled from Mecca to Medina, he took shelter in a cave in a mountainside. A spider spun a web over it that no one could penetrate, according to legend, to keep him safe from the enemies pursuing him.

In Selbu, the spider motif was often used for the bridegroom's stockings, writes Annemor Sundbø. The spider in a net of evergreen twigs symbolizes eternal youth. An endless pattern is one which has no beginning or end. It continues for all eternity.

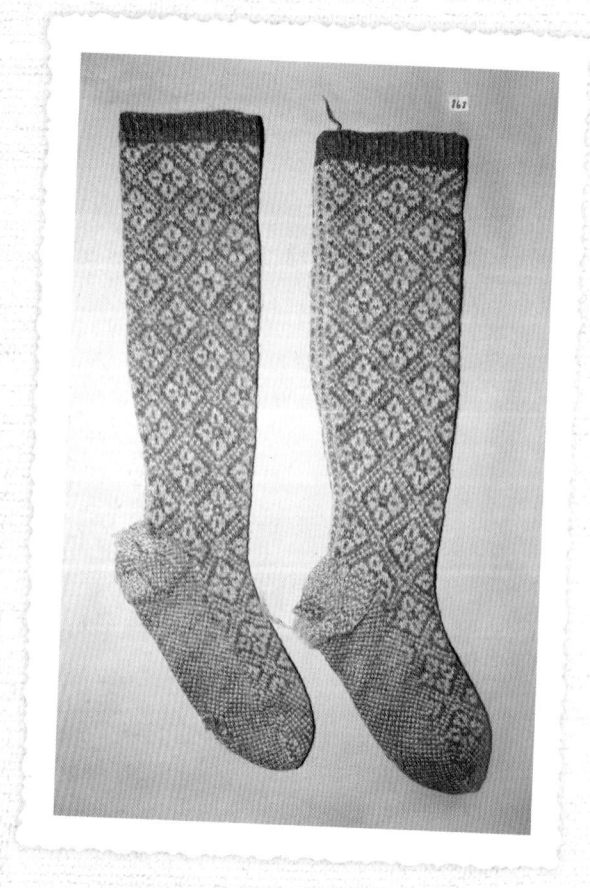

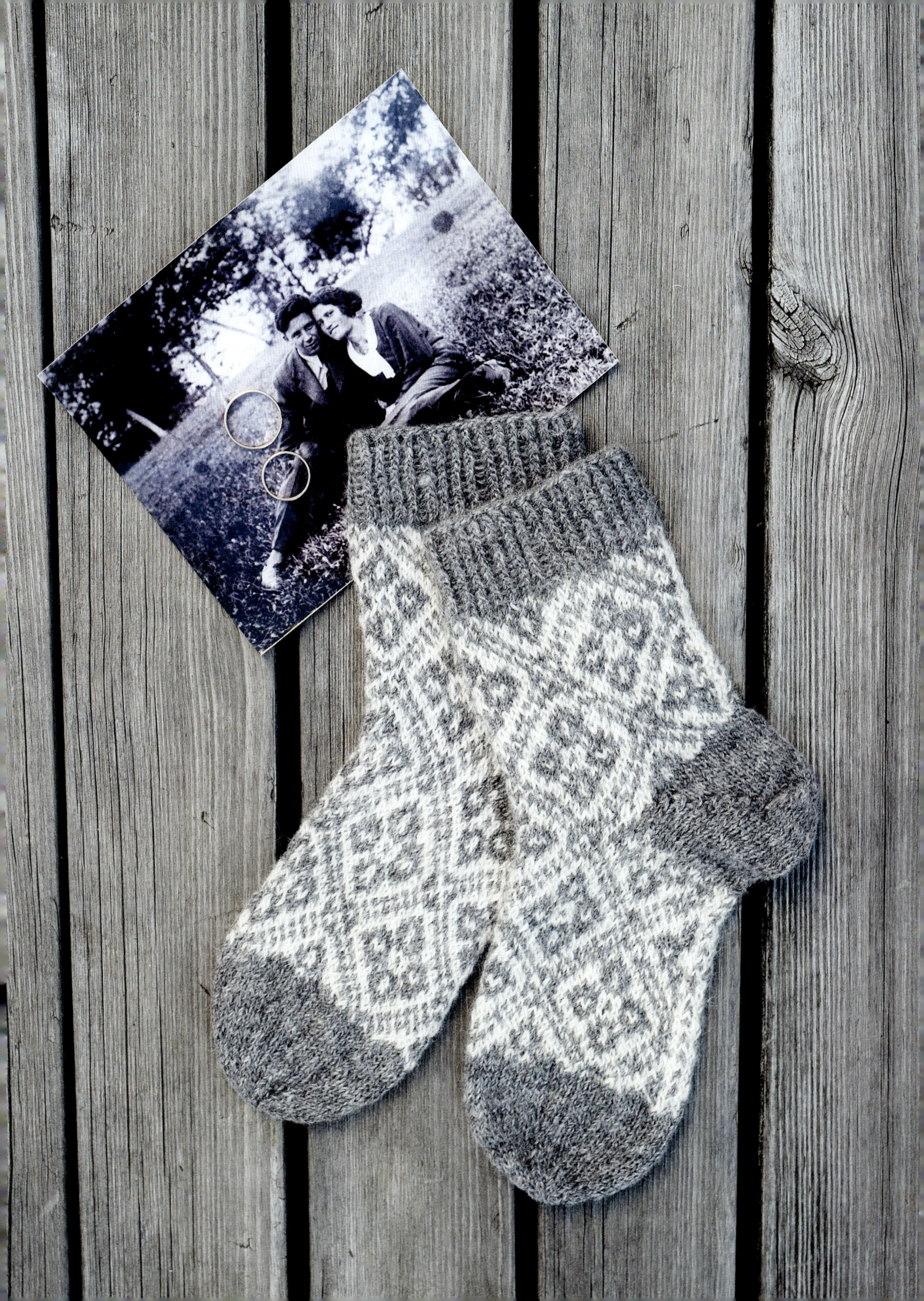

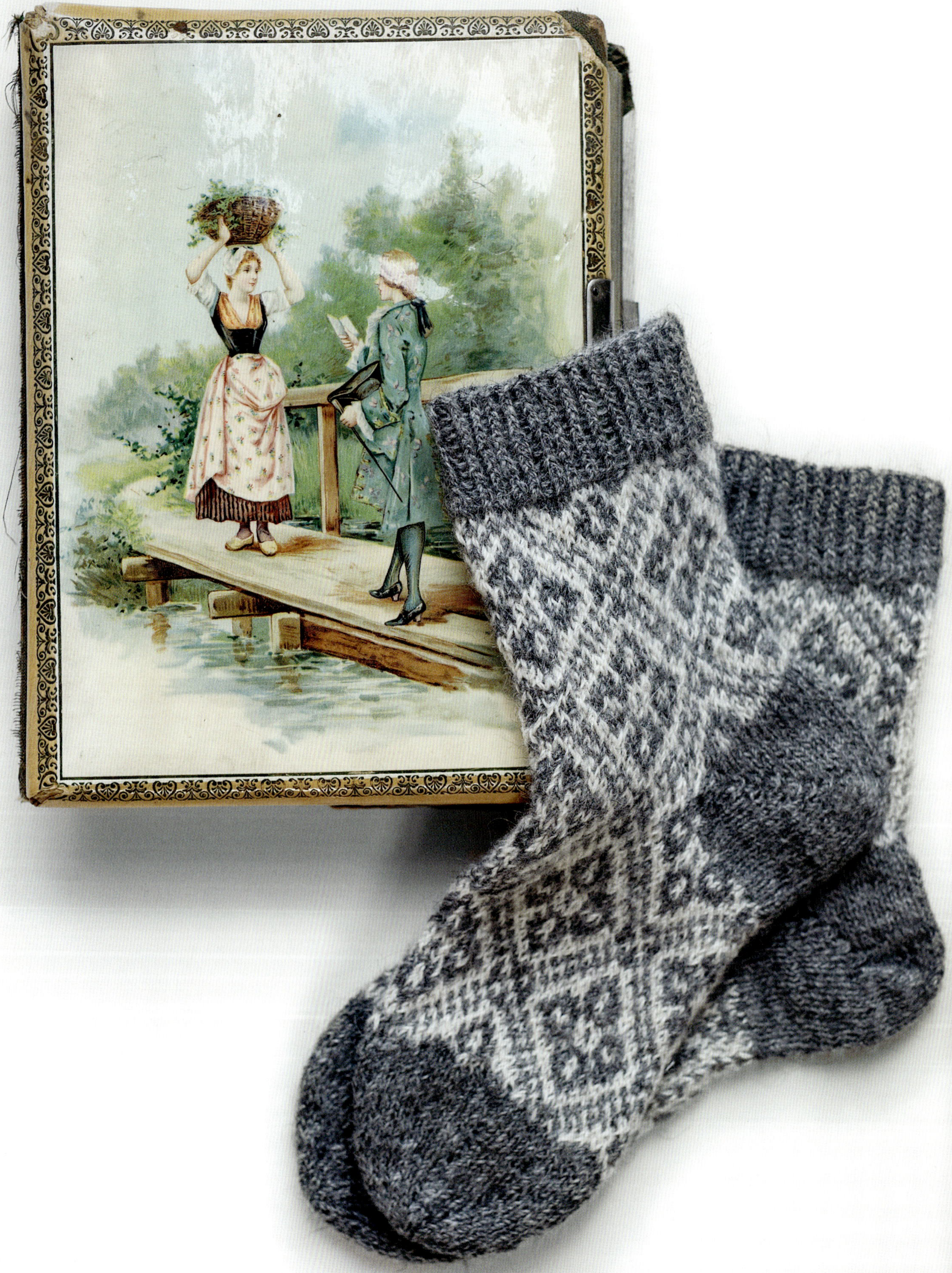

☐ Dark Gray—knit
☐ Light Gray—knit

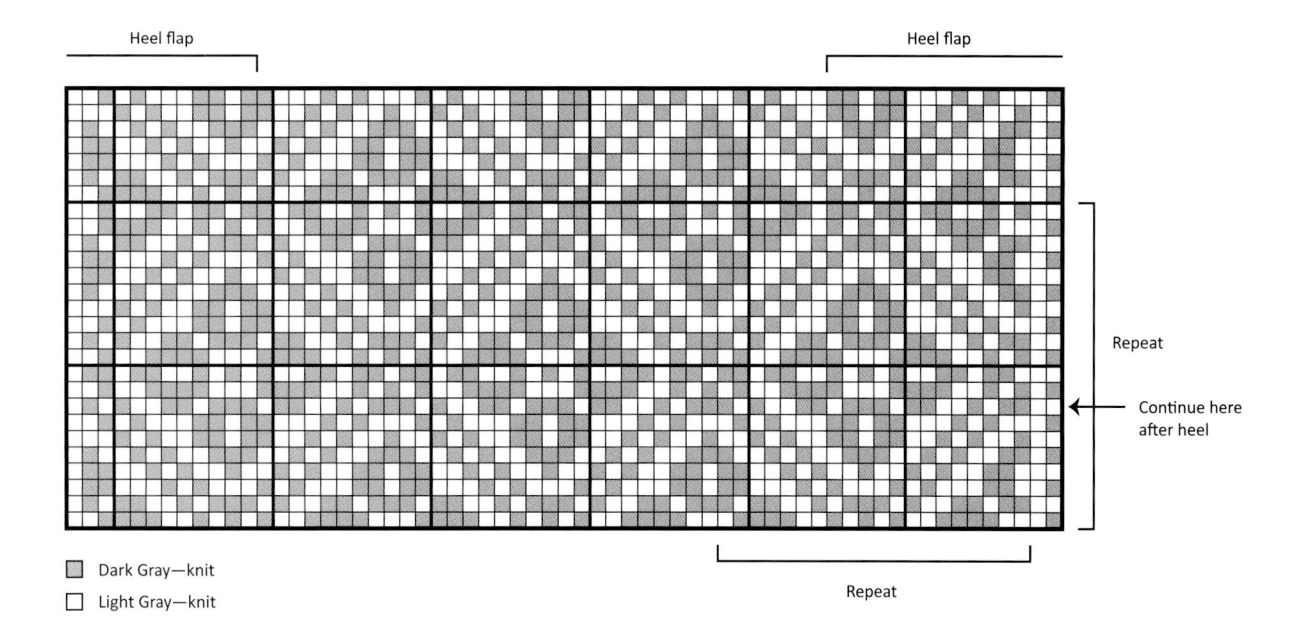

INSTRUCTIONS

Skill Level: Experienced

Sizes: Women's (men's)

MATERIALS
Yarn:
CYCA #1 (fingering/2 ply), 2-ply lamb's Rya wool from Lykkesau (100% organic lamb's wool, 284 yd/260 m / 100 g)
Or, substitute:
CYCA #1 (fingering/2 ply), 2-ply Gammelserie from Rauma (100% wool, 175 yd/160 m / 50 g)

Yarn Colors and Amounts:
Natural Dark Gray: 100 (100) g
Natural Light Gray: 100 (100) g

Needles: U. S. size 2.5 (4) / 3 (3.5) mm: set of 5 dpn

Gauge: 28 (26) sts in pattern = 4 in / 10 cm. Adjust needle size to obtain correct gauge if necessary.

LEG
With Dark Gray, CO 62 sts. Divide sts as evenly as possible onto 4 dpn. Join, being careful not to twist cast-on row; pm for beginning of rnd. Work around in (k1tbl, p1) ribbing for 1½ in / 4 cm. Knit 1 rnd, increasing 1 st at center back = 63 sts. Continue, following chart.

HOURGLASS HEEL
After completing charted rows for leg, divide the sts, placing 35 sts for the instep on scrap yarn. These sts will "rest" until the heel is finished. Arrange rem 28 sts at center back (see chart) on one dpn and work back and forth with Dark Gray.

Row 1 (RS): Knit across; turn.
Row 2: Sl 1 purlwise wyf, purl until 1 st rem; turn.
Row 3: Sl 1, knit until 1 st rem; turn.
Row 4: Sl 1, purl until 2 sts rem; turn.
Row 5: Sl 1, knit until 2 sts rem; turn.
Continue the same way with 1 less st before each turn until 10 sts rem at the center of the heel. The last row is on RS.
Sl 1, purl as many sts as were last knitted. Pick up the strand between the last and next st, twist it and purl it tog with the next st; turn.
Sl 1, knit as many sts as last worked. Pick up the strand between the last st and the next, twist it and knit it together with the next st; turn.
Continue, repeating these 2 rows. You should have 1 more st each time before you turn.
NOTE: Tighten the yarn a bit each time you turn to avoid holes.
Continue with 1 more st on each row until you work across all the sts on the last row.

Now work around on all sts following chart, a total of 32 rnds. Make sure the pattern on the foot matches the leg pattern. If necessary, add or subtract rounds to lengthen or shorten foot.

STAR TOE
Begin at the center of the sole.
Rnd 1: (K5, k2tog) around.
Rnds 2-6: Knit.
Rnd 7: (K4, k2tog) around.
Rnds 8-11: Knit.
Rnd 12: (K3, k2tog) around.
Rnds 13-15: Knit
Rnd 16: (K2, k2tog) around.
Rnds 17-18: Knit.
Rnd 19: (K1, k2tog) around.
Rnd 20: Knit.
Rnd 21: (K2tog) around.

FINISHING
Cut yarn and draw end through rem sts; tighten. Weave in all ends neatly on WS. Make the second sock the same way.

Sports Socks from Alta

After WWII, sports socks with a patterned band that could be folded down over ski boots became very popular. The socks were called *beksøm* socks. A worn pair from Komagfjord in Alta was registered with the Norwegian Handcrafts Association when it collected information about knitted garments in 1983-84.

There are few traces of socks in Finnmark. In the fall of 1944, the entire population of the district was forcibly evacuated by the Germans, and everything east of Lyngenfjord was burned. Anything valued that people couldn't take with them fell to the flames.

The Sami make many decorative and pretty mittens, although they don't have a sock-knitting tradition—they stuff sedge grass into their moccasins instead to keep feet warm and dry.

These socks from Komagfjord have a pretty pattern panel around the cuff and were knitted with gray, light blue, and sheep's natural brown wool. The registration card states that they were knitted by Signe Hvitbro in 1946. She was born in Oslo around 1895.

Signe was most likely Signe Kamilla Hvitbro, born in Christiana (former name for Oslo) on the 19th of September, 1896. She was confirmed on the 23rd of April, 1911, in Greenland Church and lived at Grønlandsleret 69. In the 1923 census, she's listed as an unmarried hair cutter.

At the turn of the century, six sisters lived at home. In 1911, Signe Ingeborg immigrated to Ohio. Two years later, Margit Ingeborg immigrated to Chicago. That could mean that opportunities in the capital were few and circumstances were difficult. But how the socks Signe knitted ended up in Alta is a mystery. Perhaps she traveled northwards?

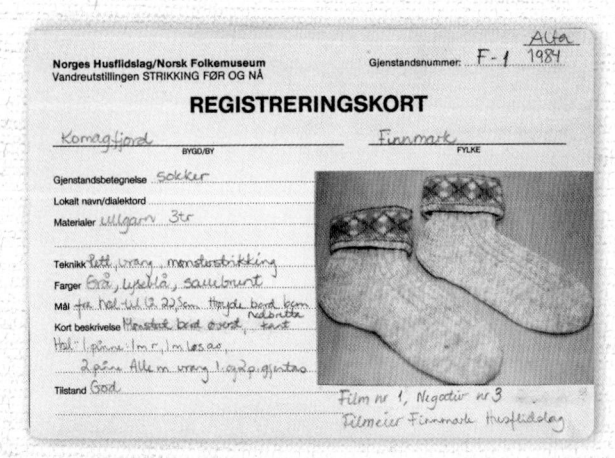

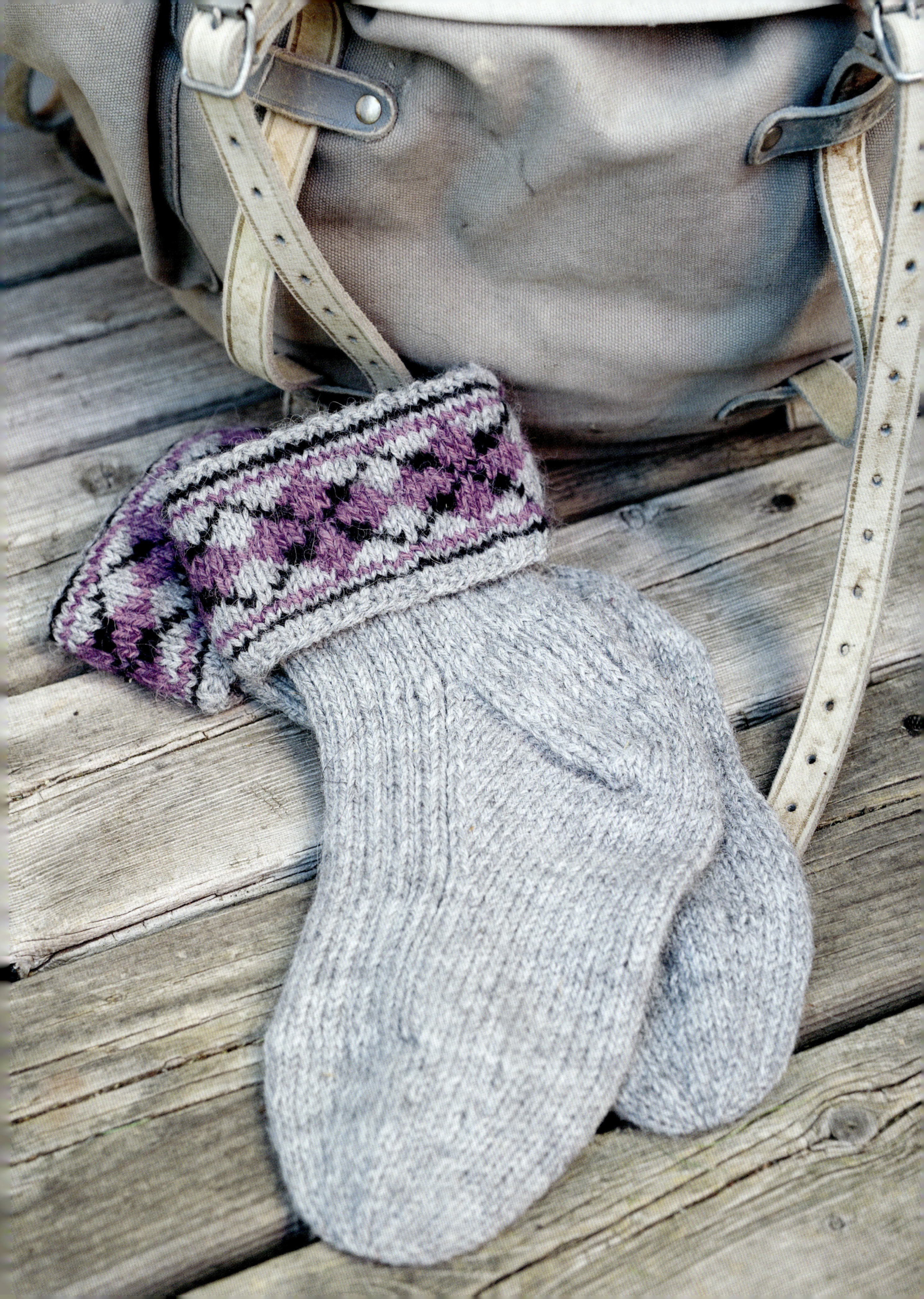

Repeat = 12 sts

☐ Gray—knit
☐ Purple—knit
■ Black—knit

182

INSTRUCTIONS

Skill Level: Experienced

Sizes: Women's (men's)

MATERIALS
Yarn:
CYCA #3 (DK, light worsted), Sterk from Du Store Alpakka (40% Merino wool, 40% alpaca, 20% nylon, 150 yd/137 m / 50 g)

Yarn Colors and Amounts:
Gray Heather 822: 100 (100) g
Black 809: 50 (50) g
Purple Heather 818: 50 (50) g

Needles: U. S. size 2.5 (4) / 3 (3.5) mm: set of 5 dpn

Gauge: 26 (24) sts in pattern = 4 in / 10 cm. Adjust needle size to obtain correct gauge if necessary.

LEG
With Gray, CO 72 sts. Divide sts evenly onto 4 dpn. Join, being careful not to twist cast-on row; pm for beginning of rnd. Work around in (k2, p2) ribbing for 2 rnds.
Continue in st st and charted pattern. End with knit 1 rnd with Gray. Turn the work inside out so the WS faces. Continue with Gray only.
Knit 1 rnd, decreasing evenly spaced around to 60 sts [= (k4, k2tog) around].
Now work around in k2, p1 ribbing until the piece measures 4¼ in / 11 cm from Black rnd.

After completing sock leg, divide the sts with 31 sts for the instep and 29 sts for the sole. Make sure that there is a p1 at each side of the instep. Place instep sts on a holder to "rest" until the heel is finished.

Heel Flap
Arrange the 29 sole sts on one needle and work the heel flap back and forth. Begin with WS facing.
Row 1 (WS): Sl 1 purlwise wyf, purl to end of row.
Row 2: Sl 1 purlwise wyb, *k1, sl 1*; rep * to * until 2 sts rem and end with k2.
Repeat these 2 rows until there are 15 chain sts on each side of the flap.

Shaping the Heel
Continue in the heel flap pattern as you work the heel gusset.
Row 1 (WS): Sl 1, purl until 10 sts rem on the needle, p2tog, p1; turn.
Row 2: Sl 1, (k1, sl 1) until 10 sts rem on needle, ssk, k1; turn.
Row 3: Sl 1, purl until 1 st before gap, p2tog, p1; turn.
Row 4: Sl 1, (k1, sl 1) until 1 st rem before gap, ssk, k1; turn.
Repeat Rows 3-4, keeping slip and knit sts aligned, until all the side sts have been eliminated.

FOOT
Divide the instep sts from the holder onto 2 dpn; divide the sole sts onto 2 dpn with half of the sts on each. With RS facing, begin working in the round. Begin rnd at center of sole. With Ndl 1, knit to heel flap; pick up and knit 1 st in each chain up side of flap. You can pick up the chain sts through back loops or knit them tbl on the next rnd. With Ndls 2-3, work k2, p1 ribbing as est across the instep sts. Make sure the ribbing aligns with previous work. Next, with Ndl 4, pick up and knit sts down opposite side of flap as for the first side. Knit to center of sole.

Gusset Shaping
On the next rnd, begin decreasing to shape gusset: Knit until 2 sts rem on Ndl 1, k2tog. Work across instep sts on Ndls 2-3 in ribbing as est. With Ndl 4, ssk and then knit to end of rnd. Work next rnd without decreasing.
Repeat these 2 rnds until 60 sts rem. Continue around in st st on sole and ribbing on instep until sock foot measures approx. 6¼ (7½) in / 16 (19) cm or desired length to toe shaping. Now work in st st st all around foot/toe.

STAR TOE
Begin at the center of the sole.
Rnd 1: (K5, k2tog) around. The 4 sts rem on Ndl 4 will be decreased in subsequent rnds.
Rnds 2-6: Knit.
Rnd 7: (K4, k2tog) around.
Rnds 8-11: Knit.
Rnd 12: (K3, k2tog) around.
Rnds 13-15: Knit
Rnd 16: (K2, k2tog) around.
Rnds 17-18: Knit.
Rnd 19: (K1, k2tog) around.
Rnd 20: Knit.
Rnd 21: (K2tog) around.

FINISHING
Cut yarn and draw end through rem sts; tighten. Weave in all ends neatly on WS. Make the second sock the same way.

Shell Pattern

Helmer: You knit?
Mrs. Linde: Oh, yes.
Helmer: Well, it would be better if you did embroidery.
Mrs. Linde: So? Why?
Helmer: Yes, because it is much prettier. Look, one holds the embroidery just so with the left hand and then guides the needle in with the right hand.
And then out in an easy, long graceful arch, isn't that so—?
Mrs. Linde: Yes, that may well be.
Helmer: While, when one knits—it can't be other than ugly—see here; your arms are clamped to your side, the knitting needles go up and down—it has something Chinese about it.

This question-and-answer repartee is taken from Act 3 of Henrik Ibsen's play, *A Doll's House* (1879), and tells us that knitting wasn't well regarded in finer circles at the end of the 19th century. According to Professor Jorunn Veiteberg, it also implies that knitting wasn't considered particularly feminine. "Ugly" movements were the same as unwomanly movements in the 19th-century way of speaking. To work for money was also "ugly" for women in the upper and middle classes. However, for unmarried women, widows, and divorced women, handwork could provide income. By working at home, they didn't expose themselves to public notice.

A range of typical upper-class textiles has been preserved—for example, silk bags, and handwork bags that are knitted with fine yarn. However, without a doubt, the technique of knitting was first and foremost used by common people to make everyday clothing.

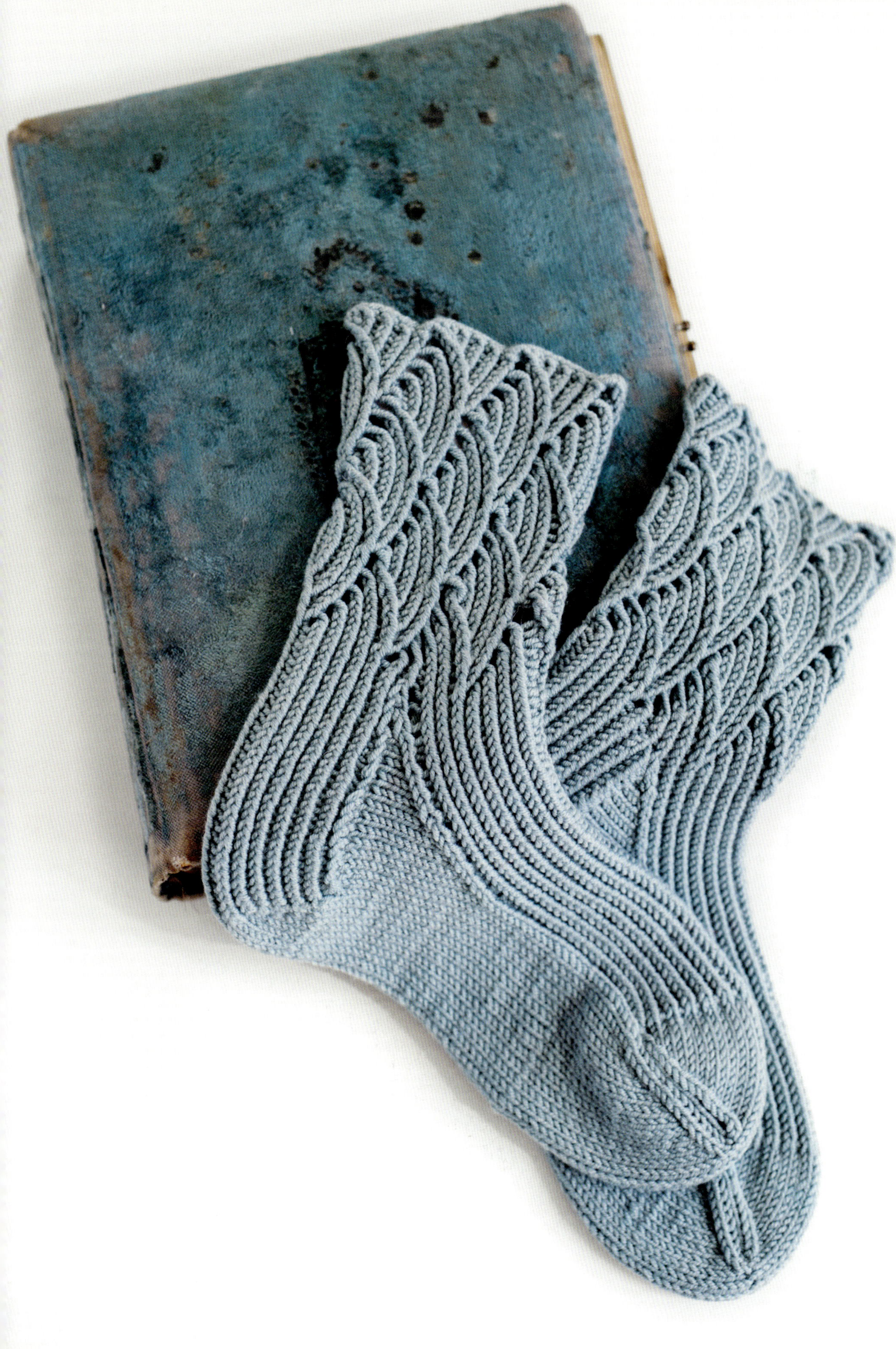

- ◯ Yarnover (yo)
- ℞ Twisted knit = k1tbl
- ⊠ Purl
- ◺ K2tog tbl

Repeat
Repeat

INSTRUCTIONS

Skill Level: Experienced

Size: Women's

MATERIALS
Yarn:
CYCA #3 (DK, light worsted), Merinoull from Sandnes Garn (100% Merino wool, 114 yd/104 m / 50 g), Light Green 7741: 150 g

Needles: U. S. size 2.5 / 3 mm: set of 5 dpn

Gauge: 24 sts in pattern = 4 in / 10 cm. Adjust needle size to obtain correct gauge if necessary.

LEG
With Gray, CO 63 sts. Divide sts evenly onto 4 dpn. Join, being careful not to twist cast-on row; pm for beginning of rnd. Purl 1 rnd. Now continue in pattern following chart or the description below.

Pattern
Rnd 1: *Yo, k2tog tbl, (k1tbl, p1) 3 times, k1tbl*; rep * to * around.
Rnd 2: *Yo, p1, k2tog tbl, (p1, k1tbl) 3 times, *; rep * to * around.
Rnd 3: *Yo, k1tbl, p1, k2tog tbl, (k1tbl, p1) 2 times, k1tbl*; rep * to * around.
Rnd 4: *Yo, p1, k1tbl, p1, k2tog tbl, p1, k1tbl, p1, k1tbl*; rep * to * around.
Rnd 5: *Yo, k1tbl, p1, k1tbl, p1, k2tog tbl, k1tbl, p1, k1tbl*; rep * to * around.
Rnd 6: *Yo, p1, k1tbl, p1, k1tbl, p1, k2tog tbl, p1, k1tbl*; rep * to * around.
Rnd 7: *Yo, (k1tbl, p1) 3 times, k2tog tbl, k1tbl*; rep * to * around.
Rnd 8: *Yo, (p1, k1 tbl) 3 times, p1, k2tog tbl*; rep * to * around.

GUSSET HEEL
After completing the leg, divide the sts, placing the 31 instep stitches onto scrap yarn. These instep stitches will "rest" until the heel is complete.
Place the remaining 32 sts onto one needle and work back and forth.
Begin with the WS facing you.
Row 1 (WS): Sl 1 purlwise wyf, (k1, p1tbl) to last st and end k1 (make sure that the patterning matches that on the RS).
Row 2: Sl 1 purlwise wyb, (k1tbl, p1) to last st and end k1 tbl.
Repeat these 2 rows until there are 15 chain sts at each side of the flap.

Shaping the Heel
Row 1 (WS): Sl 1, purl until 10 sts rem on the needle, p2tog, p1; turn.
Row 2: Sl 1, knit until 10 sts rem on needle, ssk, k1; turn.
Row 3: Sl 1, purl until 1 st before gap, p2tog, p1; turn.
Row 4: Sl 1, knit until 1 st rem before gap, ssk, k1; turn.
Repeat Rows 3-4 until all the side sts have been eliminated.

FOOT
Divide the instep sts from the holder onto 2 dpn; divide the sole sts onto 2 dpn with half of the sts on each. With RS facing, begin working in the round, with st st on the sole and twisted rib on the instep. Begin rnd at center of sole. With Ndl 1, knit to heel flap; pick up and knit 1 st in each chain up side of flap. You can pick up the chain sts through back loops or knit them tbl on the next rnd. With Ndls 2-3, work across the instep sts with (p1, k1tbl) rib, ending with p1. Make sure the twisted rib pattern matches previous work. Next, with Ndl 4, pick up and knit sts down opposite side of flap as for the first side. Knit to center of sole.

Gusset Shaping
On the next rnd, begin decreasing to shape gusset: Knit until 2 sts rem on Ndl 1, k2tog. Work across instep sts on Ndls 2-3 in twisted rib. With Ndl 4, ssk and then knit to end of rnd. Work next rnd without decreasing.
Repeat these 2 rnds until 56 sts rem. Continue around in twisted rib (instep) and st st (sole) until sock foot measures approx. 7 in / 18 cm or desired length to toe shaping.

WEDGE TOE
Divide sts evenly over 4 dpn.
Rnd 1:
Ndl 1: Knit until 3 sts rem on needle, k2tog, k1.
Ndl 2: K1, ssk, knit to end of needle.
Ndl 3: Work as for Ndl 1.
Ndl 4: Work as for Ndl 2.
Rnd 2: Knit without decreasing.
Repeat these two rounds 4 times and then decrease on every rnd until 3 sts rem on each needle. Move all sts from Ndl 1 to Ndl 4, and from Ndl 3 to Ndl 2 = 6 sts on each of 2 needles. Carefully turn work inside out and hold the 2 needles parallel. Bind off with 3-needle BO: K2tog with 1st st of each needle, *k2tog with next 2 sts (1 from each needle), pass first st over 2nd. Rep from * until 1 st loop rem.

FINISHING
Cut yarn and draw end through rem st; tighten. Weave in all ends neatly on WS. Make second sock the same way.

Heart Socks

Marie Rosing (1831-1911) was a handcraft pioneer in Norway. She became internationally recognized for her original teaching programs and, in 1889, she was awarded the Gold Medal at the World's Fair in Paris.

Her lessons were an important aid for teaching up until the 1970s, and perhaps even longer. When I began school in 1967, I remember that we had a series of lessons in elementary school.

Knitting has been an important part of handcraft teaching in Norway up to the modern day. In 1860, the county administration allowed public schools in the countryside to give boys instruction in gym, with handcraft lessons for the girls—this had been permitted in towns since 1848. That also gave the green light for establishing so-called "needlework schools" for servant girls. Handcrafts first became a required subject in 1889.

Marie Rosing called her handcraft pedagogy "the self-help method". With contributions from the public, she was able to publish her book *Handcrafts as a School Subject: A Guide for Teachers* in 1880. From the very beginning, students had to learn what they were doing so they could plan, organize, and produce crafts themselves.

There were no other such aids. Rosing developed sewing and knitting guidelines, teaching plans, and systems for using a blackboard. Handcraft instruction should proceed systematically and step-by-step. Doll-size models were chosen so the work wouldn't become too boring or take too long. These were assembled in boxes together with drawings and sample fabrics so the students could follow along and use the results as templates for later work.

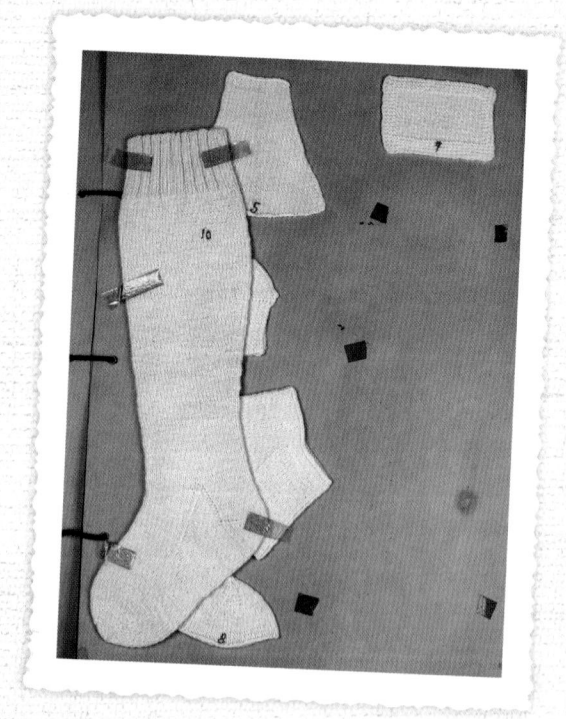

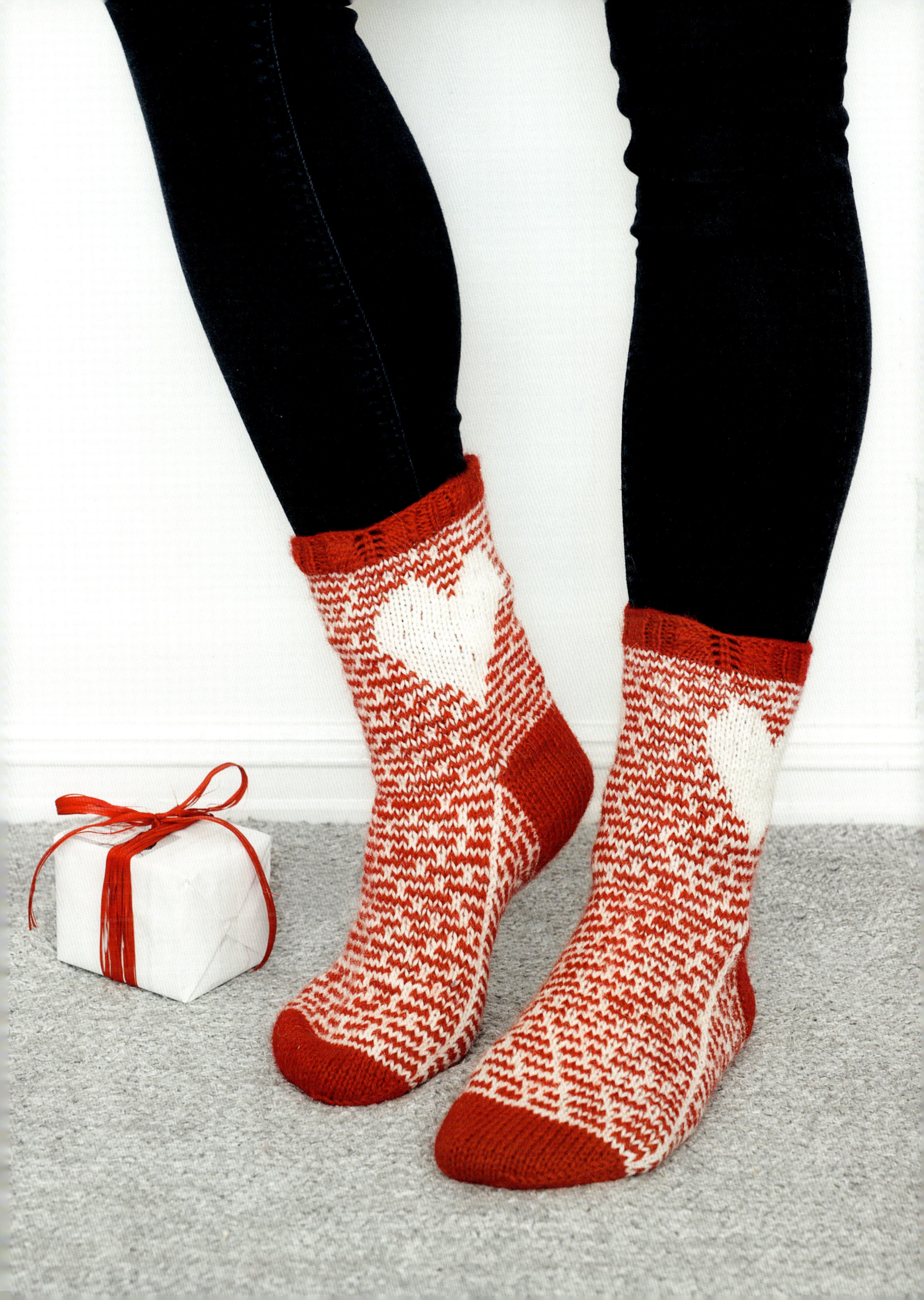

FOOT

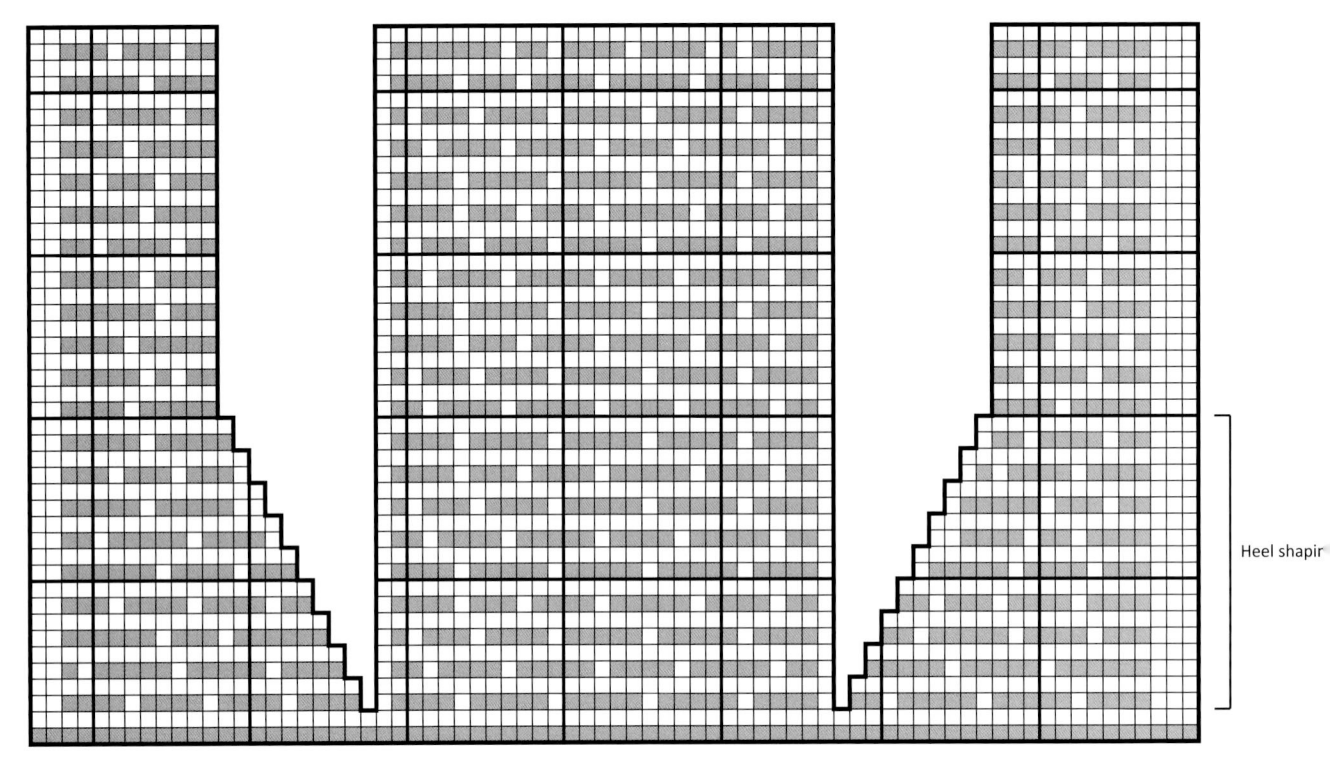

LEG

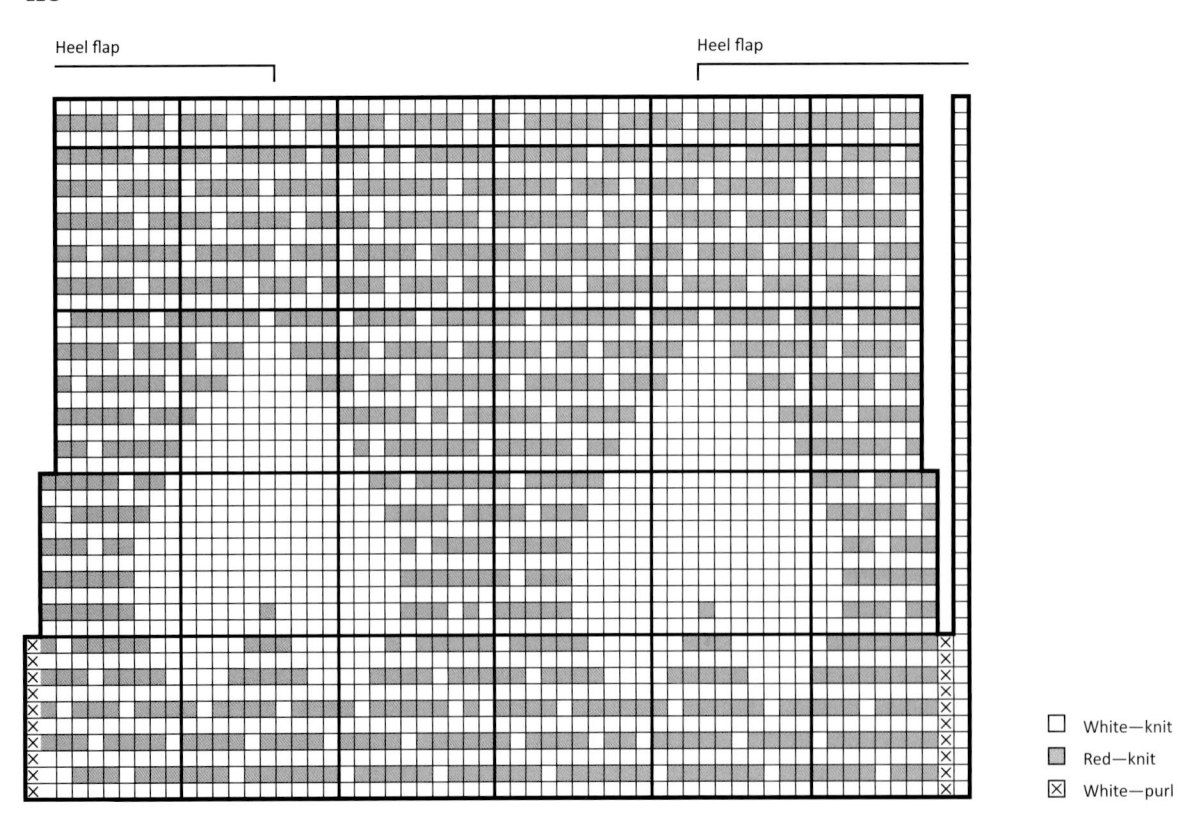

Heel flap

Heel flap

Heel shaping

☐ White—knit
▦ Red—knit
☒ White—purl

INSTRUCTIONS

Skill Level: Experienced

Sizes: Women's

MATERIALS
Yarn:
CYCA #3 (DK, light worsted), Sterk from Du Store Alpakka (40% Merino wool, 40% alpaca, 20% nylon, 150 yd/137 m / 50 g)

Yarn Colors and Amounts:
Natural White 806: 50 g
Red 828: 100 g

Needles: U. S. size 2.5 / 3 mm: set of 5 dpn

Gauge: 24 sts in pattern = 4 in / 10 cm.
Adjust needle size to obtain correct gauge if necessary.

LEG
With Red, CO 60 sts. Divide sts evenly onto 4 dpn. Join, being careful not to twist cast-on row; pm for beginning of rnd. Work lace pattern as follows:
Rnd 1: K1, p1, k1, p1, *k2tog, k3, yo, k1, yo, k3, p2tog, p1, k1, p1*; rep * to * 4 times.
Rnd 2: K1, p1, k1, p1, *k11, p1, k1, p1*; rep * to * 4 times.
Rep Rnds 1-2 a total of 4 times.
On the next rnd, decrease 2 sts at center back and work the rest of the leg as shown on the chart. There are long floats at the hearts, so be sure to twist the yarns around each other after every 3 or 4 sts. Do *not* stack the twists round to round to avoid strands showing through.

GUSSET HEEL
After completing the leg, divide the sts, placing the 27 instep stitches onto scrap yarn. These instep stitches will "rest" until the heel is complete.
Place the remaining 29 sts (sts indicated on chart) onto one needle and work back and forth.
Begin with Red and the WS facing you.
Row 1 (WS): Sl 1 purlwise wyf, purl to end of row.
Row 2: Sl 1 purlwise wyb, knit to end of row.
Repeat these 2 rows until there are 14 chain sts at each side of the flap.

Shaping the Heel
Row 1 (WS): Sl 1, purl until 10 sts rem on the needle, p2tog, p1; turn.
Row 2: Sl 1, knit until 10 sts rem on needle, ssk, k1; turn.
Row 3: Sl 1, purl until 1 st before gap, p2tog, p1; turn.
Row 4: Sl 1, knit until 1 st before gap, ssk, k1; turn.

Repeat Rows 3-4 until all the side sts have been eliminated.

FOOT
Divide the instep sts from the holder onto 2 dpn; divide the sole sts onto 2 dpn with half of the sts on each. With RS facing, begin working in the round with Red. Begin rnd at center of sole. With Ndl 1, knit to heel flap; pick up and knit 1 st in each chain up side of flap. You can pick up the chain sts through back loops or knit them tbl on the next rnd. With Ndls 2-3, knit across the instep sts. Next, with Ndl 4, pick up and knit sts down opposite side of flap as for the first side. Knit to center of sole.

Gusset Shaping
On the next rnd, begin working in charted pattern and, *at the same time*, decreasing to shape gusset. Work all decreases with Natural. Knit until 2 sts rem on Ndl 1, k2tog. Work across instep sts in pattern on Ndls 2-3. With Ndl 4, ssk and then knit to end of rnd. Work next rnd without decreasing. Repeat these 2 rnds until 54 sts rem. Continue around in charted pattern until chart pattern is complete or desired length to toe shaping.

WEDGE TOE
Divide sts over 4 dpn with a total of 28 sts for sole and 26 sts for instep. Knit the toe with Red only.
Rnd 1:
Ndl 1: Knit until 3 sts rem on needle, k2tog, k1.
Ndl 2: Knit to end of needle.
Ndl 3: Knit to end of needle.
Ndl 4: K1, ssk, knit to end of needle.
Rnd 2: Knit without decreasing.
Rnd 3:
Ndl 1: Knit until 3 sts rem on needle, k2tog, k1.
Ndl 2: Ssk, knit to end of needle.
Ndl 3: Knit until 2 sts rem on needle, k2tog.
Ndl 4: K1, ssk, knit to end of needle.
Rnd 4: Knit without decreasing.
Repeat Rnds 3-4 4 times. Now decrease the same way on every rnd until 4 sts rem on each needle. Move all sts from Ndl 1 to Ndl 4, and from Ndl 3 to Ndl 2 = 8 sts on each of 2 needles. Carefully turn work inside out and hold the 2 needles parallel. Bind off with 3-needle BO: K2tog with 1st st of each needle, *k2tog with next 2 sts (1 from each needle), pass first st over 2nd. Rep from * until 1 st loop rem.

FINISHING
Cut yarn and draw end through rem st; tighten. Weave in all ends neatly on WS. Make second sock the same way.

Socks with Larger Lice Pattern

Until the 1920s and 1930s, when hygiene improved and treatments became more effective, the plague of lice was common. Smoke, quicksilver, plant extractions, and boiling water were just a few of the substances used for centuries to fight these pests. Lice combs and lice "boards" were used in hopes of capturing head lice, body lice, and flat lice. Lice suck blood and dig in, and are itchy, unsanitary, and irritating. Nevertheless, we call some of our most beloved knitting garments lice sweaters. Single contrast-color stitches over a solid background undoubtedly look like small tiny insects, and that's likely how this pattern element got its name.

The earliest use of the phrase "lice sweater" that we know of comes from Setesdal. This typical sweater has been worn since the middle of the 19th century and is just as popular now, almost 200 years later.

Lice have also been used as a pattern element on mittens and stockings. A large number of lice-embellished stockings from Vestlandet have been preserved. Many of them have pretty ankle roses—eight-petal roses at the ankles or on the leg. The Norwegian Museum of Cultural History also has a pair of stockings with lice. They were knitted with natural white yarn at the top, heels, and toes. In the black and white photo, it looks as if there are dark lice on a red or blue background. I decided to make slightly larger lice for my version.

In Birkenes, in East Agder, they don't think stockings should be white. But "a sock should have white cuffs and white for the heels and toes." Many thought it was common in other places in the country. And many of the stockings that have been preserved were designed precisely this way—with a light cuff at the top and light-colored heels and toes.

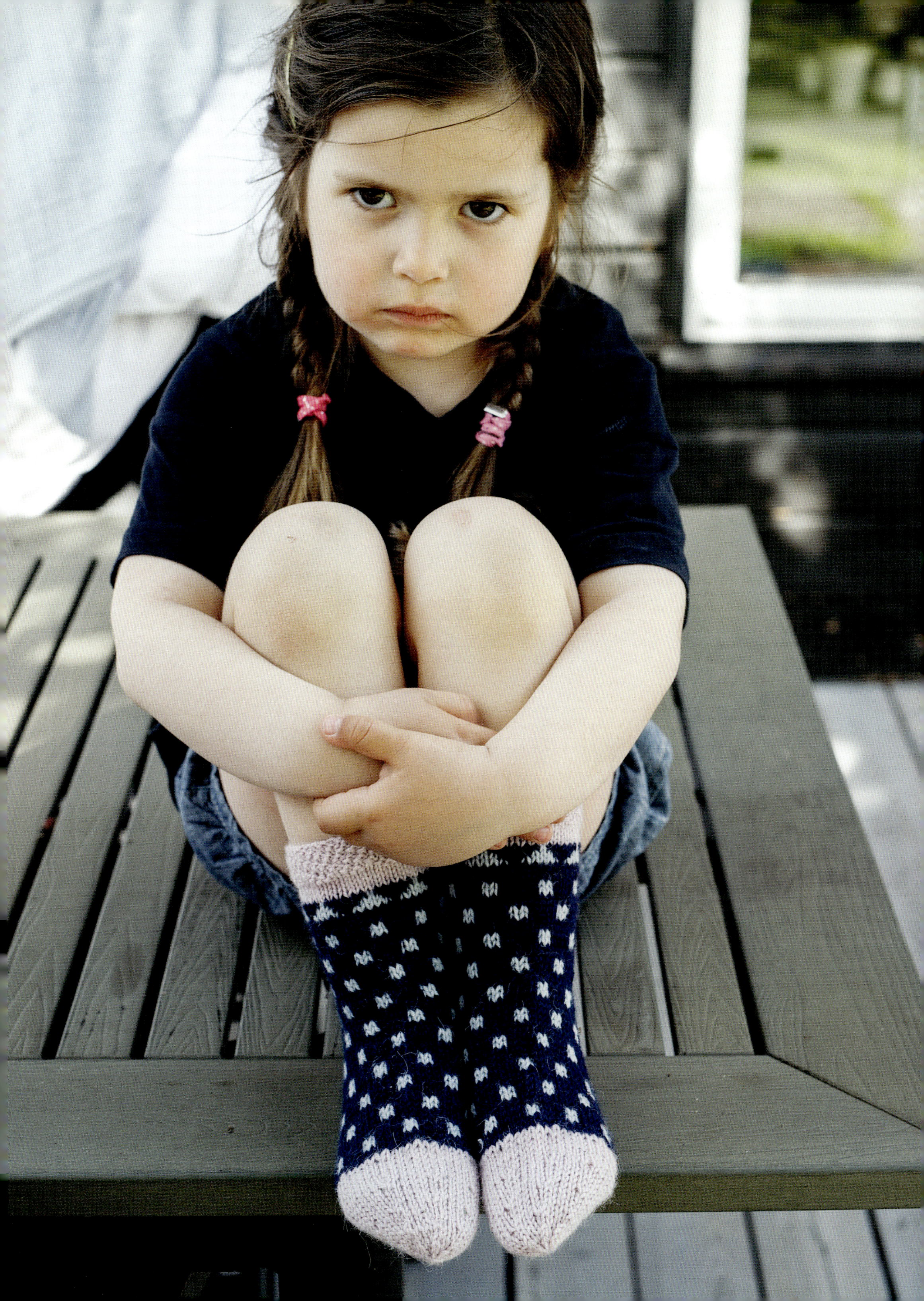

FOOT

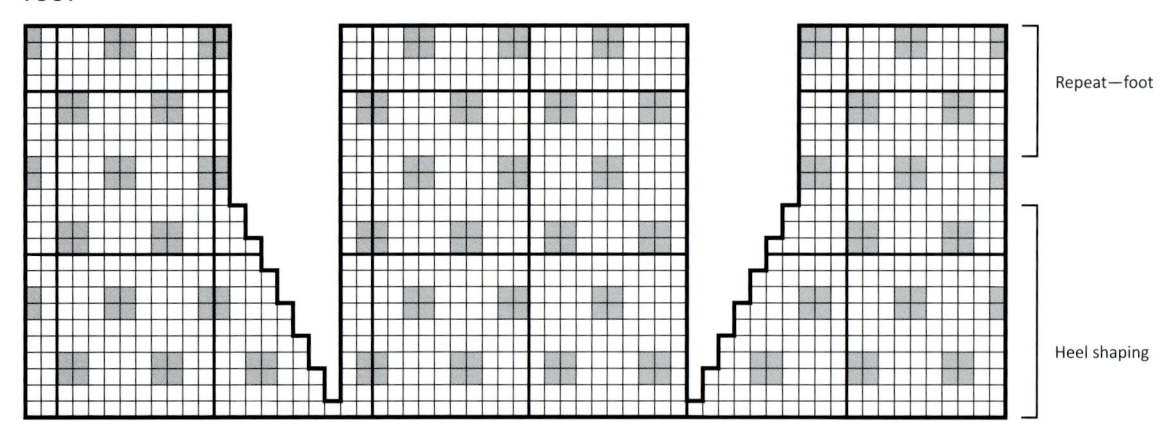

Repeat—foot

Heel shaping

LEG AND HEEL FLAP

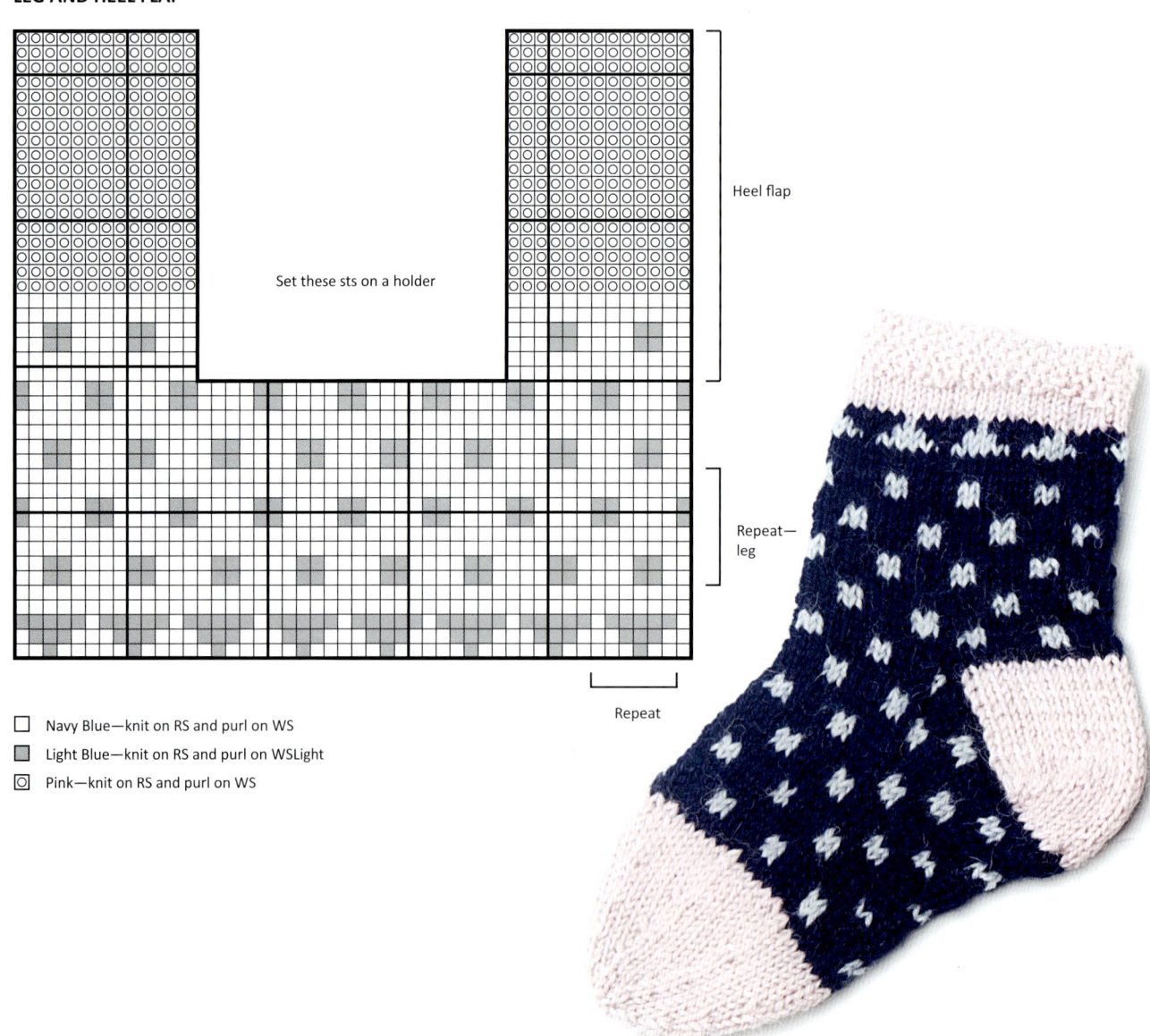

Heel flap

Set these sts on a holder

Repeat—leg

Repeat

☐ Navy Blue—knit on RS and purl on WS
▨ Light Blue—knit on RS and purl on WSLight
⊙ Pink—knit on RS and purl on WS

194

INSTRUCTIONS

Skill Level: Experienced

Sizes: 3-4 (5-6, 7-8, 9-12) years

MATERIALS
Yarn, Sizes 3-4 and (5-6) years:
CYCA #1 (fingering/2 ply), Mini Sterk from Du Store Alpakka (40% alpaca, 40% Merino wool, 20% polyamide, 182 yd/166 m / 50 g)

Yarn Colors and Amounts:
Light Pink 850: 50 (50) g
Navy Blue 827: 50 (50) g
Light Blue 848: 50 (50) g

Needles: U. S. size 0 (1.5) / 2 (2.5) mm: set of 5 dpn

Gauge: 28 (26) sts in pattern = 4 in / 10 cm. Adjust needle size to obtain correct gauge if necessary.

Yarn, Sizes 7-8 and (9-12) years:
CYCA #3 (DK, light worsted), Sterk from Du Store Alpakka (40% Merino wool, 40% alpaca, 20% nylon, 150 yd/137 m / 50 g)

Yarn Colors and Amounts:
Light Pink 850: 50 (50) g
Navy Blue 827: 50 (50) g
Light Blue 848: 50 (50) g

Needles: U. S. size 2.5 (4) / 3 (3.5) mm: set of 5 dpn

Gauge: 24 (22) sts in pattern = 4 in / 10 cm. Adjust needle size to obtain correct gauge if necessary.

LEG
With Light Pink, CO 47 sts. Divide sts evenly onto 4 dpn. Join, being careful not to twist cast-on row; pm for beginning of rnd. Work around in spiral ribbing as follows:
Rnd 1: (K2, p2) to last st and end p1.
Rnd 2: Shift the pattern by one st: P1, *k2, p2*; rep * to * until 2 sts rem and end k2.
Rnd 3: P2, *k2, p2*; rep * to * until 1 st rem, end k1.
Rnd 4: K1, *p2, k2*; rep * to * until 2 sts rem and end p2.
Repeat these 4 rnds until cuff measures approx. ¾ in / 2 cm.
On the next rnd, increase 1 st at center back and knit 4 rnds total. Now work in pattern as shown on the chart.

GUSSET HEEL
After completing the leg, divide the sts, placing the 22 instep stitches onto scrap yarn. These instep stitches will "rest" until the heel is complete.
Place the remaining 26 sts (sts indicated on chart) onto one needle and work back and forth in pattern as shown on chart.

Begin with WS facing you.
Row 1 (WS): Sl 1 purlwise wyf, purl to end of row.
Row 2: Sl 1 purlwise wyb, knit to end of row.
Repeat these 2 rows until there are 12 chain sts at each side of the flap.

Shaping the Heel
Row 1 (WS): Sl 1, purl until 8 sts rem on the needle, p2tog, p1; turn.
Row 2: Sl 1, knit until 8 sts rem on needle, ssk, k1; turn.
Row 3: Sl 1, purl until 1 st before gap, p2tog, p1; turn.
Row 4: Sl 1, knit until 1 st rem before gap, ssk, k1; turn.
Repeat Rows 3-4 until all the side sts have been eliminated.

FOOT
Divide the instep sts from the holder onto 2 dpn; divide the sole sts onto 2 dpn with half of the sts on each. With RS facing, begin working in the round with Navy Blue. Begin rnd at center of sole. With Ndl 1, knit to heel flap; pick up and knit 1 st in each chain up side of flap. You can pick up the chain sts through back loops or knit them tbl on the next rnd. With Ndls 2-3, knit across the instep sts. Next, with Ndl 4, pick up and knit sts down opposite side of flap as for the first side. Knit to center of sole.

Gusset Shaping
On the next rnd, begin working in charted pattern and, *at the same time*, decreasing to shape gusset. Knit until 2 sts rem on Ndl 1, k2tog. Work across instep sts on Ndls 2-3. With Ndl 4, ssk and then knit to end of rnd. Work next rnd without decreasing. Repeat these 2 rnds until 48 sts rem. Continue around in charted pattern until foot measures approx. 4 (4¾, 5½, 6¼) in / 10 (12, 14, 16) cm or desired length to toe shaping. End with 2 rnds Navy Blue. Change to Light Pink and knit 1 rnd.

STAR TOE
Begin at the center of the sole.
Rnd 1: (K5, k2tog) around. The 6 sts rem on Ndl 4 will be decreased in subsequent rnds.
Rnds 2-6: Knit.
Rnd 7: (K4, k2tog) around.
Rnds 8-11: Knit.
Rnd 12: (K3, k2tog) around.
Rnds 13-15: Knit
Rnd 16: (K2, k2tog) around.
Rnds 17-18: Knit.
Rnd 19: (K1, k2tog) around.
Rnd 20: Knit.
Rnd 21: (K2tog) around.
Rnd 15: (K2tog) around.

FINISHING
Cut yarn and draw end through rem sts; tighten. Weave in all ends neatly on WS. Make the second sock the same way.

YARN

Name	Producer	Fiber Content
2-ply Gammelserie	Rauma Ullvarefabrikk	100% wool
2-ply Lamull	Lykkesau	100% organic lamb's wool
Alpakka Silke	Sandnes Garn	70% baby alpaca, 30% mulberry silk
Ask Hifa 2	Hillesvåg Ullvarefabrikk	100% wool
Baby Panda	Rauma Ullvarefabrikk	100% superwash Merino wool
Baby Ull	Dale Garn	100% superwash Merino wool
Blacker Samite Silk Blend	Blacker Yarns	80% pure new wool, 20% silk
Finullgarn	Rauma Ullvarefabrikk	100% wool
Fjord Sock yarn 2	Hillesvåg Ullvarefabrikk	80% wool, 20% nylon
Hot Socks Pearl	Gründl	75% Merino wool, 20% polyamide, 5% cashmere
Marigarn	Telespinn	80% Kid mohair, 20% Merino wool
Merino DK	Hedgehog fibres	100% superwash Merino wool
Merinoull	Sandnes Garn	100% superwash Merino wool
Mini Sterk	Du Store Alpakka	40% alpaca, 40% Merino wool, 20% nylon
Pure Eco Baby Wool	Dale Garn	100% organic wool
Røros embroidery yarn	Rauma Ullvarefabrikk	100% Spelsau wool
Sand	Lofoten wool	100% Spelsau wool
Sheila's Gold	Wool2Dye4	80% superwash Merino wool, 20% nylon
Sisu	Sandnes Garn	80% superwash wool, 20% nylon
Sterk	Du Store Alpakka	40% alpaca, 40% Merino wool, 20% nylon
Sølje	Hillesvåg Ullvarefabrikk	100% wool
Hand-dyed Yarn		
Superfine Merino / nylon From The Happy Little Dye Pot (426 yd/390 m per 100 g), hand-dyed		
Kate's Favorite for Socks	Kate sin Design	80% superwash Merino Wool, 20% nylon

A variety of additional and substitute yarns are available from:
Webs – America's Yarn Store
75 Service Center Road
Northampton, MA 01060
800-367-9327
www.yarn.com

LoveKnitting.com
www.loveknitting.com/us

If you are unable to obtain any of the yarn used in this book, it can be replaced with a yarn of a similar weight and composition. Please note, however, the finished projects may vary slightly from those

Yards/Meters per 100 g	Additional Information	Distributed in North America by
350 yd/320 m	6.5/2	theyarnguys.com
284 yd/260 m		facebook.com/lykkesau/
437 yd/400 m		sandnesgarn.com
344 yd/315 m	6.3/2	nordicfiberarts.com
383 yd/350 m	4-ply	theyarnguys.com
361 yd/330 m	4-ply	dalegarnnorthamerica.com
503 yd/460 m	3-ply	thewoollythistle.com
383 yd/350 m	7/2	theyarnguys.com
273 yd/250 m	5/2	
437 yd/400 m		loveknitting.com
350 yd/320 m	2-ply	
191 yd/175 m		hedgehogfibres.com (ships worldwide)
230 yd/210 m		sandnesgarn.com
363 yd/332 m		knitwithattitude.com (ships worldwide)
350 yd/320 m		dalegarnnorthamerica.com
546 yd/500 m	10/2	theyarnguys.com
142 yd/130 m	2.3/2	
399 yd/365 m	2-ply twist	wool2dye4.com
383 yd/350 m		sandnesgarn.com
300 yd/274 m		knitwithattitude.com (ships worldwide)
383 yd/350 m	7/2, 2-ply	
		facebook.com/TheHappyLittleDyePot

shown, depending on the yarn used. Try www.yarnsub.com for suggestions.

For more information on selecting or substituting yarn, contact your local yarn shop or an online store; they are familiar with all types of yarns and would be happy to help you. Additionally, the online knitting community at Ravelry.com has forums where you can post questions about specific yarns. Yarns come and go so quickly these days and there are so many beautiful yarns available.

BIBLIOGRAPHY

Gravjord, Ingebjørg. *Bunadsokker frå Tinn* [Bunad Socks from Tinn]. Pattern Instructions from The Norwegian Institute of Bunad and Folk Costume.

Kjellberg, Anne, Ingebjørg Gravjord, Gerd Aarsland Rosander, Anne-Lise Svendsen. *Strikking i Norge* [Knitting in Norway]. Landsbruksforlaget, 1987.

Lerche, Adéle (editor). *Gyldendals Store Sy- & Håndarbeidsbok* [Gyldensal's Big Sewing- and Handwork Book]. Gyldendal norsk forlag, 1963.

Noss, Aagot. *Med ein fot in mellomaldern. Vadmålsokker og annan slag fotbunad i Tinn i Telemark* [With a Foot in the Middle Ages: Vadmal Socks and Other Bunad Footwear in Tinn in Telemark]. By og Bygd. Yearbook 1987-88 of the Norwegian Museum of Cultural History. Volume XXXII.

Rutt, Richard. *A History of Hand Knitting*. Batsford, 1987 and Interweave, 1987.

Sundbø, Annemor. *Kvardagsstrikk: Kulturskatter frå fillehaugen*. Det Norske Samlaget, 1994. *Everyday Knitting: Treasures from a Ragpile*. Torridal Tweed, 2000.

Sæther, Nina Granlund. *Votter*. Cappelen Damm, 2016. *Mittens from Around Norway: Over 40 Traditional Knitting Patterns Inspired by Norwegian-Folk-Art Collections*. Trafalgar Square, 2017. *Mittens from Norway.* Search Press, 2017.

Veiteberg, Jorunn. *Broderi og kjønn. Geriljabroderi* [Embroidery and Gender: Guerrilla Embroidery]. Magikon forlag, 2010.

Wildfeld, Elna Arbo. *Minder fra Guldskoven: Til min søn Hemming* [Memories from Guldskoven: To my son Hemming]. Hemming Arbo Windfeld-Hansen, Oslo, 1975.

Winsnes, Hanna. *For Tjenestepiger* [For Servant Girls]. Malling, Christiana, 1868.

Archive:
www.arkivverket.no/arkivverket/Brukarkivet/Nettutstillinger/Fruentimmer-Kaage-og-Farvebog

PHOTOGRAPHY CREDITS

With the exception of the following credits, all photographs in the book were taken by Guri Pfeifer.

Historic photo of Striped socks from Østfold, p. 24—The Norwegian Institute of Bunad and Folk Costume
Historic photo of Star socks, p. 28—National Museum of Norway
Photo, p. 33—Nina Granlund Sæther
Historic photo of Oslo socks, p. 38—Norwegian Museum of Cultural History
Historic photo of Stockings from 1868, p. 42—Norwegian Museum of Cultural History
Historic photo of Rose Ankle socks, p. 46—Norwegian Museum of Cultural History
Historic photo of Striped stockings from Glåmdalen, p. 50—Glåmdal Museum
Historic photo of Color Party, p. 54—State Archives in Stavangar
Historic photo of Stockings from Valdres, p. 58—The Norwegian Institute of Bunad and Folk Costume
Historic photo of Stockings from Valdres, p. 60—C. G. Rude/Valdres Museum
Historic photo of Stockings from Gausdal, p. 62—Norwegian Museum of Cultural History
Historic photos of Barleycorn (*Byggkorn*) socks from Numedal, p. 66—Norwegian Museum of Cultural History and The Norwegian Institute of Bunad and Folk Costume
Historic photo of Halling socks, p. 70—The Norwegian Museum of Cultural History
Historic photo of Larvik socks, p. 74—Larvik Museum
Historic photos of Long Lace stockings, p. 78—The National Library
Historic photos of Telemark socks, p. 84—Norwegian Museum of Cultural History and The Norwegian Institute of Bunad and Folk Costume
Historic photo of Cable stockings from Tinn, p. 88—Norwegian Institute of Bunad and Folk Costume
Historic photo of Setesdal *Krot* stockings, p. 92—Kari Benedikte Bjercke/Telemark Museum
Historic photo of Zigzag Pattern socks, p. 96—Free use, original in the National Portrait Gallery
Historic photo of Cable socks from Marnardal, p. 100—Historic Photo—Marnardal and Audnedal/agderbilder.no
Historic photo of Leftover Party socks, p. 104—Norwegian Museum of Cultural History
Historic photo of Bridegroom's socks from Vindafjord, p. 108—Norwegian Museum of Cultural History
Historic photo of Rose socks with Lace Patterns, p. 112—Anne-Lise Reinsfeldt/ Norwegian Museum of Cultural History
Historic photo of Stockings from Voss, p. 118—Norwegian Museum of Cultural History
Historic photo of Short *Skakareiker* socks from Austevoll, p. 122—Norwegian Museum of Cultural History
Historic photo of Kroneleistar from Øygarden, p. 126—Coast Museum Øygarden
Historic photo of Hardanger socks, p. 130—Norwegian Museum of Cultural History
Historic photo of Sunnfjord socks, p. 134—The Norwegian Institute of Bunad and Folk Costume
Historic photo of Spiral socks from Nordfjord, p. 138—Nordfjord Museum
Historic photo of Child's socks from Nordmøre, p. 142—Institute of the Nordmøre Museum
Historic photo of Socks from Budalen, p. 146—Anne-Lise Reinsfeldt/ Norwegian Museum of Cultural History
Historic photo of *Ragg* socks from Hitra, p. 150—Coast Museum in Trøndelag
Historic photo of Striped socks from Orkladalen, p. 154—The Norwegian Institute of Bunad and Folk Costume
Historic photo of Maria's stockings from Lierne, p. 158—The Norwegian Institute of Bunad and Folk Costume
Historic photo of Trønder socks, p. 164—Sverresborg Trøndelag Folk Museum
Historic photo of Child's socks from Helgeland, p. 168—Nordland Museum's Photography Collection
Historic photo of Entrelac stockings from Helgeland, p. 172—Free use, photographed by Margrethe Christensen, reproduced by Geir Vea
Historic photo of Spider socks from Troms, p. 176—The Norwegian Institute of Bunad and Folk Costume
Sports socks from Alta, p. 180—Norwegian Museum of Cultural History
Shell Pattern, p. 184—Norwegian Museum of Cultural History
Historic photo of Heart socks, p. 188—Glomdal Museum
Historic photo of Socks with Larger Lice Pattern, p. 192—Norwegian Museum of Cultural History

TRIKOTAS
UNDERTØ
STRØMPE